FREE MONEY®
and Services for Seniors
and Their Families

FREE MONEY®
and Services for Seniors and Their Families

Laurie Blum

John Wiley & Sons, Inc.
New York · Chichester · Brisbane · Toronto · Singapore

Copyright © 1995 by Laurie Blum
Published by John Wiley & Sons, Inc.

Library of Congress Cataloging-in-Publication Data:

Blum, Laurie.
    Free money and services for seniors and their families / Laurie Blum.
        p.   cm.
    Includes bibliographical references and index.
    ISBN 0-471-11489-8 (alk. paper)
    1. Aged—Services for—United States—Directories. 2. Aged—Care—United States—Finance—Directories. 3. Caregivers—United States—Life skills guides.   I. Title.
    HV1461.B58   1995
    362.6'3'02573—dc20   94-40816

Printed in the United States of America

10 9 8 7 6 5 4 3 2 1

I would like to briefly but sincerely thank Maggie Dana, my wonderful editor PJ Dempsey, Lachell Glaspie, Chris Jackson, and Bob Tabian.

Preface

This book came out of my own experience of caring for my grandmother who, at 87, could no longer care for herself. She skipped meals, claiming she was just too tired to cook. Although my mom and I brought her a cane, she rarely used it, and both of us worried about her falling down as she had several years before, when she broke her wrist. My grandmother has always been fiercely independent, so my mom and I were not surprised when my grandmother refused to allow us to arrange for a Meals-On-Wheels program for her.

After much discussion, my family decided that perhaps we could convince my grandmother to enter a retirement home. That was the easy part. The hard part was trying to find out what homes existed in our area, figuring out if she fit qualifications, filling out applications, and trying to find the money to pay for her care.

Over and over during that difficult year when my grandmother's health first started to decline to the point where she entered the retirement home, my family and I faced many decisions that had to be made. Yet, we were often baffled about where to turn for information, for advice, for support.

As a fundraiser and author who often works in the area of health care, I am accustomed to identifying a problem that needs to be solved, sifting through data that are often nearly inaccessible and many times mired in layers of bureaucracy, filling out applications, and trying to find money. Because of my professional background, I was able to help my grandmother. After you read this book, you too will be able to help a senior relative or friend get the assistance he or she needs.

I hope you will read the entire book, but you can also get help by turning to the particular chapter or chapters that address the specific problem you face.

The book is divided into two parts. Part One explains how to get organized, how to prepare a patient profile (both medical, financial, and legal), how to assess the problem at hand to determine what's needed as well as how to gather information in order to evaluate the services and/or facilities that need to be procured. It also contains the specific chapters on various services and facilities. Check the chapters that apply to you. Part Two is your Rolodex, a resource section of information. This section will tell where to get the help you need and how to pay for it.

Don't get discouraged, because help is out there. You simply need to find out where it is and how to get it.

By the time this book is published, some of the information contained here will have changed. No reference book can be as up-to-date as the reader or author would like. Names, addresses, dollar amounts, telephone numbers, and other data are always in flux; however, most of the information will not have changed.

Good luck.

Contents

Introduction

LAYING THE GROUNDWORK

Begin this process early. Don't make the mistake of seeking help for an elderly parent or loved one after a problem or crisis has occurred. Don't put yourself in the position of making crucial decisions hurriedly and then regretting them. Give yourself the time in advance to grapple with the financial, medical, and emotional implications of caring for a senior.

Determining the Level of Care Needed

To do this in a systematic way, you will first need to determine how much assistance is actually needed. The following questionnaire is designed to give you the answers to the questions a social worker or geriatric-care manager would ask you about this senior in order to identify specific problems and determine what actions to take in administering care.

Can the senior:	YES	NO
Take medications on time and in the correct dosage?	____	____
Shop for food and clothing?	____	____
Prepare meals?	____	____
Visit friends?	____	____
Drive a car?	____	____
Travel by bus or taxi?	____	____
Do light housekeeping?	____	____
Do heavy housekeeping?	____	____

Can the senior:	YES	NO
Do the laundry?	_____	_____
Do yard work?	_____	_____
Afford to pay the bills?	_____	_____
Write checks and pay bills efficiently?	_____	_____
Take care of legal matters?	_____	_____
Maintain personal cleanliness?	_____	_____
Dress without aid?	_____	_____
Use the toilet?	_____	_____
Tell time?	_____	_____
Sleep through the night?	_____	_____
Safely climb stairs?	_____	_____
Look up telephone numbers and make calls without help?	_____	_____
Be left alone?	_____	_____

Once you have checked off what this person can and cannot do, you can start a plan for seeking out the type of services and care that is required. This care may come from visiting nurses, home companions, volunteers from your church or synagogue, Meals-On-Wheels programs, home health aides, or even federally funded home maintenance services if the senior person otherwise is able to handle most of the normal day-to-day living experiences. If you have answered no to the majority of the questions above, the senior needs more around-the-clock care. In this case, you may need to find more intensive types of care, such as alternative housing arrangements which can range from a continuous-care retirement community to a nursing home. The next few chapters will explain the various services and facilities that do exist and how to find and pay for them. But first, you'll need to get organized and put together more information about the senior.

GET ORGANIZED

Before you delve into the wide array of services that are available for the elderly, some careful organizing has to be done. The task of finding services and planning care will be frustrating for you unless you pull together information about the senior's personal affairs including health status, insurance coverage, financial status, and personal records. You will need to be armed with very specific information. When phoning around town and visiting agencies, strangers will ask you all kinds of questions. Being organized and having quick access to answers will save you time, frustration, and money.

If the person you are helping is still mentally alert, you may find it awkward gaining access to that person's more personal information. This is understandable. Most people, no matter what their age, often resist anyone meddling in their personal affairs. But they will usually come around if you gently explain that only with this information can you find out if they are eligible for the help that they need, if they will be able to get insurance reimbursement, and, if not, to figure out how these services can be paid for. You also need to explain that documents must be put in order so that you can have access to them in case the person becomes sick or incapacitated.

POWER OF ATTORNEY

Lawyers and advocators for the elderly think it essential for a friend or relative to have power of attorney, a document in which a senior designates someone who will be able to perform tasks such as paying bills and writing checks. An individual who becomes incapacitated without having assigned power of attorney may end up having decisions made by a state-appointed guardian. A health-care proxy is also recommended, which allows the designated person to make decisions about medical treatment should a senior be unable to participate in such decisions. A lawyer usually draws up these documents although forms are available from any stationery store specializing in legal forms. Experts do urge great care; power of attorney is a highly potent instrument that can be easily abused.

Once you have obtained the senior's personal information, organize it in four file folders using the following categories:

1. *The Medical-Information File*
   - List all doctors. Be sure to include each doctor's specialty and the problem(s) being treated, as well as the doctor's phone number and address.
   - List chronic health problems of the older person with dates of diagnoses.
   - List any surgeries, with the date of surgery.
   - List any tests beyond those done during routine checkups, such as

x rays, CAT scans, cardiac tests. Also include the name of the doctor who did the test, where the test was performed, and copies of the test findings.

- List all medications. Include the name and phone number of pharmacy and pharmacists, the strength and frequency of dosage of each medication, who prescribed it, and the date of first prescription. State allergies and past drug reactions.
- Identify what to do in a medical emergency. Note which hospital to go to, including emergency-room phone number, which ambulance service to call, and include phone numbers of doctors to call. Note family members and friends to call.

Also include brochures, newspaper articles, and any other information on the senior's condition or disease.

2. *The Financial-Information File*

- List all bank accounts (checking, savings, money markets). Also include the names and phone numbers of bankers, stockbrokers, financial advisors, and accountants.
- Put together a monthly income statement with any of the following that apply:
  - ☐ Salaries, wages
  - ☐ Social Security benefits for both husband and wife
  - ☐ Pensions for both husband and wife
  - ☐ Annuities for both husband and wife
  - ☐ Stock dividends
  - ☐ Rents
  - ☐ Royalties
  - ☐ IRAs
  - ☐ Mutual funds
- Estimate monthly expenses with any of the following that apply:
  - ☐ Mortgage or rent
  - ☐ Utilities
  - ☐ Telephone
  - ☐ Housekeeping services
  - ☐ Any equipment rentals
  - ☐ Insurance premiums
  - ☐ Food
  - ☐ Clothing
  - ☐ Transportation

☐ Unreimbursed medical and dental expenses
☐ Medicines
☐ Miscellaneous

3. *The Health-Insurance File*

• Include Medicare card and any other hospital or clinic cards.
• Put together all private insurance policies including major medical and medigap policies and list names of insurance agents with phone numbers, addresses, and company names.

4. *The Legal File*

• The will
• Power of attorney
• Health-care proxy
• Name, address, and phone number of lawyer

Keep Accurate Notes

The maze of health-care services is not an easy one to navigate, so here are some pointers to help you. I developed this system after I found it necessary to call all over town, asking questions of an unconnected assortment of social workers, volunteers, and staff at elder care agencies. I found myself becoming frustrated as I dealt with unsympathetic, people who at times gave me incorrect information, were condescending if I didn't understand what they had said, failed to call me back, or put me on hold indefinitely.

Here's how to make your own search for information easier. Before you make that first phone call, do the following.

Keep an Index Card File

You need to be able to know what questions to ask as well as to keep track of the information you obtain. The index-card file is a flexible way of keeping track of ideas and information. You can use any size index cards. You'll also need a number of index tabs so that you can make separate categories for referrals, contacts, services, and so forth. Whenever some useful information is obtained from a telephone call, a newspaper article, or whatever, jot it down on a card and add it to your file. Every few weeks go through these cards and activate information that seems useful or discard information that is out of date. I find this system much easier to use than a journal or even a looseleaf binder, which fills up with obsolete material and keeps you constantly flipping back and forth. It's simple to discard and add cards, and the index tabs make it easy to find what you're looking for.

Stock Up on Manila File Folders

You will need a box of manila file folders. You should open one file for what I call investigative research. You'll also want to put together the previously mentioned files on medical, financial, health insurance, and legal information.

When you find relevant articles in newspapers and magazines, clip them and drop them in the appropriate file. If you don't organize papers in this way, soon piles of brochures, documents, bills and more bills will grow insurmountable.

As you get into your research, you'll definitely need some kind of filing system. This doesn't have to be an enormous file cabinet. You can begin with one of those large plastic portable file boxes, a cardboard file box, or a drawer.

How to Network by Telephone

When you begin your search for care for a loved one, you enter a kind of maze, a hall of mirrors if you will, with a multitude of options and requirements. You will also have to cope with a bureaucratic system, that will undoubtedly frustrate you at a time when it is essential that you know the correct way of using the system. You will not find quick and easy solutions to your problems.

Prepare for the worst so that you won't get discouraged. Unsympathetic, people may steer you in the wrong direction, give you the wrong information, speak in a condescending manner to you if you don't understand what they mean, fail to call back, stay out to lunch interminably, and, most annoying of all, put you on hold indefinitely. You may find yourself tempted to slam down the phone in frustration more than a few times. Don't.

To help you be effective in getting the information that you need when making phone calls, get out your index card and follow these tips.

- *Make a call only after you organize you thinking.* Calling back with further questions can be awkward.

- *Be precise.* The person on the other end of the phone will appreciate if you are concise and very specific about what you need.
- *Write everything down.* If the person you need to talk to is out, write down his or her name and extension in case your call is not returned.
- *Take notes on every call.* Any information you obtain may be of use later on.
- *Be assertive.* If the person on the phone seems to be less than forthcoming with information or if he or she gives you a difficult time, stay calm. Call back and politely ask to speak with a supervisor. If you still get no resolution, write down the time, date, name of the person you spoke with, and content of your call and file a complaint with the Better Business Bureau or your local Chamber of Commerce.

I suggest that you copy the following on an index card and keep it by your phone to use as a script when making your calls:

My name is _____

I'm taking care of _____

I need to find _____

Can you assist me? If not, can you give me another name or agency to call?

What type of services do you provide?

What are the costs?

What are the eligibility requirements?

Is there a waiting list, and, if so, how long is it?

Would you send me an application and brochure?

To whom am I speaking?

Thank you for your help.

Good-bye.

Part I

The Services and Products

1

Services and Products Available for the Well at Home

All home-based services have one goal in common: to help a senior remain living at home in a safe and clean environment with the basic needs of food and health care provided. Home care can be arranged for just a few hours a week, such as in services that provide hot meals or housekeeping, or for around-the-clock, such as a twenty-four-hour nurse's aide.

Although in-home services are primarily designed to help seniors who would not be able to live at home without such help, they are also a godsend for caregivers who need to take a break.

Until recently, the health-care system was widely prejudiced against paying for any in-home services. Nowadays, thanks to increased pressure from advocates for the aging and as evidence increases of the cost-effectiveness of home care, more and more temporarily disabled and chronically ill older people are being rehabilitated and maintained at home. And, unequivocally, that's where they prefer to be, rather than in a hospital or a nursing home.

It is important to note that the home health-care industry is not regulated. Anyone can open an agency, advertise, and send workers classified as health aides into people's homes. As a rule, one should stay away from such agencies because their owners have not subjected themselves to the scrutiny of state licensure and Medicare certification.

FIND A HOME-CARE AGENCY

You can find well-run agencies that meet the industry's high standards established by its membership organization, the National Association of Home Care. The following is a list of questions to ask when hiring someone so as not to be taken advantage of by an unscrupulous agency.

- Is the agency licensed by the State Department of Health?
- Is the agency Medicare certified? (Note that although this is not an essential requisite for choosing an agency, it is a good barometer of high standards. Some agencies operate only on private payments, thus avoiding the complicated procedure leading to Medicare certification. However, just because the agency is certified by Medicare does not necessarily mean that services can be reimbursed through Medicare.)
- Are employees of the agency insured and bonded?
- Does the agency provide workers' compensation to its employees?
- Is the home health-care worker supervised by a registered nurse? (A good agency will provide case management by a nurse-supervisor at least once a month.)

Record this information in your index-card file.

SERVICES PROVIDED BY HOME CARE

Telephone Reassurance Programs

Telephone reassurance programs go under different names, such as House Calls, Call-a-Day, and Care-Line. Many are staffed by volunteers working with nonprofit organizations, such as senior citizen organizations, the Visiting Nurse Association, and hospital social work departments. In some areas where volunteer programs are sparse or nonexistent, private companies have filled the void for this valuable service. Usually a client is telephoned once a day, and the caller keeps a chart, which includes daily information about medication, meals, and appointments that the senior needs to be reminded of. Some for-profit services offer twenty-four-hour reassurance programs, which allow the older person to call a central office at any time.

How Much Does It Cost?

Usually the service is free. For-profit businesses charge a monthly fee, usually based on time spent by personnel working for the telephone service.

Where to Find It

- Your local Area Agency on Aging office (please refer to Chapter 9)
- A nonprofit home health-care agency such as the Visiting Nurse Association
- A for-profit home health-care agency
- Senior centers
- Local hospitals

Handyman Programs

Handyman programs are usually provided by local youth groups, retirees, and volunteers for seniors who can no longer manage home maintenance themselves. These services do not include major improvements such as putting on a new roof or painting the house. Rather, basic home and garden maintenance is provided so that elderly people can live safely and comfortably in their own homes. This might include repairing steps, installing handrails and other safety features, putting in lightbulbs, fixing leaks, replacing windows, putting in or taking out storm windows, raking leaves, cutting down branches, and mowing lawns.

How Much Does It Cost?

Some communities have free services for seniors living on fixed incomes who are in need of assistance. If payment is involved, it is far less than it would be for a professional.

Where to Find It

- Your local Area Agency on Aging office (please refer to Chapter 9)
- Classified ads in your local paper
- Your Chamber of Commerce
- The Yellow Pages
- Your local high school
- Local churches and synagogues

The Friendly Visitor Service

The Friendly Visitor Service offers companionship to seniors. Volunteers visit them at home usually for a few hours once or twice a week. The volunteer's main purpose is to provide company (which can include chatting, playing cards, reading out loud, writing letters); the volunteer does not perform personal, medical, or housekeeping tasks).

How Much Does It Cost?

The service is usually free.

Where to Find It

- Your local Area Agency on Aging office (please refer to Chapter 9)
- Local churches or synagogues
- Retiree volunteer programs
- The Junior League
- Local high schools
- Boy and Girl Scout troops

Senior Companions

Senior companions provide company and services to older people who are unable to handle the basic tasks of daily living. They are not trained to administer medical assistance or to help with dressing, bathing, or personal hygiene. Their job description does not include heavy-duty housecleaning. They are ideal for the senior who lives alone and is not quite able to manage alone during the day.

How Much Does It Cost?

Depending on the area, costs range from the minimum wage to $12 an hour. Families pay the companion's wages out of pocket.

Where to Find It

In some communities the service can be arranged through a social worker. Most programs are set up through local Area Agency on Aging offices (see Chapter 9). Other possible sources include:

- The Visiting Nurse Association
- Private home-service employment agencies
- The Department of Social Services

- The American Association of Retired Persons
- Classified ads in your local paper

Meals-On-Wheels

Home-delivered meals, usually called Meals-On-Wheels, are a nutritional food service provided by public and nonprofit organizations. Most programs are provided with funding by the federal government under the Older Americans Act. Meals-On-Wheels programs are for seniors of all income levels who have difficulty preparing nourishing meals for themselves. In recent years, nonprofit programs have been started by churches, synagogues, and civic organizations such as the Kiwanis Clubs and Rotary International, as well as other social-service organizations.

How Much Does It Cost?

A donation is suggested to pay for the meals. For lunch the charge is usually about $3, for dinner $5. Programs that receive federal funds are not permitted to turn people away because of an inability to pay. Private programs generally charge a fee; however, sometimes meals are provided to a limited number of nonpaying clients.

Where to Find It

- Your local Area Agency on Aging Office (please refer to Chapter 9)
- Civic clubs
- Local churches and synagogues
- The National Association of Meals Programs
  101 North Alfred Street, Suite 202
  Alexandria, VA 22314
  (703) 548-5558
  (Call or write for the names of local member programs.)

Licensed Home Health-Care Agency Personnel

Health-care agencies are set up to send personnel into the homes of people who are incapacitated, ill, or recuperating from an illness. The personnel can be homemakers, home health aides, registered nurses, physiotherapists, or speech therapists.

How Much Does It Cost?

A bona fide agency supplying home health-care services will be able to determine whether or not the older person is eligible for insurance coverage and for how long.

Under specific, limited circumstances, a primary doctor can order employing a home health aide, homemaker, or a skilled professional such as a nurse or physiotherapist, so that fees will be paid by Medicare and private insurance. Usually such short-term payment applies if restorative care is needed after a hospital stay. In most states, Medicaid will pay for limited long-term home health-care services.

Insurance reimbursement should always be attempted when someone with medical problems needs paid help. If the patient is not eligible for reimbursement or if reimbursement has ended, the patient and family are left to decide whether or not to pay for home-care services out of pocket.

If a homemaker or a home health aide is needed and the older person can't afford the cost, do investigate a Pay-As-You-Can homemaker health-aide program. Available in some communities, this program is run by nonprofit agencies such as the Visiting Nurse Association for those who can prove that their income is below a certain limit.

Where to Find It

- The hospital discharge office
- Your physician
- The Visiting Nurse Association or another nonprofit home health-care agency
- A local branch of a private home health-care chain. The following are some of the largest chains, which are known for providing quality care:
  - ☐ Kimberly Quality Care
  - ☐ Medical Personnel Pool
  - ☐ Upjohn Health Care Services
  - ☐ Morrell Health Care
  - ☐ Olstein Health Care
- A locally controlled, licensed agency offering home health care

The following section will outline costs as well as job descriptions of three of the most often used types of licensed home health-care agency workers: homemakers, home health aides, and skilled home-care personnel.

Homemakers

Homemakers are trained to take care of the household needs of elderly people who cannot manage by themselves. A homemaker usually has no training in personal or nursing care.

How Much Does It Cost?

In some circumstances, after a senior has been discharged from the hospital, homemaker fees are paid for by one's insurance carrier. Otherwise, the cost varies greatly from city to city but usually will average about $8 an hour.

Home Health Aides

Home health aides are trained to provide personal care for people who have health problems. They function in the patient's home much as nurse's aides do in the hospital, but are usually supervised by a registered nurse.

Sometimes hospitals train and provide such aides for their discharged patients but more often than not they are employed by community-based, nonprofit home health-care agencies or private for-profit agencies. Although home health aides are usually ordered by a doctor as part of the hospital discharge, families can secure home health aides on their own.

How Much Does It Cost?

Under certain circumstances, a physician can order a home health aide so that the fees will be paid for by Medicare and/or private insurance. Usually some payment applies if the patient needs rehabilitative care after, for example, a stroke or hip replacement surgery. Costs vary from city to city and run from $10–$20/hour on average.

Skilled Home-Care Personnel

Skilled home care is provided by licensed health-care professionals such as nurses, practical nurses, physical or occupational therapists, respiratory therapists, and nutritionists. These professionals work with the patient's physician to perform many of the functions that are ordinarily administered in a hospital setting. All across the country, more and more insurance programs are paying for limited periods of skilled home care so that patients can leave the hospital sooner and receive care at home. The arrangement works for both the patient and the insurance carrier; the patient is able to return home sooner, and it is also cheaper for the insurance programs, which now give hospitals incentives for releasing patients as soon as possible.

How Much Does It Cost?

If a physician orders skilled care according to the guidelines set by Medicare or a private insurance company, costs are usually paid in full. The rates for skilled care vary according to the profession involved. A reputable home health-care agency will quote prices over the phone.

Medical-Alert Products

Medical-alert products allow older people who are at high risk for accidents and medical emergencies to live independently. There are three categories of products: emergency-response systems, medical-identification cards, and medical-identification jewelry tags.

Emergency-Response Systems

The response systems link people to twenty-four-hour assistance at the push of a button. A small device, the help button, is worn around the neck on a chain or strapped to clothing. Help buttons can also be installed in other convenient locations such as next to the bathtub or bed, in a wheelchair, or on a walker. Most people choose to wear help buttons around their neck. In an emergency, the wearer activates the help button, which initiates a call for help to an emergency-response center. As soon as the call is received, someone at the center calls the person in distress and talks over a speaker phone attached to the home telephone. If no answer is heard, someone at the emergency-response center next calls one of three nearby "responders" who have agreed to enter the distressed caller's home in an emergency. An ambulance can also be sent depending on circumstances and prior arrangements.

How Much Does It Cost?

Some community-based centers offer free service to seniors, although they usually have a one-time installation charge and a monthly fee. Basic service ordered directly from Lifeline costs $35 a month with a $50 installation fee. Be wary of unscrupulous companies that offer similar services at exorbitant prices. Comparison shop to see what services you get for your money.

Where to Find It

Your local Area Agency on Aging office (see Chapter 9) or a local hospital can tell you who runs the medical-alert program in your community. You can also look for programs listed in the Yellow Pages under "medical alarms." In some communities, service is arranged through local hospitals or home health agencies such as the Visiting Nurse Association.

If no such programs are available in your area or if the waiting lists for services are long, you can directly contact one of the regional or national companies that supply emergency-response centers with equipment. Such companies should be listed in the Yellow Pages.

Lifeline Emergency-Response Systems is the largest company in the business in both the United States and Canada. You can call the company at (800) 451-0525 to make arrangements for service.

Medical-Identification Cards

Wallet-sized medical cards provide vital information for medical personnel to review in an emergency. They range in cost from $2–$12 and are particularly important if the card owner loses consciousness or the ability to communicate.

Where to Find It

Check with your primary physician about a suitable card company or contact:

STAT Medical ID Company
P.O. Box 9874
Alexandria, VA 22304-9874

The STAT Company offers a credit-card size copy of a detailed application, which is reduced onto microfilm but is readable without magnification. Physicians' names and a medical history are also included.

National Medic-Card Systems
P.O. Box 4307
Oceanside, CA 92504

This company's folded card includes a patient's medical history, insurance information, and treatment-consent forms.

Medical Passport Foundation
P.O. Box 820
Deland, FL 32721

The Foundation's card provides space for a variety of general health information.

Medical-Identification Jewelry

Emergency personnel are trained to look for medical identification tags on bracelets or pendants or in clothing on incapacitated patients. Such tags are good for those with health problems. Besides the wearer's name and a few basic items of medical information, the tag carries a collect-call telephone number of a central office where vital patient information can be obtained quickly. Calls can be handled twenty-four hours a day from anywhere in the world. The service is particularly valuable for those prone to confusion, angina, diabetes, and allergies to penicillin and other medications.

How Much Does It Cost?

Medic-Alert is the leading medical signaling company; the basic service costs $10 per month and there is a one-time fee of $90. The products range from bracelets to necklaces, with a selection of precious and nonprecious metals.

Where to Find It

For information about these products call Medic-Alert at (800) 449-2944.

Lifesaver Charities offers a plastic tag free but will welcome a small donation. Send a self-addressed, stamped envelope to Lifesaver Charities, P.O. Box 125-BH & G, Buena Park, CA 90621.

2

Community-Based Services

These may be in the form of social programs for seniors who are well and want to get out of the house and meet and spend time with others of their generation. Or they may be for older people who are chronically ill and need a place to go to for minimal medical care and supervised therapy.

Some community-based programs are designed for families who need to take a break from caregiving duties. These services allow the caregiver to work outside the home, take a break, or go on vacation.

Senior Centers

Senior Centers were originally established to provide social activities for older people who were able to manage on their own and were not in need of medical services. Of the thousands of Senior Centers around the country, many of them offer much more than coffee and conversation. Some act as a clearinghouse for information about legal and financial problems. Many participate in the federally funded hot-meal program, and a large number utilize the services of a social worker who plans outings, classes, and other social events. Senior Centers are primarily for the well elderly who can get themselves to the center on their own. A limited number offer transportation services.

How Much Does It Cost?

Most services and programs at Senior Centers are free; although, they will often charge for meals.

Where to Find It

- Your local Area Agency on Aging office (please refer to Chapter 9)
- Nationality associations such as Italian-Americans, Polish-Americans, German-Americans
- Civic organizations such as the Kiwanis, Elks, or Rotary Clubs
- Local churches and synagogues
- Union clubs
- Company retirement clubs

Community-Based Programs

Community-based meal programs operate in most cities and some smaller towns throughout the United States. Most meal programs operate five days a week, although in some communities they are offered seven days a week. Meals, usually at lunchtime, are provided in a group setting at local churches and synagogues, schools, and Senior Centers. The purpose behind these programs is to keep people healthy. Most programs provide transportation for those who cannot drive or otherwise get to the site on their own.

How Much Does It Cost?

A donation for meals is suggested, usually $5 or less.

Where to Find It

- Your local Area Agency on Aging office (please refer to Chapter 9)
- Local Senior Centers
- Local churches and synagogues

Adult Day Care

Adult day-care centers take frail or demented older people who can no longer remain at home by themselves but who don't need skilled nursing care. Although adult day-care centers are a growing form of care, they are a relatively new idea and are not available in all communities. Centers within communities vary in specifying whom they will and will not take. Some centers, for example, will not take demented people, those who are incontinent, or those who use wheelchairs or walkers. Others are set up to take people suffering from specific diseases such as Alzheimer's or those with stroke damage. Besides providing a safe, structured environment, such centers give the frail elderly both contact with other adults as well as medical and rehabilitative care. Lunch is almost always provided and most centers have a space where clients can nap. Some centers provide transportation, although most do not.

How to Evaluate an Adult Day-Care Facility

1. Ask to see their written policy statement, which will spell out the target population served by the facility.
2. Find out whether there is a policy of excluding people with a history of violent or antisocial behavior.
3. Ask whether records of individual participants include: Medical and assessment information that is regularly updated, signed authorizations for medical emergency care if necessary, reports on the participants' activities.
4. The ratio of staff to participants should be one to eight. If the program serves an especially high percentage of severely impaired men and women, the ratio should be one to five. (Volunteers included in these calculations should meet the same job qualifications as paid staff members.) Staff members should include:
   - An *experienced director*, preferably one who has a professional degree in the field of health and human services.
   - A *trained social worker* or counselor who, in addition to his or her other duties, will meet with family members to provide them with information about community resources and entitlements.
   - A *registered nurse* or a licensed practical nurse supervised by an RN.
   - An *activities director* with an academic degree in a field related to occupational therapy.
   - *Licensed therapists* (who are either regular staff members or consultants) with state credentials in physical, speech, or occupational therapy.
5. Each participant's plan should include an assessment of needs and care

requirements and a regular reassessment of each patient's plan as necessary or, at the very least, every six months.

6. One midday meal should be part of every participant's program.

7. In addition to meeting the participant's physical requirements, programs should be planned around the intellectual, cultural, social, and emotional needs of the older person.

8. In evaluating the inside and outside of the facility, check for the following:

   • Accommodations for the physically handicapped
   • Adequate lighting in all parts of the facility
   • Noise levels and soundproofing
   • Comfortable furniture, cheerful furnishings, and a generally attractive decor
   • Procedures for fire safety and fire drills

Respite Care

Respite care is an offshoot of adult day care. Respite programs are for overburdened caregivers who without it are in danger of buckling under. The word derives from the Latin word, "respirare" which means "to breathe." Respite care can mean that someone comes to the home to give a family caregiver a break, a program at a hospital or nursing home where a disabled older person is dropped off, or a short stay in a nursing home.

On a nationwide basis respite programs differ widely depending on their setting and the type of services that they offer. Whether the dependent elderly person participates on an occasional and temporary basis or on a regular weekly or monthly schedule, the basic purpose of respite care is to provide a period of relief for the family member or members responsible for caring for the older person. While respite care isn't meant to replace other specialized services, it is another community-based option designed to reduce family stress and help to prevent the premature institutionalizing of older people.

How Much Does It Cost?

The daily rate for overnight respite care averages about $100. Such care is usually not reimbursable through Medicare, Medicaid, or private insurance. However, volunteer-provided services in the home are free, and drop-off respite programs are either free or handled on a pay-as-you-can basis.

Where to Find It

Finding a place that provides overnight respite care is not easy. Write to the American Association of Homes for the Aging, 1129 20th Street NW, Washington, DC 20036 for a list of their members who offer respite care. I would also suggest calling local licensed nursing homes.

Some communities have in-home and drop-off respite services, which can be found through:

- Your local Area Agency on Aging office (please see Chapter 9)
- Local civic groups
- Local churches and synagogues
- Home health agencies such as the Visiting Nurse Association

3

Services Provided at Home for the Ill

Home Care

Skilled home care, either live-in or for a certain number of hours each week, is provided by licensed health-care professionals such as nurses, practical nurses, and physical or occupational therapists. These professionals work in conjunction with the patient's physician and perform many of the functions that they were trained to carry out in a hospital setting.

Properly organized home care has a great number of advantages over prolonged hospitalization or institutionalization. These advantages include:

- The feeling of security derived from living at home. An older person, especially one who is partially disabled or increasingly frail, derives enormous benefits from being in familiar surroundings.
- Home-cooked meals. Even when conforming to the instructions of a nutritionist, this service can mean a great deal to older people who are set in their ways.
- Positive input from family members. If they can make useful and practical suggestions and contributions to the patient's well-being, they may not feel like helpless visitors in a hospital setting.

All across the country, more and more insurance programs are paying for limited periods of home care so that patients can leave the hospital sooner and return to their familiar home surroundings; it is also cheaper for the insurance programs, which now give hospitals incentives for releasing patients as soon as possible.

How Much Does It Cost?

Depending on the state in which the older person lives, his or her financial situation, and the type of care required, in-home services may be paid for partially or entirely by Medicare, Medicaid, supplementary insurance, a group insurance plan, a health maintenance organization, and/or community programs subsidized by nonprofit organizations or local efforts. If a doctor orders skilled care according to the guidelines set by Medicare or a private insurance company, costs are usually paid in full.

Veterans and their spouses and children may benefit from the Veterans Administration "improved pension program" when a need exists for assistance for a non-service-associated disability. The amount of benefits paid is determined by an individual's economic circumstances and may be used to pay for any type of home care.

Retirees and their spouses usually receive certain home-care services through corporate and union pension plans.

In many states, private health insurance plans are required by law to include coverage for home care under the same conditions that apply to Medicare. In some cases, the policy may not spell out this coverage; call your insurance carrier or speak to your agent to find out about home-care coverage.

For most families of modest or middle income, the problems of payment begin when insurance coverage for maintenance care runs out. Parents who declare that they don't want to go to their children for help didn't realize how quickly a lifetime of savings could be depleted. Even though home health care purchased for a dependent parent is deductible under the federal tax law, it's still quite costly.

The alternative for many older people is to use up their own savings to the point where they become eligible for Medicaid or to embark on a spending-down campaign, which eventually will help them achieve Medicaid eligibility. Often this calculated reduction of assets consists of transferring savings accounts, securities, and other assets to a son or daughter.

Hospice Care

Hospice care is a form of care that was developed by grass-roots organizations determined to find ways in which people could die with dignity.

Hospice care can be care in the home, in a hospital setting, or in a free-standing facility. Wherever possible, hospice care is administered in the patient's home. The underlying philosophy of all hospice programs is that for a person with a limited time to live, symptoms should be relieved and pain alleviated. Until comparatively recently, this philosophy has been and still continues to be resisted by the conventional medical establishment dedicated as it always has been to prolonging the patient's life by whatever means possible.

Whether the program is based in the home, a hospital, or a facility setting, unlimited visiting hours are usually possible, beds are often provided for friends and family members in order to stay over, young children are permitted to visit, and pets are allowed to remain at the bedside of the patient. Consultations with family members and friends occur regularly so that they are trained in as many aspects of caregiving as they can and want to handle.

Most hospice programs also do what they can to ease the pain of loss for the family. Bereavement counseling may continue for months after the patient has died. Volunteer-staffed hospice programs also exist for those who have no family member who lives nearby or even no family. Indeed, the backbone of all hospice programs is the volunteers, many of whom once cared for terminally ill relatives or friends and saw how important other volunteers were to them.

How Much Does It Cost?

Most people using hospice service are reimbursed from Medicare. Medicaid will pay for hospice care in certain states. Many private insurance companies also provide coverage. Since 1982, when the Medicare Hospice Benefit Act was passed, the federal government has allocated more and more funds for hospice care. Hospice care saves Medicare from the far greater expense of hospital or nursing home care.

Medicare-certified hospice programs will receive Medicare reimbursement only if a primary doctor and the patient sign a statement saying that the patient has less than six months to live and if the care is palliative rather than curative.

Where to Find It

Write to the National Hospice Organization, 1901 North Moore Street, Suite 901, Arlington, VA 22209, (800) 658-8898. This organization represents most hospice programs, whether Medicare-certified or independent.

4

Alternative Housing Arrangements for Older People

When an older person can no longer live at home, he or she may go to live with a relative or go into a nursing home. These, however, are not the only alternatives. Almost every city or town in America has a variety of types of intermediate housing. Before we explore the different types of housing arrangements that exist let me discuss what may be a challenging situation for you, the caregiver, to deal with: explaining to the older person why it is that he or she needs to move to a different type of housing arrangement.

A change in living arrangements is disconcerting for all of us; for an older person, however, it is much more difficult. For an older person, home represents identity, a familiar way of life, security, and, perhaps most important, independence. A change in living arrangements means not only leaving the house but separating links to the past.

If the older person denies the need to make a change, you will find this stage of caregiving particularly difficult. The following are a few suggestions that may help you convince the older person that it's in his or her best interest to make a change in residence.

- Plan with, not for, the older person. No adult likes to have decisions made for him or her.

- Try to determine why the older person is resisting making a change. Does he feel as though he'll be abandoned? Does she think a nursing home is the only alternative?

- Deal with the older person's perceptions and feelings; if he or she says that it is perfectly safe living alone, be specific in explaining why you don't think so.

- Talk with the older person about his or her desires and priorities. Determine what is important to her in a living arrangement. Does he feel uncomfortable living with other people? Does she worry about having to give up cherished possessions?

- Don't focus on the older person's limitations as a reason for moving. Avoid statements such as "You can't cook for yourself any more," and instead say, "You will eat well-prepared meals at. . . ."

- Enlist the help of another person, i.e., a friend, a doctor, or a social worker. This person may encounter less resistance in presenting problems and solutions.

Remember, however, to start networking now to find out what is available. Waiting lists are long for just about every type of housing. Be sure to ask questions over the phone and send for written information and brochures and keep accurate notes in your index-card file. Once you have determined which places to consider, visit each one. Follow your instincts about the "feel" of a place; talk to the staff and residents.

VARIOUS TYPES OF HOUSING ARRANGEMENTS

Retirement Communities

Retirement communities are self-contained complexes for older people who wish to live with others of their generation. Often such services as security, recreational choices, and a communal dining room are provided. Sometimes shops and health-service providers are located in the community. Retirement communities can consist of a multiple-unit building, a townhouse, a single-family housing development, mobile or modular homes, or even a small community. Retirement communities are for those older people who are in good health. Housing units may be for rent or for sale, and prices vary widely according to different regions of the country as well as the quality of both housing and services.

Continuous-Care Retirement Communities

Retirement communities with continuous care are set up to take care of their residents' needs throughout the remainder of their life. Because a skilled nursing home facility exists within the community, continuous-care retirement communities can offer both personal housing as in the retirement community and additional home nursing care if needed. This type of community is ideal for couples who remain in the same community even when one partner needs nursing-home care.

Many of these communities are like whole cities with a medical clinic, stores, banks, libraries, a transportation system, and recreational and education facilities. Because of the numerous services and availability of nursing-home care, continuous-care communities can be costly. They usually require a substantial entrance fee (called a founder's fee) as well as monthly charges.

Congregate Housing or Senior Housing

Congregate housing or senior housing is housing that is designed for middle-income older people and built with federal, state, or local government funding. If services are included, it is called "assisted living" or "enriched housing." It is designed for the elderly on fixed retirement incomes who are capable of living independently. Most congregate housing is rented and prices are kept affordable with some rent subsidies available. Usually apartments are in a high-rise building or a garden complex. Residents have their own private apartments including a kitchenette for light meals and snacks. Limited services usually are available, such as meals in a common dining room, housekeeping, transportation, recreation, and security.

Board-and-Care Homes

Board-and care homes are homes of ten people or fewer who need help with personal care. In a well-run home, this can be a friendly, supportive environment for the older person. These homes are usually run by someone licensed by the state health or social service department. Levels of care vary widely from home to home. It is essential that you investigate the home you choose before making a decision.

Generally, most homes provide assistance with bathing, grooming, dressing, getting in and out of bed and the bathtub, and supervision of medications. Meals, housekeeping, and laundry services are also provided. Not all facilities accept people using walkers or wheelchairs, and residents must be fairly alert mentally and able to take themselves to the toilet.

Adult Foster Care

Adult foster care may be provided by individuals who in many cases own a large home and offer foster care to bring in needed income. For a monthly fee meals, housekeeping, assistance with dressing, eating, bathing, and other personal care are provided. This arrangement is a good option for a relatively healthy older person.

Echo Housing

The idea of echo housing originated in Australia where it is known as "granny flats." Elder Cottage Housing Opportunity (ECHO) housing consists of small living units, which can be ordered and set up through a city agency to be placed on the same lot as a family member's house. The units are not mobile homes but are designed to correspond to rulings of local zoning boards. Costs vary from community to community.

Home Sharing

Home sharing is a roommate-matching service for senior citizens. Programs match up individuals of any age including students who want to live in the home of an older person who needs some services and companionship. Please see Chapter 7 for resource information.

Inviting the Senior to Live with You

Finally, another housing option is to have the older person come live with you. Before you consider this option, do some careful thinking about the advantages and disadvantages of this change. Sharing a home with an aging relative or friend almost always introduces stress into a household, and if the relative is in poor physical or mental health the stress can become unbearable. However, if careful planning is done and major adjustments are anticipated, the arrangement can mean an enriched life for all members of the family.

The decision to join households permanently should not be made hastily. Thoughtful planning now will later save everyone resentment and anger.

Before making a commitment, consider the following questions. They will help you come to a decision about whether or not living together is a sensible option. And, if you do decide to live together, the answers to these questions may help to identify potential problems that can be worked through before they occur.

- Begin by asking yourself "Is this something I truly want to do?" or "Am I thinking about doing this out of obligation, guilt, sentimentality, or because this is what others want me to do?" Above all, consider whether or not the older person really wants to live with you.

- Can you get along day after day? Examine past conflicts; pleasant and unpleasant aspects of your relationship with the older person; irritating habits and/or idiosyncrasies, which could be magnified if you lived together. Consider all aspects of potential incompatibility, food preferences, use of alcohol and cigarettes, standards of cleanliness.

- How does everyone in the household feel about a joint living arrangement? Involve your spouse and children in the decision. How good are the in-law relationships?

- Who will be in charge if the older person becomes dependent and needs care? Who will provide the care? How will tasks be delegated and divided among the household? If help is acquired, how will it be paid for? How will long-term caregiving affect the family as a whole? Is everyone aware of the sacrifices required in giving selfless care to an older, dependent, perhaps ill person?

- Does the house have enough space for another person? Is an extra room available? Is a bathroom near the room that has been designated for the older person? Is closet space adequate? Are living areas sufficient to accommodate everyone?

- How will the financial arrangements be worked out?

5

Nursing Homes

The decision to place a loved one in a nursing home is never an easy one. Mere mention of the words conjures up terrible images of neglect, abuse, abandonment, and dingy surroundings. Although there are truly awful places, many are not.

The necessity of nursing-home care may come suddenly, after a turn for the worse in a loved one's state of health or when a caregiver even with professional help can no longer manage. Finances certainly enter into a decision, for around-the-clock nursing care at home is usually prohibitively expensive compared to similar care provided in a nursing home.

Admission to a nursing home has to be arranged through a doctor, who signs papers stating that the candidate has a medical need, which requires twenty-four-hour access to skilled medical care or intermediate custodial care.

Skilled nursing care is care provided around the clock by registered nurses, licensed practical nurses, and nursing assistants. This care includes such services as oxygen therapy, feeding tubes, dressing changes, draining of body fluids, and administration of intravenous fluids. A staff physician oversees care. Only a small portion of nursing home residents receive this kind of care. Often such patients are recuperating from a serious illness, which was previously treated in a hospital, or from a serious operation.

Intermediate custodial care is for people who cannot live independently because of one or more severe disabling or chronic illnesses. This type of care is particularly suited to the Alzheimer's disease patient or the stroke victim, for example. Unfortunately, this kind of care is rarely paid for by Medicare or private insurance except in limited circumstances and then only for a few weeks. Once the patient's assets have been depleted Medicaid will sometimes pick up the tab. Most private nursing homes require two to three years of residence before payment through Medicaid is allowed. The for-profit nursing home often shuns patients on Medicaid because the program provides limited reimbursement.

The following are some of the steps the reader needs to follow in choosing a suitable nursing home for an elderly loved one. If the patient is moving from a hospital to a nursing home, the reader has the advantage of being able to use the services of the hospital's social work department. The reader should work with the discharge planner and listen to his or her suggestions. No decisions, however, should be made without the caregiver's approval. Remember, discharge planners work for the hospital, and it is their job to get patients out of the hospital by a specific discharge date in order to save the hospital from penalties for keeping the patient longer than the time allotted by Medicare. The discharge planner is more likely to come up with a quick-and-easy solution rather than the right solution.

SELECTING A NURSING HOME

Most nursing homes with good reputations have long waiting lists. Families who wait until a medical emergency arises often are shocked and distraught to hear that no places will be open for months or sometimes years in the "best" homes. I suggest that you begin looking around at nursing homes and "sign up" for those that look acceptable as soon as you begin to determine that the older person's health is deteriorating. Being on waiting lists and in contact with homes you like will allow the older person to gain easy access after a sudden illness, a debilitating condition, or when the time comes that you can no longer care for the older person at home. You can always say "no" to a nursing home if the time is not right and ask to keep the older person's name active on the waiting list. You may have to pay a deposit to get onto the list. Be sure to find out whether you forfeit the deposit in the event that you do not want a place when one becomes available.

Find out about nearby nursing homes from your doctor, a social worker, or friends who have placed relatives or friends in nursing homes. You can get a list of homes from your local Area Agency on Aging office (see Chapter 9) or a local Senior Citizen's center. Once you have compiled a list of potential homes, make arrangements to visit them. Make at least one and if possible several visits to any home you are seriously considering. Take someone along with you; two pairs of eyes are better than one.

You should try to meet the director of the home and staff members as well as several residents. A tour of the home is essential; excellent times to visit are during mealtime and on the weekend. By observing during mealtimes you can see whether or not residents are eating properly, are interacting with each other, and are being treated courteously by the staff. (Usually nursing homes have a smaller staff on weekends and by observing during this time, you can determine how well the home is run with limited staff.)

The staff is probably the most important component of a home. Observe how staff members talk to residents. Are they patient and respectful? Do they care for patients gently and kindly? In a reputable home, the staff will encourage you to be involved in your friend or relative's plan of care. Talk to residents and their families. Many homes have residents' councils and family councils; members of these councils are excellent people to contact.

Ask the following questions when evaluating a nursing home:

- Is the home licensed by the state? (This is a must.) Is the facility Medicare- and Medicaid-licensed?

- Is the facility a member of the American Health Care Association or the American Association of Homes for the Aged?

- What is the ratio of registered nurses, licensed practical nurses, and nurses' aides to patients on any shift?

- Is a physician on call twenty-four hours a day, as required by law? Is there a physician on permanent staff within the facility?

- When would a medical situation be considered beyond the staff's capabilities? What is the hospital-transfer policy?

- Is psychiatric or psychological counseling available?

- When are visiting hours?

- Can residents bring their own furniture and mementos?

- Is the neighborhood quiet?

- What are the daily activities for both mobile patients and for bedridden patients?

- Are religious services offered?

- Is a hairdressing service available?

- Is there a dietitian on staff?
- Will meals be delivered to rooms if patients don't come to the dining room?
- Are patients weighed routinely?
- What is the basic monthly fee?
- How long does someone have to live at the home to be eligible for Medicaid?

6

Arranging and Checking Care from Afar

If you live far from the older person you're caring for, you face specific problems as well as the guilt and frustration of not being able to do enough to help with day-to-day difficulties and crises when they arise. If you must manage the task of caring from afar, here are some suggestions to make your job easier.

When You Visit a Senior

- Be observant about health and safety issues.
- Notice if there is a change in health status.
- Notice if the older person is eating properly.
- Find out if friends visit.
- Notice if the house is clean and in good repair.
- Talk to neighbors, friends, and aides about how the senior copes when you're not there. You may uncover all kinds of problems needing resolution that he or she has kept from you.
- Arrange for and hire services well before you leave the older person.
- Make sure you have a network of back-up assistance for an emergency,

and give the individuals who are involved the names and phone numbers of local people to contact. Include your own name, work and home phone numbers, other family members, doctors, a private geriatric care manager if applicable, and neighbors in your network.

- Leave a house key with a trusted neighbor for use in emergencies.
- Consider hiring a private geriatric care manager (please refer to next section). Ask the manager to report to you regularly and as emergencies arise.

When You Call a Senior

- Establish a routine for telephone calls. Try to get other family members to help with the job of staying in touch with the older person.
- Be alert to any changes in physical or mental condition. Increased frequency of telephone calls, calls at odd times of the day or night, and calls for no apparent reason are tipoffs that something is not right. You need to find out what is wrong and solve the problem. Frequent repetition of information, forgetfulness, and slurred speech are also signs of a problem.

PRIVATE GERIATRIC-CARE MANAGERS

Private geriatric-care managers are a by-product of the huge growth in the elderly population. They are proving to be especially helpful for those who live far from the older person they are caring for and those who have a full-time job. Compared with caseworkers for government agencies, care managers usually are more available and more flexible about the service they offer. But their fees are hefty, averaging $80–$150 an hour depending on the task, and these fees are not covered by health insurance or Medicare. Care managers are either social workers, nurses, psychologists, or private practitioners who hold degrees in gerontology.

Care managers arrange for community-based services such as those offered by visiting nurses; occupational, physical, speech, or other therapists; homemakers; and organizations that provide home-delivered meals. Often care managers work with families, bank trust officers, or attorneys to ensure that an older person's government benefits are maintained and that assets are preserved. They may also help complete insurance or government assistance application forms and provide advocacy when disputes arise over coverage. Some care managers handle financial and bookkeeping functions to help clients organize their bills, write checks, and prepare taxes.

You can call or write to The National Association of Private Geriatric Care Managers to receive information about geriatric care management and the names and credentials of managers in your area. Call (602) 881-8008 or write to NAPGCM, 1604 North Country Club Road, Tucson, AZ 85711.

Anyone can set up a practice as a geriatric-care manager, and the number of people who do is growing. Make sure the person you hire has proper credentials. If possible, use a practitioner who has been approved for membership in the NAPGCM. Once you have found a care manager, determine if he or she is qualified by asking the following questions:

- What is your training and experience in gerontology?
- How long have you been in private practice?
- What state licenses permitting you to practice do you have?
- Who substitutes for you if you are ill or on vacation?
- What are your fees?
- What services do you provide directly and which do you arrange through outside providers?
- Can you provide references from other clients?

Part II

The Sources

7

Associations and Organizations Directed toward the Needs of Older Americans

This section is an invaluable resource guide for older Americans and their caregivers. It contains listings of associations and organizations that provide invaluable help to older Americans, their caregivers, or health-care providers. For every major disease there is an organization that will help an individual understand what treatment is appropriate and where that treatment can be found. Associations exist that assist the elderly with everything, including case management; information and referral to appropriate health, welfare, educational, social, recreational, and vacation services; government benefits and entitlements; personal counseling; and financial assistance for health and medical long-term care. There are organizations directed toward private caregivers and professional caregivers such as nurses, occupational therapists, physical therapists, and social workers.

This section is divided into three parts: advocacy, information, and research groups, caregiving services, and health-care organizations. The various associations/foundations are listed alphabetically within each section.

Older people and their caregivers will find that the members of these foundations/associations can be exceedingly helpful. Use them to your best advantage.

Cancer

Alliance for Cannabis Therapeutics
P.O. Box 21210
Washington, DC 20009
(202) 483-8595
Robert Randall, President

Advocacy group fighting to end the existing federal prohibition on the medical use of cannabis for treating seriously ill patients, including those with glaucoma, multiple sclerosis, and cancer.

AMC Cancer Information and Counseling Line
(American Medical Center)
1600 Pierce Street
Denver, CO 80214
(800) 525-3777; (303) 233-6501

Nonprofit organization. Professional counselors answer questions, send written materials, offer advice and reassurance to cancer sufferers and families. Offers laminated card to hang in shower with instructions for breast self-examination. Call (303) 239-3421.

American Cancer Society
1599 Clifton Road, NE
Atlanta, GA 30329
(404) 320-3333; Fax 325-0230
John R. Beffrin, Ph.D., Executive Vice President

A voluntary organization that funds cancer research and offers educational programs to the public and health-care professionals on cancer prevention, detection, and treatment. ACS has over 3,000 divisions across the country providing services such as self-help and support groups, transportation programs, and home-care items.

Association of Community Cancer Centers
11600 Nebel Street, Suite 201
Rockville, MD 20852
(301) 984-9496; Fax 770-1949
Lee E. Mortenson, Executive Director

Association of providers (institutions and individuals) of cancer care. Encourages professional communication. Promotes improved quality of care and clinical research, all in community settings.

R. A. Bloch Cancer Foundation
H and R Block Building
4410 Main
Kansas City, MO 64111
(816) 932-8453; Fax 753-5346
A. J. Yarmot, Contact

Organization operating the Cancer Hot Line, a telephone support system matching newly diagnosed cancer patients with volunteers (cured, in remission, or with the same diagnosis) and directing them to the Cancer Management Center for second opinions (if requested). Cancer Hot Lines in St. Louis and Kansas City, MO; Ft. Lauderdale, FL; Ft. Worth, TX; Oklahoma City, OK; Cleveland, OH; and Pittsburgh, PA.

Cancer Care
1180 Avenue of the Americas
New York, NY 10036
(212) 221-3300; Fax (212) 719-0263
Diane Blum, Executive Director

Organization promoting social services for cancer patients and their families. Offers social work counseling guidance and professional consultation/education. Supports social research on the impact of catastrophic illness (emotional, financial, etc.). Provides financial assistance for home care, child care, transportation, and medical treatment.

Cancer Control Society

2043 North Berendo Street
Los Angeles, CA 90027
(213) 663-7801
Norman Fritz, President

Association of patients/physicians/others promoting the prevention and control of cancer through nontoxic alternative therapies, including: wheat grass, enzymes, Koch, Hoxsey, Gerson, immunology, mega-vitamins, and laetrile. Maintains 24-hour information hotline and direct mail information service. Provides physician and patient lists.

Cancer Federation, Inc.

21250 Box Springs Road, No. 209
Moreno Valley, CA 92387
(800) 982-3720; Fax (714) 682-0169
John Steinbacher, Executive Director

Organization promoting cancer research and education. Provides counseling to cancer patients and their families. Sponsors charitable programs.

Cancer Guidance Institute

1323 Forbes Avenue, Suite 200
Pittsburgh, PA 15219
(412) 261-2211
Estelle Weissburg, Executive Director

Organization addressing the psychological impact of cancer, and the healing power of attitudes/emotions in recovery. Offers consulting service, self-help groups, speakers' bureau, lectures, and workshops.

Corporate Angel Network (CAN)

Westchester County Airport
Building One
White Plains, NY 10604
(914) 328-1313; Fax (800) 328-4226
Judith Haims, Administrator

Transportation service offered by U.S. corporations that own aircraft. Empty seats are given to cancer patients needing transportation to or from recognized treatment centers. One attendant or family member may accompany the patient without charge. Patient must meet certain self-care requirements and must have medical authorization for the flight.

Foundation for Advancement in Cancer Therapy
Box 1242, Old Chelsea Station
New York, NY 10113
(212) 741-2790
Ruth Sackerman, President

Organization of individuals promoting nutrition, detoxification, and mind-body cohesion as complements to traditional cancer therapies. Encourages public education on nontoxic biological alternatives to surgery, chemotherapy, and radiation. Supports cancer/nutrition research. Fights for the elimination of environmental carcinogens.

International Association of Cancer Victors and Friends
7740 West Manchester Avenue, No. 110
Playa Del Rey, CA 90293
(213) 822-5032; Fax (213) 822-5132
Ann L. Cinquina, Executive Director

Organization promoting independent cancer research. Provides information on nontoxic chemotherapies. Offers one-on-one support services to cancer patients. Maintains library and sponsors educational programs on topics such as environmental carcinogens.

International Health Council
P.O. Box 151
Fairbanks, AK 99707
Walter Ermer, President

Organization supporting early detection and treatment of cancer in order to prevent cancer deaths. Promotes public awareness.

Make Today Count, Inc.
P.O. Box 6063
Kansas City, KS 66106-0063
Sandra Butler Whyte, Executive Director

A nonprofit organization with over 150 chapters across the country providing information and emotional support to people with life-threatening illnesses and to their caregivers. MTC, Inc., publishes a bimonthly newsletter, holds group support meetings, offers a telephone "buddy" system, home and hospital visits, and emergency transportation.

National Cancer Institute
Cancer Information Service
NCI/NIH, Building 31, Room 10A24
9000 Rockville Pike
Bethesda, MD 20892
(800) 4-CANCER; Fax (301) 402-0555
Kate Duffy, Chief

NCI is the government's principal agency for funding cancer research and distributing information about cancer to health-care professionals and the public. Through its toll-free number, the institute provides the latest information about cancer treatment and where to get it. You can also call to obtain a list of publications about different forms of cancer.

National Coalition for Cancer Survivorship
1010 Wayne Avenue, Suite 300
Silver Spring, MD 20910
(301) 585-2616; Fax (301) 588-3408
Catherine Logan, Executive Director

The coalition's mission is to let those who are victims of cancer know that there can still be a vibrant and productive life to lead after diagnosis. It has an information clearinghouse and referral service on all aspects of cancer and its accompanying life problems. Free publications and resources available upon request.

National Committee for Radiation Victims
6935 Laurel Avenue, Suite 202
Takoma Park, MD 20912
(301) 891-3990; Fax (301) 891-3992
E. Cooper Brown, Director

Information clearinghouse on radiation exposure, victims' organizations, legislation, and existing radiation standards/practices. Provides public service information on the effects of manmade ionizing radiation. Offers speakers' bureau.

Nevada Test Site Radiation Victim Association
953 East Sahara, Suite E-15A
Las Vegas, NV 89104
(702) 737-6009
Bennie F. Levy, President

Legal advocacy organization serving the widows and survivors of individuals exposed to radiation at the Nevada Test Site. Seeks compensation for contracted employees who work/have worked in that area. Collects research data on cancer deaths among individuals who have worked at the site.

United Cancer Council
8009 Fishback Road
Indianapolis, IN 46298-1047
Randall B. Grove, President

Alliance of cancer agencies promoting direct service provision for cancer patients and their families. Supports public education.

We Can Do!
c/o Jackalyn Rainosek
5373 West Alabama, Suite 250
Houston, TX 77056
(713) 780-1057
Jackalyn Rainosek, Executive Officer

Support organization concentrating on the psychological aspects of cancer. Offers no medical advice or services. Promotes emotional well-being of cancer patients. Offers weekly educational program and support group. Provides therapy program for stress reduction, relaxation, biofeedback. Holds classes for spouses. Provides referral service.

Well Spouse Foundation
P.O. Box 28876
San Diego, CA 92128
(619) 673-9043
Barbara Drucker, President

Support group for relatives/spouses of chronically ill individuals. Provides advocacy services.

BRAIN TUMORS

American Brain Tumor Association (ABTA)
3725 North Talman Avenue
Chicago, IL 60618
(312) 286-5571; Fax 549-5561; (800) 886-2282
Naomi Berkowitz, Executive Director

Alliance of health-care professionals, patients, and families promoting the treatment of brain tumors. Raises funds for research. Provides patient education; seeks to increase public awareness. Offers referral service to medical specialists, treatment centers, and support groups.

BREAST CANCER

Breast Cancer Advisory Center
P.O. Box 224
Kensington, MD 20895
Fax (301) 949-1132
Rose Kushner, Executive Director

Information clearinghouse on breast cancer. Provides referral service. Features library, lectures, and informative materials.

Susan J. Komen Breast Cancer Foundation
5005 LBJ, Suite 370
Dallas, TX 75244
(214) 450-1777; Fax (214) 450-1710; (800) IM-AWARE
Patrick McDonough, Executive Director

Organization promoting early detection, research, and treatment of breast cancer. Provides political advocacy services in seeking insurance coverage for breast cancer examination. Offers education and speakers' bureau. Promotes self-examination.

National Alliance of Breast Cancer Organizations
1180 Avenue of the Americas, Second Floor
New York, NY 10036
(212) 719-0154; Fax (212) 768-8828
Amy Langer, Administrative Director

Resource center for information about breast cancer, breast diseases, detection, care, and research. Offers health policy advocacy services and advice on political legislation. Provides educational materials, as well as information on support groups, breast-care centers, and hospital programs.

Reach to Recovery
c/o American Cancer Society
1599 Clifton Road, NE
Atlanta, GA 30329
(404) 320-3333
Jerilynn Jones, Contact

Peer-support program for women with breast cancer. Offers short-term visitation by volunteers (at physician's request) to discuss physical, emotional, and cosmetic needs and to provide preoperative and postoperative support and information to the patient and her family.

Society for the Study of Breast Disease
Sammons Tower
3409 Worth
Dallas, TX 75246
(214) 821-2962; Fax (214) 827-7032
George N. Peters, M.D., Secretary

Association of health-care professionals involved in the study of breast diseases. Provides information on diagnosis and treatment developments to physicians and other health-care professionals. Promotes research. Encourages professional discussion.

Y-Me National Organization for Breast Cancer Information and Support
c/o Sharon Green
18220 Harwood Avenue
Homewood, IL 60430
(708) 799-8338; Fax (708) 799-5937; (800) 221-2141,
    weekdays; (708) 799-8228, 24-hour hotline
Sharon Green, Executive Director

Peer-support organization for women with breast cancer. Offers information, counseling, referral service, hotline, and library.

INNER EAR TUMORS

Acoustic Neuroma Association
P.O. Box 12402
Atlanta, GA 30355
(404) 237-8023; Fax (404) 237-8023
Sally Anderson, Contact

Patient-support organization for those who have had acoustic neuroma (inner ear tumor) or other tumors affecting cranial nerves and neural tissue. Provides rehabilitation information to health-care professionals. Encourages research and public awareness.

INTESTINAL CANCER

United Ostomy Association
36 Executive Park, Suite 120
Irvine, CA 92714
(714) 660-8624; Fax (714) 660-9262
Darlene Smith, Executive Director

Patient-support organization for those who have undergone ostomy (colostomy, ileostomy, ileal conduit, or ureterostomy surgery). Provides moral support and practical advice. Sponsors patient-to-patient visits. Encourages public education.

LEUKEMIA

Leukemia Society of America
600 Third Avenue
New York, NY 10016
(212) 573-8484; Fax (212) 972-5776; (800) 955-4LSA
Rudolph F. Badum, Acting President & CEO

Organization providing patients and families with information, telephone counseling, and literature. Financial aid awarded to qualified outpatients being treated for leukemia, lymphomas, multiple myelomas and Hodgkin's disease; support groups.

National Leukemia Association
585 Stewart Avenue, Suite 536
Garden City, NY 11530
(516) 222-1944; Fax (516) 222-0457
Allan D. Weinberg, Executive Director

Organization promoting research and public awareness of leukemia. Offers financial assistance to families in need. Provides referral service and children's service.

LUNG CANCER

American Lung Association
1740 Broadway
New York, NY 10019-4374
(212) 315-8700; Fax (212) 265-5642
John R. Garrison, Managing Director

A voluntary organization, which funds research and conducts educational programs about lung diseases, including influenza, pneumonia, emphysema, chronic bronchitis, and lung cancer. Smoking-cessation programs are also provided. A list of free publications by the association is also available upon request.

Spirit and Breath Association
8210 Elmwood Avenue, Suite 209
Skokie, IL 60077
(708) 673-1384
Morton Liebling, Founder and Director

Support organization for lung cancer patients and their families. Provides moral and physical support. Encourages information exchange. Supports physical and psychological rehabilitation. Offers volunteer visitation program to hospitalized patients. Maintains speakers' bureau.

PROSTATE CANCER

American Foundation for Urologic Disease
300 West Pratt Street, Suite 401
Baltimore, MD 21201
(410) 727-2908; Fax (410) 783-1566; (800) 243-2383
Sandra K. Wiseman, Executive Director

Medical research/education organization concerned with urologic diseases. Offers education programs to the public on such topics as childhood urologic problems and prostate cancer. Supports research.

National Kidney and Urologic Diseases Information Clearinghouse
P.O. Box NKUDIC
9000 Rockville Pike
Bethesda, MD 20892
(301) 468-6345
Elizabeth H. Singer, Director

Referral and resource information clearinghouse on kidney and urologic diseases. Distributes educational information to patients, health-care professionals, and the public. Responds directly to written and telephone inquiries.

SKIN CANCER

Skin Cancer Foundation
245 Fifth Avenue, Suite 2402
New York, NY 10016
(212) 725-5176; Fax (212) 725-5751
Perry Robins, President

Foundation concerned with the prevention and early detection of skin cancer. Funds research and sponsors medical symposia. Provides public education programs. Assesses sunscreen products for effectiveness as skin-damage prevention agents.

Caregiving

Aging in America
1500 Pelham Parkway South
Bronx, NY 10461
(718) 824-4004; Fax (718) 597-1524
Ralph Hall, President

Research and service organization for professionals in gerontology. Objectives are to produce, implement, and share effective and affordable programs and services to improve the quality of life for the elderly and to better prepare professionals and students interested in or currently involved with aging and the aged.

Alliance for Aging Research
2021 K Street, NW, Suite 305
Washington, DC 20006
(202) 293-2856; Fax (202) 785-8574
Daniel Perry, Executive Director

Includes gerontologists and other medical professionals who work to increase private and public research into aging. Supports policies concerning productive aging and independence for older Americans.

American Federation for Aging Research
1414 Avenue of the Americas, Eighteenth Floor
New York, NY 10019
(212) 752-2327; Fax (212) 832-2298
Stephanie Lederman, Executive Director

Purpose is to stimulate and fund research on the aging.

American Foundation for Aging Research
North Carolina State University
Biochemistry Department
128 Polk Hall
Raleigh, NC 27695-7622
(919) 737-5679; Fax (919) 737-5679
Paul F. Agris, President

Supports basic research and educational opportunities for the study of age-related diseases and the biology of aging.

American Longevity Association

1000 West Carson Street
Torrance, CA 90509
(310) 544-7057
Robert J. Morin, M.D., President

Scientists and laypersons interested in the acceleration of research programs that study the mechanisms of aging including arteriosclerosis, heart attack, and stroke, and other areas relevant to longevity such as the use of artificial hearts and the cryopreservation of organs.

American Society on Aging

833 Market Street, Suite 512
San Francisco, CA 94103
(415) 882-2910; Fax (415) 882-4280
Gloria H. Cavanaugh, Executive Director

Works to enhance the well-being of older individuals and to foster unity among those who work for and with the elderly. Offers 25 continuing education programs for professionals in aging-related fields.

Association for Adult Development and Aging

c/o American Counseling Association
5999 Stevenson Avenue
Alexandria, VA 22304
(703) 823-9800; Fax (703) 823-0252
Theodore P. Remley, Executive Director

Seeks to improve the competence and skills of A.A.C.D. and A.A.D.A. members and expand professional work opportunities in adult development and aging counseling.

Center for the Study of Aging

706 Madison Avenue
Albany, NY 12208
(518) 465-6927; Fax (518) 462-1339
Robert L. Lowry, President

Promotes education, research, training, and provides leadership in the field of health and fitness for older people.

Center for the Study of Pharmacy and Therapeutics for the Elderly

c/o Peter P. Lamy, Ph.D.
School of Pharmacy
20 North Pine Street, Room 352
Baltimore, MD 21201
(301) 328-3011; Fax (301) 328-4012
Peter P. Lamy, Director

Conducts research in geriatrics and gerontology, particularly as they relate to pharmacotherapy and pharmacodynamics.

Children of Aging Parents

Woodbourne Office Campus, Suite 302A
1609 Woodbourne Road
Levittown, PA 19057
(215) 945-6900

National, nonprofit organization, offering information and referrals. Self-help group devoted to education, support, and the development of coping skills of caregivers to the elderly. Workshops encourages development of support groups; provides referrals to appropriate professionals. Most activities in Pennsylvania and New Jersey, but acts as national clearinghouse for information, guidance, advice, and networking to groups and individuals. Newsletter, publications.

Dependent Care Connection Inc.

P.O. Box 2783
Westport, CT 06880
(203) 226-2680

National dependent-care assistance company providing direct referrals to local child-care and elder-care service providers in communities throughout the United States. A service for employers as a benefit to employees.

Eldercare America, Inc.

1141 Loxford Terrace
Silver Spring, MD 20901
(301) 593-1621

Lobbying group for people who care for elderly, caretakers, to get benefits.

Family Caregivers of the Aging
c/o National Council on the Aging
409 Third Street, SW, Second Floor
Washington, DC 20024
(800) 424-9046; (202) 479-1200

Offers practical help to caregivers and serves as a resource for referrals to adult day-care centers, senior centers, support groups, and other programs. Newsletter and guidebooks.

Families USA Foundation
1334 G Street, NW
Washington, DC 20005

A health-care consumer advocate group. Focuses on improving living conditions for elderly, families, and minorities. Issues of interest: nursing home insurance, prescription drug cost, health insurance coverage, and rising health costs. Develops projects and educational activities designed to help older adults. Information or publication list available upon written request.

Gerontological Society of America
1275 K Street, NW, Suite 350
Washington, DC 20005
(202) 842-1275
John M. Cornman, Director

Professionals interested in improving the well-being of older people by promoting scientific study of the aging process, publishing information for older professionals about aging, and bringing together groups interested in aging research.

Health Promotion Institute
409 Third Street, NW, Second Floor
Washington, DC 20024
(202) 479-1200
Mary Connolly, Program Manager

Seeks to aid professionals who are interested in developing and implementing health promotion programs for senior citizens and in serving older consumers. Advocates for and empowers older adults to achieve health and well-being through a multidisciplinary approach.

InterCare

P.O. Box 8561
Moscow, ID 83843
(509) 229-3259; Fax 229-3259
Theodore Carcich, Jr., President

Aims are to improve long-term health care and to encourage high standards of professional care and administration. InterCare interacts with professional groups, academic institutions, and government agencies to discover solutions to the problems of the aged, chronically ill, and disabled.

International Federation on Aging

601 E Street, NW
Washington, DC 20049-1170
(202) 434-2430; Fax (202) 434-6494
Charlotte Nusberg, Secretary General

Purposes are to serve as an international advocate for the aging in order to exchange information on cross-national levels of development in aging, which are of primary interest to the practitioner, and to assist in the creation of associations for the aging.

Leadership Council of Aging Organizations

c/o National Council of Senior Citizens
1331 F Street, NW
Washington, DC 20004-1171
(202) 347-8800
Daniel J. Schulder, Chairman

Objective is to further the public's understanding of the potential and needs of older persons. Acts as coordinating body in reviewing and acting on public policy issues.

Lifespan Resources

1212 Roosevelt
Ann Arbor, MI 48104
(313) 663-9891
Carol Tice, President

Designs, develops, and implements innovations for programs involving interaction between youth and senior citizens. Develops policy initiatives to assist states in determining their intergenerational program needs.

Disabilities

Adventures in Movement for the Handicapped (AIM)
945 Danbury Road
Dayton, OH 45420
(513) 294-4611; (513) Fax 294-3783
Dr. Jo A. Geiger, Executive Director

Support organization, which developed and promotes the AIM Method of Specialized Movement Education, to improve muscle control and coordination through rhythmic exercises of gross- and fine-motor movements. The program is suitable/adaptable to various handicaps, including visual impairment, hearing impairment, learning disabilities, emotional problems, and orthopedic problems.

The Association for Persons with Severe Handicaps (TASH)
11201 Greenwood Avenue North
Seattle, WA 98133
(206) 361-8870; Fax (206) 361-9208
Liz Lindley, Executive Director

Organization that publishes a monthly newsletter and quarterly journal reporting innovations and research for persons with handicaps. Also makes referrals.

Clearinghouse for Disability Information
U.S. Department of Education
Office of Special Education and Rehabilitative Services
Switzer Building, Room 3132
Washington, DC 20202-2524
(202) 205-8241

Information clearinghouse that answers questions about persons with disabilities. Provides referrals to local organizations. Responds to a wide range of inquiries. Focuses on federally funded programs serving disabled persons and on federal legislation affecting the disabled community. Provides a publication, *A Pocket Guide to Federal Help for Individuals with Disabilities*, upon request.

Coalition on Sexuality and Disability
122 East Twenty-third Street
New York, NY 10010
(212) 242-3900; Fax (516) 737-5547
Lou Markowitz, President

Organization providing education, training, and advocacy for sexual health-care services for individuals with disabilities. Fosters sexuality/disability research. Promotes exchange of information and increased public awareness of the issue.

Foundation for Hospice and Home Care
519 C Street, NE
Washington, DC 20002
(202) 547-6586; Fax (202) 546-8968
Bill Halamandaris, CEO

Dedicated to helping people set up quality home care and hospices, as an alternative to institutional care. It provides certification programs and workshops for home health aides and publishes educational materials.

National Association for Hearing and Speech Action
10801 Rockville Pike
Rockville, MD 20852
(800) 638-8255 (Voice/TDD); Consumer Helpline (301) 897-8682

Toll-free number to ask questions about hearing and speech; makes referrals to certified audiologists; offers free brochures about hearing, hearing aids, communication disorders, and aging.

National Library Service for the Blind and Physically Handicapped
1291 Taylor Street, NW
Washington, DC 20542
(800) 424-8567; (202) 287-5100

Provides materials to visually impaired, blind, and handicapped people by mail through local libraries. Material can be ordered through toll-free number.

Diseases of Aging

ALZHEIMER'S DISEASE

Alzheimer's Association
919 North Michigan Avenue, Suite 1000
Chicago, IL 60611
(312) 335-8700; Fax (312) 335-1110; (800) 621-0379
Edward Truschke, President

Believes that long-term care should be geared toward individual needs and provided in a spectrum ranging from nursing care to independent living. Attempts to determine the cause, treatment, and cure for the disease; provides educational programs; represents the continuing care needs of the affected population before government and social service agencies. Works to develop family support systems for relatives of victims of the disease.

Alzheimer's Disease International
919 North Michigan Avenue, Suite 1000
Chicago, IL 60611
(312) 335-5777; Fax (312) 335-1122
Edward Truschke, Secretary General

Group of physicians and other individuals interested in discovering treatments and a cure for Alzheimer's disease. Sponsors organ donation program.

ARTHRITIS

Arthritis Foundation
1314 Spring Street, NW
Atlanta, GA 30309
(404) 872-7100; Fax (404) 872-0457
Don L. Riggin, CAE, President

A volunteer organization supporting research for a cure for arthritis and providing support services for people with arthritis and other rheumatic diseases. Services provided include exercise programs, support groups, physician referrals, and courses in arthritis management.

National Arthritis and Musculoskeletal and Skin Disease Information Clearinghouse
9000 Rockville Pike
P.O. Box AMS
Bethesda, MD 20892-2903
(301) 495-4484; Fax (301) 587-4352

Provides information about federal programs related to rheumatic and musculoskeletal diseases and skin diseases. Also provides a number of free publications.

EMPHYSEMA

Emphysema Anonymous, Inc.
P.O. Box 3224
Seminole, FL 34642
(813) 391-9977
William E. Jaeckle, Executive Director

Support organization concerned with emphysema. Offers education and assistance to patients and provides nonmedical counseling to patients and their families.

GLAUCOMA

Foundation for Glaucoma Research
490 Post Street, Suite 830
San Francisco, CA 94102
(415) 986-3162; Fax (415) 986-3763
Tara L. Steele, Executive Director

Research-supporting organization fighting glaucoma. Provides clinical programs, promotes public awareness, and maintains support network for informal counseling from experienced patients and relatives.

National Eye Care Project
P.O. Box 429098
San Francisco, CA 94142-9098
(415) 561-8520; (800) 222-EYES
B. Thomas Hutchinson, M.D., Chairman

A project of the Foundation of the American Academy of Ophthalmology, this 7,000-member group of ophthalmologists provides free medical and surgical eye care to economically disadvantaged and elderly individuals. Provides referrals and information on participating physicians. Offers information on eye diseases related to aging.

HEARING LOSS

Association of Late-Deafened Adults
P.O. Box 641763
Chicago, IL 60664-1763
(815) 549-5741 (Voice/TDD); Fax (815) 459-5753
Bill Graham, President

Information and support for individuals who have become deaf as adults. Offers self-help groups, social events, workshops, seminars, speakers' bureau, and research programs.

OSTEOPOROSIS

National Osteoporosis Foundation (NOF)
1150 Seventeenth Street, Suite 500
Washington, DC 20037
(202) 223-2226; Fax 223-2237
Sandra C. Raymond, Executive Director

NOF is dedicated to reducing the widespread prevalence of osteoporosis. A list of free publications is available upon request. Membership entitles you to the quarterly newsletter, *The Osteoporosis Report*, containing information on diagnosis, prevention, treatment, and support groups.

PROSTATE DISEASES

American Foundation for Urologic Disease
300 West Pratt Street, Suite 401
Baltimore, MD 21201
(410) 727-2908; Fax (410) 783-1566; (800) 243-2383
Sandra K. Wiseman, Executive Director

Medical research/education organization concerned with urologic diseases. Offers education programs to the public on such topics as childhood urologic problems and prostate cancer. Supports research.

American Urological Association
1120 North Charles Street
Baltimore, MD 21201
(301) 727-1100; Fax (301) 625-2390
G. James Gallagher, Executive Director

Encourages research on treatment of conditions of the urinary tract. Contact the association for names of local board-certified urologists.

Continence Restored, Inc.
785 Park Avenue
New York, NY 10021
(212) 879-3131
Anne Smith-Young, President

The organization has established a network of support groups throughout the country and disseminates information on incontinence. Provides information on local support groups and will direct you to sources of care.

Help for Incontinent People (HIP)
P.O. Box 544
Union, SC 29379
(803) 579-7900; Fax (803) 579-7902; (800) BLADDER
Katherine F. Jeter, Director

A nonprofit advocacy organization for people with urinary incontinence. Its mission is to educate the public and health-care professionals about causes, diagnosis, treatment, and management of this problem. Call for information and referral services. Personal questions about incontinence will be answered by mail when accompanied by a business-size, stamped, self-addressed envelope. A list of publications is available upon request.

International Association for Enterostomal Therapy
2755 Bristol Street, Suite 110
Costa Mesa, CA 92626
(714) 476-0268
Debi Dahlman, Executive Director

An organization of nurses who specialize in the prevention and treatment of pressure ulcers and the management of incontinence, wounds, and ostomies. Call for names of nurses in your area.

National Kidney and Urologic Diseases Information Clearinghouse
P.O. Box NKUDIC
9000 Rockville Pike
Bethesda, MD 20892
(301) 468-6345
Elizabeth H. Singer, Director

Referral and resource information clearinghouse on kidney and urologic diseases. Distributes educational information to patients, health-care professionals, and the public. Responds directly to written and telephone inquiries.

The Simon Foundation for Incontinence
Box 815
Wilmette, IL 60091
(708) 864-3913; Fax (708) 864-9758; (800) 23SIMON
Cheryle B. Gartley, President

Educates the public and professionals about incontinence and its management. The toll-free number provides information about basic membership. You can also order a free information kit about incontinence issues and a copy of *The Informer*, a quarterly magazine for those interested in incontinence control.

RESPIRATORY DISEASES

National Association for Ventilator Dependent Individuals
3601 Poplar Street
P.O. Box 3666
Erie, PA 16508
(814) 455-6171
Daniel W. Dubowski, President

Support group for respiratory patients requiring long- or short-term ventilator use. Educates health-care service personnel. Works to increase public awareness. Distributes information on resources, services, and education.

National Jewish Center for Immunology and Respiratory Medicine
1400 Jackson Street
Denver, CO 80266
(303) 388-4461; (800) 222-LUNG
Leonard Perlmutter, President

A teaching and research center providing clinical care for patients with respiratory diseases. The toll-free number offers information about these diseases and their treatment, and names of doctors who have completed the training program at the center.

OTHER AGING-RELATED ASSOCIATIONS

American Aging Association
c/o Denham Harman, M.D.
600 South Forty-second Street
Omaha, NE 68198-4635
(402) 559-4416
Denham Harman, Executive Director

Dedicated to "helping people live better longer" by promoting bio-medical aging studies directed toward slowing down the aging process, informing the public of the progress of aging research and of practical means of achieving a long and healthy life, and increasing the knowledge of gerontology among physicians and other health workers.

Foundation for Hospice and Home Care
519 C Street, NE
Washington, DC 20002
(202) 547-6586; Fax (202) 546-8968
Bill Halamandaris, CEO

Dedicated to helping people set up quality home care and hospices as an alternative to institutional care. It provides certification programs and workshops for home health aides and publishes educational materials.

Hospice Association of America
519 C Street, NE
Washington, DC 20002
(202) 546-4759; Fax (202) 547-3540
Janet E. Neigh, Executive Director

Organization made up of health-care professionals and organizations involved in hospice care. Promotes the use of hospice care for terminally ill individuals. Provides hospice referral service, Medicare reimbursement assistance, and hospice start-up guidance. Holds AIDS workshops. Offers speakers' bureau.

National Hospice Organization
1901 North Moore Street, Suite 901
Arlington, VA 22209
(703) 243-5900; Fax (703) 525-5762; (800) 658-8898
John J. Mahoney, President

Promotes quality care for terminally ill people and provides information about hospices and local hospice services. A list of publications is available upon request.

Well Spouse Foundation
P.O. Box 28876
San Diego, CA 92128
(619) 673-9043
Barbara Drucker, President

Support group for relatives/spouses of chronically ill individuals. Provides advocacy services.

Diseases of the Blood and Blood-Forming Organs

ANEMIA

Aplastic Anemia Foundation of America
P.O. Box 22689
Baltimore, MD 21203
(800) 747-2820; Fax (410) 955-0247
Marilyn Baker Kuipers, Executive Director

Organization concerned with aplastic anemia. Supports expansion of clinical treatment options. Offers public education, patient/family assistance, and family support groups.

HEMOPHILIA

National Hemophilia Foundation
110 Green Street, Suite 303
New York, NY 10012
(212) 219-8180; Fax (212) 966-9247
Alan P. Brownstein, Executive Director

Health organization of volunteers concerned about hemophilia.
Supports research, distributes educational material, offers referral
services, and sponsors children's summer camp.

HISTIOCYTOSIS

Histiocytosis Association of America
609 New York Road
Glassboro, NJ 08028
(609) 881-4911; Fax (609) 589-6614
Jeffrey M. Toughill, President

Support organization made up of patients, families, and medical
professionals concerned about histiocytosis (a rare blood disease in
which white blood cells attack organs or bones). Promotes research,
offers patient/family support, provides speakers' bureau, and offers
referral service.

HYPOGLYCEMIA

Adrenal Metabolic Research Society of the
Hypoglycemia Foundation
153 Pawling Avenue
Troy, NY 12180
(518) 272-7154
Marilyn H. Light, President and Director

Society of physicians and research scientists studying the metabolic
anomalies involved in hypoglycemia (low blood sugar). Conducts
medical seminars. Provides information to the public on a nationwide basis.

National Hypoglycemia Association
P.O. Box 120
Ridgewood, NJ 07451
(201) 670-1189
Lenore L. Cohen, Founder and Director

Support organization for hypoglycemics, composed of patients, health-care professionals, and family members. Offers support groups, speakers' bureau, seminars, and workshops. Provides physician referrals, evaluations, and consultation services.

Dr. John W. Tintera Memorial Hypoglycemia Lay Group
149 Spindle Road
Hicksville, NY 11801
(516) 731-3302
Elaine Arnstein, President and Secretary

Parent/patient-support organization for individuals with hypoglycemia. Shares information on this metabolic disorder. Promotes research.

SICKLE CELL DISEASE

National Association for Sickle Cell Disease
3345 Wilshire Boulevard, Suite 1106
Los Angeles, CA 90010-1880
(213) 736-5455; Fax (213) 736-5211; (800) 421-8453
Lynda King Anderson, Contact

Network of local community groups involved in sickle cell anemia programs in the United States. Promotes public awareness, distributes educational materials, promotes service programs, and encourages research. Provides blood banks, workshops, counselor training, vocational rehabilitation, and children's camps.

Sickle Cell Disease Foundation of Greater New York
127 West 127th Street, Room. 421
New York, NY 10027
(212) 865-1500
Dick Campbell, Executive Director

Health agency supporting research and education designed to control and, ultimately, to conquer sickle cell anemia. Assists in the establishment of other local chapters to maintain screening and counseling clinics. Offers speakers' bureau. Provides information on support groups, research, and advocacy services. Provides referrals, counseling, blood bank, and social service assistance.

Diseases of the Heart and Circulatory System

BUNDLE BRANCH BLOCK

International Bundle Branch Block Association
6631 West Eighty-third Street
Los Angeles, CA 90045-2899
(213) 670-9132
Rita Kurtz Lewis, Executive Director

Support and information organization concerned with the rare heart condition "bundle branch block" (BBB). Responds to inquiries, distributes information, and works to increase public awareness.

CARDIOVASCULAR DISEASE

American Heart Association
7272 Greenville Avenue
Dallas, TX 75231-4596
(214) 373-6300; Fax (214) 706-1341
Dudley H. Hafner, Executive Vice President

The nation's largest voluntary health organization funding research and sponsoring educational programs about the prevention and treatment of heart disease and stroke. The association and its affiliates offer programs in stroke clubs as well as exercise, diet, and smoking-cessation programs. It publishes pamphlets on heart disease and stroke.

Coronary Club
9500 Euclid Avenue
Cleveland, OH 44106
(216) 444-3690
Kathryn E. Ryan, Administrative Assistant

A 9,000-member organization of health-care professionals and patients. Publishes bulletin on heart care and rehabilitation in easy-to-understand language.

Heart Disease Research Foundation
50 Court Street
Brooklyn, NY 11201
(718) 649-6210
Dr. Yoshiaki Omura, Medical Research Director

Research-promoting organization seeking early diagnosis and effective treatment of cardiovascular disease. Conducts and supports studies in such fields as acupuncture, electrotherapeutics, and noninvasive early diagnostic methods. Offers public education programs. Responds to inquiries.

Heartline
The Cleveland Clinic Foundation
9500 Euclid Avenue
Cleveland, OH 44195
(216) 444-3690

Worldwide organization. Publishes *Heartline,* a monthly newsletter for heart patients and their families, as well as other publications.

Mended Hearts
7272 Greenville Avenue
Dallas, TX 75231
(214) 706-1442
Darla Bonham, Executive Director

Peer-support organization for individuals with heart disease and their families and friends. Offers advice, services, and encouragement.

National Heart Savers' Association
9140 West Dodge Road
Omaha, NE 68114
(402) 398-1993; Fax (402) 398-1994
Phil Sokolof, President

Organization working to educate the public about the dangers of a
high-cholesterol diet. Conducts public cholesterol screening program.
Encourages major food processors and fast-food chains to discon-
tinue use of items high in saturated fats (e.g., palm oil, coconut oil,
lard, and beef tallow). Promotes improved public school nutrition.

HYPERTENSION

Citizens for Public Action on Blood Pressure and Cholesterol
7200 Wisconsin Avenue, Suite 1002
Bethesda, MD 20814
(301) 907-7790; Fax (301) 907-7792
Gerald Wilson, Director

Public education/advocacy organization targeting health-policy officials, medical professionals, and the public on the need to fund
efforts to reduce blood pressure and cholesterol in order to prevent
heart attacks and strokes.

National Hypertension Association
324 East Thirtieth Street
New York, NY 10016
(212) 889-3557; Fax 447-7032
William M. Manger, M.D., Chair

Professional organization concerned with control of hypertension.
Promotes education, conducts research, sponsors seminars, offers
hypertension and hypercholesterol detection programs, and provides
medical consultations.

National Institute of Hypertension Studies—Institute of Hypertension School of Research

295 Mount Vernon
Detroit, MI 48202
(313) 872-0505; Fax (313) 872-0505
Dr. Herbert R. Lockett, Executive Director

Organization working to combat hypertension. Conducts research, offers public education, and provides public seminars and detection clinics. Seeks to diagnose, counsel, and refer individuals with hypertension for treatment and follow-up. Extends research to fields of psychosocial and occupational stress.

National Stroke Association

8480 East Orchard Road, Suite 1000
Englewood, CO 80111-5015; (800) 787-6537; (303) 771-1700

Nonprofit organization dedicated to educating stroke survivors, families, health professionals, and the general public. Provides workshops, research, and clearinghouse services. Publishes newsletter, educational material.

Diseases of the Nervous System

AMYOTROPHIC LATERAL SCLEROSIS

ALS and Neuromuscular Research Foundation

c/o California Pacific Medical Center
2351 Clay Street, No. 416
San Francisco, CA 94115
(415) 923-3604
Dee Holden, R.N., Executive Director

Research information clearinghouse on neuromuscular diseases, including ALS. Provides monthly patient/family support groups in the San Francisco Bay area.

Amyotrophic Lateral Sclerosis Association
21021 Ventura Boulevard, Suite 321
Woodland Hills, CA 91364
(818) 340-7500; Fax (818) 340-2060; (800) 782-4747
Joseph M. Aguayo, President and CEO

Support organization for patients and families of patients with ALS.
Provides information and assistance. Funds research and conducts
support meetings.

ATAXIA

National Ataxia Foundation
750 Twelve Oaks Center
15500 Wayzata Boulevard
Wayzata, MN 55391
(612) 473-7666; Fax (612) 473-9289
Donna Gruetzmacher, Executive Director

Health organization concerned with ataxia, a genetic neurologic
disease. Promotes early diagnosis, public education and awareness,
and research. Provides screening and diagnosis clinics. Offers information and services to patients and their families.

CEREBRAL PALSY

Sister Kenny Institute
800 East Twenty-eighth Street at Chicago Avenue
Minneapolis, MN 55407
(612) 863-4457
N. Rehkamp, Executive Director

Organization supporting rehabilitation projects. Specializes in
trauma patients (stroke, spinal cord, brain injury, amputation), but
also provides treatment to patients with arthritis, cerebral palsy,
Parkinson's disease, and polio residuals.

United Cerebral Palsy Associations
1522 K Street, NW, Suite 1112
Washington, DC 20005
(202) 842-1266; Fax (202) 842-3519; (800) USA-4UCP
John D. Kemp, Executive Director

National affiliation of state and local organizations serving individuals with cerebral palsy and their families. Supports research, public education, and welfare efforts for the handicapped. Local organizations provide medical, therapeutic/social services, special education, vocational training, family counseling, and supervised independent-living facilities.

United Cerebral Palsy Research and Educational Foundation (UCPREF)
7 Penn Plaza, Suite 804
New York, NY 10001
(212) 268-5962; Fax (212) 268-5960; (800) USA-1UCP
Leon Sternfeld, M.D., Medical Director

Grant-making organization that funds prevention/treatment research on cerebral palsy and fellowships for medical and dental specialists in CP.

EPILEPSY

American Epilepsy Society
638 Prospect Avenue
Hartford, CT 06105
(203) 232-4825; Fax (203) 232-0819
Susan C. Berry, Executive Director

Professional organization of physicians and researchers involved in epilepsy treatment and study. Encourages improved care. Funds research fellowships, grants, and awards.

Epilepsy Concern Service Group
1282 Wynnewood Drive
West Palm Beach, FL 33417
(407) 683-0044; Fax (407) 881-5085
George L. McKay, Executive Director

Self-help network of regional "council" groups, each of which includes one Friends Group (for support), one or more Epilepsy Groups (for persons with epilepsy), and one or more Love Groups (for family members). Maintains long-distance pen-pal program. Encourages formation of new regional councils.

Epilepsy Foundation of America (EFA)
4351 Garden City Drive
Landover, MD 20785
(301) 459-3700; Fax (301) 577-2684; (800) EFA-1000
William McLin, Executive Vice President

National health agency fighting epilepsy. Sponsors research and services as government liaison. Supports medical, educational, and advocacy programs. Local organizations provide patient/family assistance and counseling. Maintains national information and referral service. Offers mail-order pharmacy program.

International League Against Epilepsy
c/o Dr. Roger Porter
National Institutes of Health
Building 31, Room 8A52
Bethesda, MD 20892
(301) 496-3167
Dr. Roger Porter, Secretary

Thirty-two-member federation of organizations supporting research and encouraging improved treatment of epilepsy.

HUNTINGTON'S DISEASE

Hereditary Disease Foundation
1427 Seventh Street, Suite 2
Santa Monica, CA 90401
(310) 458-4183; Fax (310) 458-3937
Nancy S. Wexler, Ph.D., President

Grant-making organization supporting biomedical research on genetic diseases, with focus on Huntington's disease (a neurological disorder). Distributes information to organizations and individuals.

Huntington's Disease Society of America

140 West Twenty-second Street, Sixth Floor
New York, NY 10011-2420
(212) 242-1968; Fax (212) 243-2443; (800) 345-4372; (800)
   345-HDSA, outside New York; info line 9:00 A.M. to 5 P.M.
   weekdays
Steve Bajardi, Executive Director

Volunteer-support organization concerned with Huntington's disease, an inherited neurological disorder. Supports research and increased public awareness. Offers patient service programs and community services. Provides legislative advocacy for government clinics. Provides crisis intervention.

MULTIPLE SCLEROSIS

Alliance for Cannabis Therapeutics

P.O. Box 21210
Washington, DC 20009
(202) 483-8595
Robert Randall, President

Advocacy group fighting to end the existing federal prohibition on the medical use of cannabis for treating seriously ill patients, including those with glaucoma, multiple sclerosis, and cancer.

National Multiple Sclerosis Society

733 Third Avenue
New York, NY 10017
(212) 986-3240; Fax (212) 986-7981; (800) 624-8236
Gen. Michael Dugan, President and CEO

Organization providing services and assistance to individuals with MS. Offers on-line computer search services for biomedical databases. Provides 24-hour tape message with information about resources. Helps to establish treatment clinics. Encourages public education.

MUSCULAR DYSTROPHY

Muscular Dystrophy Association
3300 East Sunrise Drive
Tucson, AZ 85718
(602) 529-2000; Fax (602) 529-5300
Robert Ross, Executive Director

National health agency concerned with eight categories of neuromuscular disease: (1) muscular dystrophies; (2) motor neuron
diseases, such as ALS and Werdnig-Hoffmann; (3) inflammatory
myopathies; (4) diseases of neuromuscular junction, such as myasthenia gravis; (5) diseases of the peripheral nerve, such as Friedreich's
ataxia; (6) metabolic diseases of muscle, such as McArdle's disease;
(7) myopathies due to endocrine abnormalities; (8) other myopathies.
Supports research and 230 outpatient hospital clinics. Provides diagnostic patient exams, follow-up medical evaluations, physical
therapy, summer camps, and orthopedic appliances.

NARCOLEPSY

American Narcolepsy Association
425 California Street, No. 201
San Francisco, CA 94104
(415) 788-4793; Fax 788-4795; (800) 222-6085
Mary Lee Keane, President

Support organization for individuals experiencing narcolepsy or sleep
apnea. Provides public information and education. Conducts and
fosters research. Encourages earlier medical diagnosis. Offers practical guidance and assistance to afflicted individuals. Conducts
mutual support and self-help programs.

Narcolepsy and Cataplexy Foundation of America
445 East Sixty-eighth Street, No. 12L
New York, NY 10021
(212) 628-6315
Helen Demitroff, Ph.D., Executive Vice President

Support organization for individuals with narcolepsy or cataplexy. Provides educational information to the public and to medical professionals. Encourages neurological evaluation at onset of symptoms. Promotes rehabilitation and occupational safety guidelines. Maintains speakers' bureau and library.

NEUROFIBROMATOSIS

National Neurofibromatosis Foundation
141 Fifth Avenue, Suite 7S
New York, NY 10010
(212) 460-8980, within New York; (800) 323-7938
Peter R. W. Bellerman, President

Foundation supporting research on neurofibromatosis (also called von Recklinghausen's disease). Provides referrals to medical and social services as well as for genetic counseling. Educates patients, families, and health-care professionals; works to establish diagnostic standards and protocols.

Neurofibromatosis, Inc.
3401 Woodridge Court
Mitchellville, MD 20721-8878
(301) 577-8984; Fax (301) 577-8984; (410) 461-5213 (TDD);
    (800) 942-6825
Paul Mendelsohn, President

Alliance of support groups for individuals with NF (a genetic neurologic disorder) and their families. Supports research and legislative advocacy. Distributes information, identifies local support groups, and provides referrals.

PARKINSON'S DISEASE

American Parkinson's Disease Association
60 Bay Street, Suite 401
Staten Island, NY 10301
(718) 981-8001; Fax (718) 981-4399; (800) 223-2732
Mario Esposito, President

Promotes research and supports patient care for people with Parkinson's disease and for their families. The toll-free number puts you in touch with one of the 43 referral and information centers in hospitals throughout the country. The association provides free publications, including *The Parkinson's Disease Handbook,* upon request.

National Parkinson Foundation
1501 NW Ninth Avenue
Miami, FL 33136
        and
122 East Forty-second Street
New York, NY 10017
        and
9911 West Pico Boulevard
Los Angeles, CA 90035
(305) 547-6666
Physician and support group referral lines: (800) 327-4545;
    (800) 433-7022, in Florida; (800) 544-4882, in California

Professional organization concerned with Parkinson's disease. Supports research, provides therapy services, and offers education. Sponsors regional patient support groups. Makes referrals.

Parkinson's Disease Foundation
William Black Medical Research Building
Columbia Presbyterian Medical Center
650 West 168th Street
New York, NY 10032
(212) 923-4700; Fax (212) 923-4778; (800) 457-6676
Lewis P. Rowland, M.D., President

Research-supporting organization for Parkinson's disease. Publishes patient-care and rehabilitation information. Publishes list of treatment clinics and patient support groups. Provides counseling and advocacy groups.

Parkinson's Educational Program—USA
3900 Birch Street, No. 105
Newport Beach, CA 92660
(714) 250-2975; Fax (714) 250-8530; (800) 344-7872
Charlotte Jayne Drake, Executive Director

Information clearinghouse on Parkinson's disease. Fosters the establishment of local support groups nationwide. Supports research.

Sister Kenny Institute
800 East Twenty-eighth Street at Chicago Avenue
Minneapolis, MN 55407
(612) 863-4457
N. Rehkamp, Executive Director

Organization supporting rehabilitation projects. Specializes in trauma patients (stroke, spinal cord, brain injury, amputation), but also provides treatment to patients with arthritis, cerebral palsy, Parkinson's disease, and polio residuals.

United Parkinson Foundation and International Tremor Foundation
360 West Superior Street
Chicago, IL 60610
(312) 664-2344

Membership organization for patients, their families, and health professionals. Supports research, makes referrals, distributes exercise information.

POST-POLIO SYNDROME

International Polio Network
5100 Oakland Avenue, No. 206
St. Louis, MO 63110
(314) 534-0475
Joan Headley, Director

Organization made up of polio survivors and rehabilitation healthcare professionals. Encourages research and information exchange concerning the long-term effects of polio.

Polio Society
P.O. 106273
Washington, DC 20016
(202) 897-8180
Stanley L. Lipshultz, President

Organization of health-care professionals and polio survivors (3,500 members) interested in the long-term health of individuals who have had polio. Reports on postpolio syndrome (PPS). Operates outreach and referral services. Provides disability/benefit advocacy services.

SPINA BIFIDA

Spina Bifida Association of America (SBAA)
4590 MacArthur Boulevard, Suite 250
Washington, DC 20007
(202)944-3285; Fax (202) 944-3295; (800) 621-3141
Steve Laubacher, Executive Director

Support organization concerned with spina bifida, a birth defect. Provides information and promotes research. Encourages vocational training programs and legislative advocacy. Promotes public education and trains health-care personnel. Provides referral services.

TUBEROUS SCLEROSIS

National Tuberous Sclerosis Association (NTSA)
8000 Corporate Drive, Suite 120
Landover, MD 20785
(301) 459-9888; Fax (301) 459-0394; (800) 225-NTSA
Chuck Paradise, President

Research-funding organization concerned with tuberous sclerosis. Maintains national support network for families and for information distribution.

Tuberous Sclerosis Association of America
97 Vernon Street
Middleborough, MA 02346
(508) 946-1649
Linda Connors, Co-Director

Support organization concerned with tuberous sclerosis, a genetic neurologic disease. Provides public education and patient services. Supports early detection and identification. Provides advocacy services. Supports genetic research and counseling. Encourages the formation of support groups.

OTHER NEUROLOGIC DISORDERS

Avenues, National Support Group for Arthrogryposis Multiplex Congenita
c/o Mary Anne Schmidt
P.O. Box 5192
Sonora, CA 95370
(209) 928-3688
Mary Anne Schmidt, Director

Support organization for health-care professionals, family members, and individuals with arthrogryposis multiplex congenita (AMC, a neuromuscular birth defect). Encourages communication about coping techniques and self-help ideas.

Benign Essential Blepharospasm Research Foundation
P.O. Box 12468
Beaumont, TX 77726
(409) 832-0788; Fax (409) 832-0890
Mattie Loukoster, Contact

Advocacy group (5,000 members) made up of victims of benign essential blepharospasm (BEB, a neurologic disorder causing involuntary eyelid closure). Promotes research, supports increased public awareness, and promotes interdisciplinary cooperation among medical specialists. Compiles patient data. Offers seminars and continuing education activities.

Charcot-Marie-Tooth Association
c/o Crozer Mills Enterprise Center
600 Upland Avenue
Upland, CA 19105
(215) 499-7486
Karol B. Hitt, President

Patient/professional–support organization concerned with CMT disease, also known as peroneal muscular atrophy. Provides patient/family education and support groups. Fosters research and provides telephone referral services.

Charcot-Marie-Tooth International
One Springbank Drive
St. Catherine's, Ontario,
Canada L2S 2K1
(416) 687-3630
Linda Crabtree, Executive Director and President

Multinational group of individuals concerned about Charcot-Marie-Tooth disease (also known as peroneal muscular atrophy). Promotes distribution of information on CMT to the public and to health-care professionals. Encourages research. Maintains an international network of information/counseling services for persons with CMT. Funds research and scholarships.

Dystonia Medical Research Foundation
8383 Wilshire Boulevard, Suite 800
Beverly Hills, CA 90211
(312) 755-0198
Nancy Harris, Services Director

Support and research-funding organization interested in dystonia, a neurologic muscular disorder. Encourages increased public awareness. Sponsors support programs.

Guillain-Barré Syndrome Foundation International
P.O. Box 262
Wynnewood, PA 19096
(215) 667-0131
Robert and Estelle Benson, Founders

Support organization for Guillain-Barré syndrome, acute idiopathic polyneuritis, a rare neurologic disorder. Supports public education and research. Establishes support groups nationwide. Arranges patient-to-patient communications.

International Joseph Diseases Foundation
P.O. Box 2550
Livermore, CA 94551-2550
Rose Marie Silva, Executive Director

Support organization for Joseph disease, a genetic neurologic disorder resembling multiple sclerosis, Parkinson's disease, and spinocerebellar degeneration. Maintains free clinics for diagnosis and treatment. Offers genetic counseling and public/professional education. Conducts research.

International Research Council of Neuromuscular Disorders

1434 Pleasantville Road
Lancaster, OH 43130
(614) 653-1098
James R. Grilliot, D.C., Executive Director

Medical professional organization interested in the prevention and cure of neuromuscular disorders. Promotes research and interdisciplinary communication. Distributes information and prepares educational materials. Offers speakers' bureau.

Myasthenia Gravis Foundation

53 West Jackson Boulevard, Suite 660
Chicago, IL 60604
(312) 427-6252; Fax (312) 427-8437; (800) 541-5454
Anna El-Qudsi, Executive Director

Support organization for patients with myasthenia gravis and for their families. Raises funds for research. Offers public/professional education. Sponsors low-cost prescription service.

Myoclonus Families United

1564 East Thirty-fourth Street
Brooklyn, NY 11234
(718) 252-2133
Sharon Dobkin, President

Thirty-member group of individuals interested in myoclonus and other movement disorders. Promotes public/medical education. Serves as family support group. Offers speakers' bureau.

National Organization for Rare Disorders

P.O. Box 8923
New Fairfield, CT 06812-1783
(203) 746-6518; Fax (203) 746-6481; (800) 999-NORD
Abbey S. Meyers, Executive Director

Information and referral clearinghouse providing assistance to individuals with rare disabilities/diseases. Maintains patient support network. Monitors the Orphan Drug Act.

National Spasmodic Torticollis Association
P.O. Box 476
Elm Grove, WI 53122
Howard Thiel, Vice President, Operations

Support organization made up of individuals with spasmodic torticollis (ST, a rare neurologic syndrome in which muscles on one side of the neck contract and pull the head to one side). Offers public education and awareness activities. Provides support and communication forum for ST sufferers.

Reflex Sympathetic Dystrophy Association
P.O. Box 821
Haddonfield, NJ 08033
(215) 955-5444
Audrey F. Thomas, R.N., Co-Founder and President

Organization made up of health-care professionals and individuals with reflex sympathetic dystrophy syndrome (RSDS, a neurologic disorder usually preceded by minor trauma and involving severe pain, bone softening, and loss of muscle use in affected areas). Fosters increased public/medical awareness. Supports research. Assists in formation of support groups. Provides referral services. Offers speakers' bureau.

Sturge-Weber Foundation
P.O. Box 460931
Aurora, CO 80046
(303) 690-9735; (800) 627-5482
Karen L. Ball, President

Information clearinghouse and support organization concerned with Sturge-Weber syndrome, a congenital neurologic disorder. Funds research.

Tardive Dyskinesia/Tardive Dystonia National Association

4244 University Way, NE
P.O. Box 45732
Seattle, WA 98145
(206) 522-3166
S. K. Kjaer, Executive Director

Organization made up of legal and health-care professionals, relatives of afflicted individuals, and individuals with Tardive Dyskinesia and Tardive Dystonia (muscular disorders, which are side effects of certain antipsychotic drugs). Provides legislative advocacy services in support of patients being advised of potential side effects of such drugs, and in support of requiring signed patient informed consent before administration of the drugs. Supports research; fosters increased public awareness. Offers referral services, support, and guidance.

Tourette Syndrome Association

42-40 Bell Boulevard
Bayside, NY 11361
(718) 224-2999; Fax (718) 279-9596; (800) 237-0717
Steven M. Friedlander, Executive Officer

Support organization for Tourette syndrome, a neurologic disorder. Promotes education and awareness. Stimulates research funding, makes physician referrals, and maintains support groups. Provides advocacy services.

Well Spouse Foundation

P.O. Box 28876
San Diego, CA 92128
(619) 673-9043
Barbara Drucker, President

Support group for relatives/spouses of chronically ill individuals. Provides advocacy services.

Diseases of the Sensory Organs

Alliance for Cannabis Therapeutics
P.O. Box 21210
Washington, DC 20009
(202) 483-8595
Robert Randall, President

Advocacy group fighting to end the existing federal prohibition on the medical use of cannabis for treating seriously ill patients, including those with glaucoma, multiple sclerosis, and cancer.

American Academy of Ophthalmology
655 Beach Street
San Francisco, CA 94019
(415) 561-8500; Fax (415) 561-8533; (800) 222-EYES
Bruce E. Spivey, M.D., Executive Vice President

Professional organization of physicians who specialize in the diagnosis and treatment of eye disease. Toll-free number gives names of ophthalmologists nationwide who provide free or low-cost eye care to financially disadvantaged older adults. Publications available upon request.

American Hearing Research Foundation
55 East Washington Street, Suite 2022
Chicago, IL 60602
(312) 726-9670
William L. Lederer, Executive Director

Nonprofit organization of otolaryngologists (ear, nose, and throat specialists). Call for names of otolaryngologists in your area and for information about hearing disorders.

American Optometric Association
243 North Lindbergh Boulevard
St. Louis, MO 63141
(314) 991-4100; Fax (314) 991-4101
Earle L. Hunter, O.D., Executive Director

A professional organization of optometrists and primary eye-care providers who diagnose and treat conditions of the eyes and vision system. Contact them for information about finding a local low-vision specialist. Free written materials available upon request.

American Speech-Language-Hearing Association (ASHA)
10801 Rockville Pike
Rockville, MD 20852
(301) 897-5700; Fax (301) 571-0457; (800) 638-8255 (out-of-state calls)
Frederick T. Spahr, Ph.D., Executive Director

Membership association of over 6,400 audiologists and speech language pathologists. Publishes pamphlets on communication disorders and aging, hearing aids, assistive listening devices, and tinnitus. Call toll-free number for publications, referral services, and other information.

American Tinnitus Association (ATA)
P.O. Box 5
Portland, OR 97207
(508) 248-9985
Gloria E. Reich, Executive Director

Voluntary organization supporting research to find a cure for tinnitus. ATA distributes information about tinnitus, sponsors self-help groups, and offers a referral service. ATA publications available upon request.

Association for Macular Diseases
210 East sixty-fourth Street
New York, NY 10021
(212) 605-3719
Nikolai Stevenson, President

Support organization for individuals with macular diseases (including tumors, inflammations, retinal growths, and degenerative diseases). Fosters increased public awareness, research, and eye donations for research purposes. Provides information on low-vision resources and aids. Offers group support and counseling services.

Better Hearing Institute
P.O. Box 1840
Washington, DC 20013
(703) 642-0580; Fax (703) 750-9302; (800) 327-9355
Joseph J. Rizzo, Executive Director

Educates the public about the issue of uncorrected hearing problems and available medical, surgical, hearing aid, and rehabilitation assistance. Free pamphlets about related information available upon request by calling the toll-free number.

Ear Foundation
2420 Castillo Street
Santa Barbara, CA 93105-4346
(805) 569-6833; (805) OUR-EARS (telephone hearing screening test)
Joseph R. DiBartolomeo, M.D., Director

Organization promoting increased professional/public understanding of ear diseases and their treatment. Provides educational programs; lectures on tinnitus, vertigo, and other ear disorders; seminars and workshops. Conducts research on laser surgery.

Eye Care
1319 F Street, NW
Washington, DC 20004
(202) 628-3816
Donna A. Fujiwara, Director

Professionally staffed ophthalmic-care organization serving individuals with eye injuries or eye diseases who might not otherwise have access to care. Has three operating suites, seven clinics, and a rehabilitation program in Haiti.

Foundation for Glaucoma Research
490 Post Street, Suite 830
San Francisco, CA 94102
(415) 986-3162; Fax (415) 986-3763
Tara L. Steele, Executive Director

Research-supporting organization fighting glaucoma. Provides clinical programs, promotes public awareness, and maintains support network for informal counseling from experienced patients and relatives.

International Myopia Prevention Association
RD 5, Box 171
Ligonier, PA 15658
(412) 238-2101
Donald S. Rehm, President

Individuals and organizations united to educate the public about the concept that myopia (a condition of progressive nearsightedness) is caused by excessive close work, rather than being an inherited condition. Promotes preventive measures, such as periodic vision testing of children, proper reading habits, adequate home/office/school lighting. Solicits funds for educational activities and publications.

Ménière's Network
c/o Ear Foundation at Baptist Hospital
2000 Church Street, Box 111
Nashville, TN 37236
(615) 329-7807; Fax (615) 340-7935; (800) 545-HEAR
Dr. Eddie Thompson, Executive Director

Peer-support group network for persons with Ménière's syndrome, an inner-ear disorder. Offers an educational program, a pen-pal program, and a "phone buddies" program.

Myopia International Research Foundation
1265 Broadway, Room 608
New York, NY 10001
(212) 684-2777
Sylvia N. Rachlin, President

Organization made up of physicians, health-care professionals, families, and individuals with myopia (a condition of progressive nearsightedness) working to promote international, cooperative, interdisciplinary research on myopia.

National Eye Care Project

P.O. Box 429098
San Francisco, CA 94142-9098
(415) 561-8520; (800) 222-EYES
B. Thomas Hutchinson, M.D., Chairman

Group of ophthalmologists (7,000 members) working under a
project of the Foundation of the American Academy of Ophthalmology, to provide free medical and surgical eye care to economically disadvantaged and elderly individuals. Provides referrals and
information on participating physicians. Offers information on eye
diseases related to aging.

National Eye Research Foundation

c/o Pamela Baker
910 Skokie Boulevard, No. 207A
Northbrook, IL 60062
(708) 564-4652
Pamela Baker, Executive Director

Public information center on questions about eye care. Conducts
and sponsors research.

National Society to Prevent Blindness

500 East Remington Road
Schaumburg, IL 60173
(708) 843-2020; Fax (708) 843-8458; (800) 331-2020
Robert Bolan, Executive Director

Aims to educate the public about preserving sight and preventing
blindness. The toll-free information line provides answers to questions. Free written materials on eye diseases, including glaucoma,
cataracts, and macular degeneration, and its free publication available upon request.

RP Foundation Fighting Blindness

1401 Mt. Royal Avenue, Fourth Floor
Baltimore, MD 21217
(410) 225-9400; Fax (410) 225-3936; (410) 225-9409 (TDD);
   (800) 638-5555
Robert M. Gray, Executive Director

Research-supporting organization fighting retinal degenerative diseases (retinitis pigmentosa, macular degeneration, Usher's syndrome, Laurence-Moon-Biedl syndrome). Coordinates retina donor program, operates self-help support networks, and provides information and referral services.

BLINDNESS AND VISUAL IMPAIRMENT

Adventures in Movement for the Handicapped (AIM)
945 Danbury Road
Dayton, OH 45420
(513) 294-4611; Fax (513) 294-3783
Dr. Jo A. Geiger, Executive Director

Support organization, which developed and promotes the AIM Method of Specialized Movement Education, to improve muscle control and coordination through rhythmic exercises of gross- and fine-motor movements. The program is suitable/adaptable to various handicaps, including visual impairment, hearing impairment, learning disabilities, emotional problems, and orthopedic problems.

Affiliated Leadership League of and for the Blind of America (ALL)
1101 Seventeenth Street, NW, Suite 803
Washington, DC 20036
(202) 833-0092; Fax (202) 833-0086
Robert R. Humphreys, Administrator

Advocacy organization working to protect the consumer rights and legislative rights of blind and visually impaired persons.

American Council of the Blind
1155 Fifteenth Street, NW, Suite 720
Washington, DC 20005
(202) 467-5081; Fax (202) 467-5085; (800) 424-8666
Oral O. Miller, Representative

Seeks to improve the lifestyles of those who are blind or visually impaired. Toll-free referral service provides up-to-date information on low-vision services, treatment, and services. List of publications is available upon request.

American Foundation for the Blind
15 West Sixteenth Street
New York, NY 10011
(212) 620-2000; Fax (212) 727-1279; (800) 232-5463 (NY State
    residents call [212] 620-2147)
Carl Augusto, Executive Director and President

Nonprofit foundation offering services to the blind or visually impaired and their families, as well as educational and training programs to educators, health-care workers, and other professionals
and volunteers who work with them. Toll-free number provides
information about blindness and low vision, informative publications and videos, local community services, and low-vision products sold through the foundation. Catalog of free publications and
products available upon request.

Associated Blind
135 West Twenty-third Street
New York, NY 10011
(212) 255-1122
Ed Sternstein, Executive Director

Support and advocacy organization interested in the socioeconomic
welfare of blind and physically disabled persons. Provides rehabilitation referral and follow-up, family counseling and guidance, recreation services, and support for independent-living programs.

Associated Services for the Blind
919 Walnut Street
Philadelphia, PA 19107
(215) 627-0600; Fax (215) 922-0692
Vincent McVeigh, Executive Director

Service agency for blind and visually impaired individuals, with the
goal of promoting independent living. Features retail store, Braille
printing house, counseling service, radio reading service, referral,
and job placement services.

Association for Advancement of Blind and Retarded
164-09 Hillside Drive
Jamaica, NY 11432
(718) 523-2222
Christopher Weldon, Executive Director

Organization serving multihandicapped blind and severely retarded adults. Operates intermediate care facilities, short-term treatment centers, and summer camp. Provides information and referral services.

Blind Veterans Association
477 H Street, NW
Washington, DC 20001
(202) 371-8880; Fax (202) 371-8258; (800) 669-7079
Ronald L. Miller, Ph.D., Executive Director

Support organization for blind U.S. veterans. Provides assistance in areas of employment, benefits, and community reintegration. Funds scholarship and grant awards. Supports research.

Carroll Center for the Blind
770 Centre Street
Newton, MA 02158
(617) 969-6200; Fax (617) 969-6204; (800) 852-3131
Rachel Ethier Rosenbaum, Executive Director

Rehabilitation facility providing services to adults who have become blind. Offers evaluation, adjustment training, informa·ion, and referral services. Maintains library and charitable program.

Guide Dog Foundation for the Blind
371 East Jericho Turnpike
Smithtown, NY 11787
(516) 265-2121; Fax (516) 361-5192; (800) 548-4337
Wells B. Jones, CAE, CFRE, Executive Director

Organization giving qualified blind applicants trained guide dogs, free of charge. Provides a 26-day residential training for the individual and dog. Guarantees free service for life.

Guiding Eyes for the Blind
611 Granite Springs Road
Yorktown Heights, NY 10598
(914) 245-4024; Fax (914) 245-1609
Dr. John Kullberg, President

Accredited service organization providing trained guide dogs to blind individuals. Offers 4-week training programs to blind individuals in proper care of guide dogs.

National Association for Visually Handicapped (NAVH)
22 West Twenty-first Street
New York, NY 10010
(212) 889-3141; Fax (212) 727-2931
Lorraine Marchi, Executive Director

Only nonprofit national organization devoted to those who are not totally blind but who do not have adequate vision, even with the best corrective lenses. NAHV distributes more than 1,600 free titles in large-print book form as well as a large-print newspaper and provides counseling in the use of low-vision aids. Contact NAHV for a kit, including a visual aids catalog, large-print library catalog, and listings of low-vision clinics and services in your state.

National Center for Vision and Aging
Information and Resources Service
800 Second Avenue
New York, NY 10017
(800) 334-5497; (800) 808-5544; (212) 808-0077 (TTD)

To promote understanding of vision problems of the aging. Toll-free number to answer questions and provide referrals. Publications.

National Federation of the Blind
1800 Johnson Street
Baltimore, MD 21230
(410) 659-9314; Fax (410) 685-5653; (800) 638-7518 (job
   opportunity line)
Marc Maurer, President

National advocacy organization supporting the legislative rights and social integration/equality of blind individuals. Funds scholarships for blind students. Distributes information and supports research. Works to improve public policy as it affects blind individuals.

Recording for the Blind
20 Roszel Road
Princeton, NJ 08540
(609) 452-0606; Fax (609) 987-8116; (800) 221-4792
Ritchie Geisel, Executive Director

Association of studios, which records and lends educational books
to blind/visually impaired students and employed adults. Record-
ings are made upon individual request, free of charge, by volunteers. Approximately 3,000 titles are recorded annually. Does not
duplicate titles offered by the Library of Congress Talking Book
Program.

Vision Foundation
818 Mount Auburn Street
Watertown, MA 02172
(617) 926-4232
Barbara R. Keller, Executive Director

Self-help organization serving the newly blinded, the partially sighted,
and those with progressive eye disease. Provides referral services,
individualized advocacy, a "buddy" telephone network to share
information, and self-help support groups for persons recently
blinded and becoming blind. Operates the Visually Impaired Elders
Project.

DEAFNESS AND HEARING IMPAIRMENT

Adventures in Movement for the Handicapped (AIM)
945 Danbury Road
Dayton, OH 45420
(513) 294-4611; Fax (513) 294-3783
Dr. Jo A. Geiger, Executive Director

Support organization, which developed and promotes the AIM
Method of Specialized Movement Education, to improve muscle
control and coordination through rhythmic exercises of gross- and
fine-motor movements. The program is suitable/adaptable to various handicaps, including visual impairment, hearing impairment,
learning disabilities, emotional problems, and orthopedic problems.

Association of Late-Deafened Adults
P.O. Box 641763
Chicago, IL 60664-1763
(815) 549-5741 (Voice/TDD); Fax (815) 459-5753
Bill Graham, President

Information and support for individuals who have become deaf as adults. Offers self-help groups, social events, workshops, seminars, speakers' bureau, and research programs.

Hearing Helpline
The Better Hearing Institute
5021-B Backlick Road
Annandale, VA 22003; (800) 327-9355

Nonprofit educational organization. Helpline answers questions about symptoms, hearing loss, hearing aids, surgery, finances. Referrals to specialist and self-help groups. Informative publications.

Hear Now
4001 South Magnolia Way, Suite 100
Denver, CO 80237
(303) 758-4919; (800) 648-HEAR (Voice/TDD)
Bernice Dinner, Ph.D., President

Organization providing financial assistance (through a national lottery) to hearing-impaired persons who need hearing-assistive devices.

National Information Center on Deafness
Gallaudet University
800 Florida Avenue, NE
Washington, DC 20002-3625
(202) 651-5051; Fax (202) 651-5054; (202) 651-5052 (TDD)
Loraine DiPietro, Director

Resource and information clearinghouse on all aspects of deafness. Maintains library and referral services.

Self Help for Hard of Hearing People, Inc.
c/o Lori A. Ropa
7800 Wisconsin Avenue
Bethesda, MD 20814
(301) 657-2248; Fax (301) 913-9413; (301) 657-2249 (TDD)
Lori A. Ropa, Membership Coordinator

Volunteer organization with 280 chapters nationwide helping those who are hard of hearing to help themselves. Membership includes a copy of their bimonthly magazine, *SHH Journal*, and information about conventions for the hard of hearing, self-help groups, and publications. Call or write for membership fee information.

Endocrine, Metabolic, and Immune System Disorders

DIABETES

American Association of Diabetes Educators
444 North Michigan Avenue, Suite 1240
Chicago, IL 60611-3901
(312) 644-2233; Fax (312) 644-4411
Kate Doyle, Executive Director

A professional organization of certified diabetes educators who counsel people with diabetes about disease management.

American Association of Kidney Patients
111 South Parker Street, Suite 405
Tampa, FL 33606
(800) 749-2257; Fax (813) 254-3270
Erwin Hytner, Executive Director

Support organization for patients on hemodialysis, peritoneal dialysis, or with kidney transplants, as well as for family members and friends. Offers patient/public education about kidney disease. Promotes donor program.

American Diabetes Association (ADA)
P.O. Box 25757
1660 Duke Street
Alexandria, VA 22314
(703) 549-1500; Fax (703) 836-7439; (800) 232-3472
John H. Graham IV, CEO

Voluntary organization supporting diabetes research and seeking to improve the lives of people with diabetes and of their caregivers. ADA offers seminars for those with Type II diabetes, support groups for the elderly and their families, and health screenings. Toll-free number service provides free publications and a quarterly newsletter.

American Kidney Fund
6110 Executive Boulevard, Suite 1010
Rockville, MD 20852
(301) 881-3052; Fax (301) 881-0898; (800) 638-8299
Francis J. Soldovere, Executive Director

Fundraising organization working to meet the financial needs of kidney disease patients by providing direct aid for their treatment. Also supports emergency dialysis, research, and public education.

National Diabetes Information Clearinghouse (NIH)
Box NDIC
9000 Rockville Pike
Bethesda, MD 20892
(301) 468-2162

Federal information service. Answers questions, provides referrals, and publishes information booklets.

National Kidney Foundation
30 East Thirty-third Street, Suite 1100
New York, NY 10016
(212) 889-2210; Fax (212) 689-9261; (800) 622-9010
John Davis, Executive Director

Support organization fostering research, public education, patient services, and organ donor program for kidney disease. Offers speakers' bureau, screening programs, and telephone referral service.

National Kidney and Urologic Diseases Information Clearinghouse
P.O. Box NKUDIC
9000 Rockville Pike
Bethesda, MD 20892
(301) 468-6345
Elizabeth H. Singer, Director

Referral and resource information clearinghouse on kidney and urologic diseases. Distributes educational information to patients, health-care professionals, and the public. Responds directly to written and telephone inquiries.

IMMUNE SYSTEMS DISORDERS

Immune Deficiency Foundation
P.O. Box 586
Columbia, MD 21045
(410) 461-3127; Fax (410) 461-3292; (800) 296-4433
Toni Volk, Executive Director

Organization encouraging education and research on immune deficiency diseases. Funds physician research fellowships, research awards, and patient scholarships. Provides patients and family members with educational materials.

National Coalition on Immune System Disorders
1030 Fifteenth Street, NW, Suite 468
Washington, DC 20005
(202) 371-8090; Fax (202) 371-1405
Robert R. Humphreys, Executive Director

Thirteen-member coalition of organizations interested in immune system diseases. Provides public education, education for health-care professionals, and legislative advocacy services. Supports research and distributes information.

LUPUS

The American Lupus Society
3914 Del Amo Boulevard, Suite 922
Torrance, CA 90503
(213) 542-8891; (800) 331-1802
Dr. William H. Kraus, Contact

National support organization assisting lupus erythematous patients
and their families through local chapters and support groups. Collects and distributes research funds. Encourages public education
and awareness.

L. E. Support Club
8039 Nova Court
North Charleston, SC 29420
(803) 764-1769
Harriet B. Mesic, President and Editor

Support organization for persons with lupus erythematous (and other
autoimmune diseases), their friends, and families. Offers self-help
education, emotional support, newsletters, communication, and
information on nutrition and medication. Funds research.

Lupus Foundation of America
4 Research Place, Suite 180
Rockville, MD 20850-3226
(301) 670-9292; Fax (301) 670-9486; (800) 558-0121
John M. Huber, Executive Director

Volunteer health agency serving persons with lupus erythematous
and their families. Provides patient education, services, support, and
public education. Fosters research.

Lupus Network
230 Ranch Drive
Bridgeport, CT 06606
(203) 372-5795
Linda J. Rosinsky, President

Professional/patient organization fostering education about lupus erythematous.

METABOLIC DISORDERS

Adrenal Metabolic Research Society of the Hypoglycemia Foundation
153 Pawling Avenue
Troy, NY 12180
(518) 272-7154
Marilyn H. Light, President and Director

Society of physicians and research scientists studying the metabolic anomalies involved in hypoglycemia (low blood sugar). Conducts medical seminars. Provides information to the public on a nation-wide basis.

American Celiac Society/Dietary Support Coalition
58 Musano Court
West Orange, NJ 07052
(201) 325-8837
Annette Bentley, Executive Officer

Organization of individuals and health-care professionals interested in the diagnosis and care of gluten-sensitive intestinal disease and gluten-sensitive enteropathy (celiac sprue). Offers information on gluten-free diet and special gluten-free food products. Provides speakers' bureau.

American Porphyria Foundation
P.O. Box 22712
Houston, TX 77227
(713) 266-9617
Desiree H. Lyon, Executive Director

Support organization concerned about porphyrias (seven rare, usually inherited metabolic disorders). Funds research, fosters education, locates porphyria patients. Supports 17 self-help groups.

Association for Glycogen Storage Disease
P.O. Box 896
Durant, IA 52747
(319) 785-6038; Fax (319) 785-6038
Hollie Swain, President

Support organization concerned about glycogen storage disease, a hereditary metabolic disorder. Provides information exchange forum and encourages communication. Distributes medical information. Raises money and helps patients obtain home-care equipment. Plans to provide referral services for treatment.

Celiac Sprue Association/U.S.A.
P.O. Box 31700
Omaha, NE 68103-0700
(402) 558-0600
Leon H. Rottmann, President

Support network for individuals and families with celiac sprue (a genetic disorder causing digestive malabsorption of the protein in cereal grains) and dermatitis herpetiformis (a gluten-related skin disorder also involving problems with cereal grain diet). Supports research. Provides information on gluten-free foods and maintaining a gluten-free diet.

Cystinosis Foundation
17 Lake
Piedmont, CA 94611
(510) 601-6940
Jean Hotz, President

Support organization concerned about cystinosis. Promotes increased public awareness. Serves as patient support group. Funds research.

Gluten Intolerance Group of North America
P.O. Box 23053
Seattle, WA 98102-0353
(206) 325-6980
Elaine I. Hartsook, Ph.D., Director

Organization composed of 1,500 individuals with celiac sprue (gluten-sensitive enteropathy) and their families, health-care professionals, and smaller celiac sprue organizations. Offers psychological support, patient/public education, and nutritional guidance. Conducts research. Encourages food product labeling (on gluten content) and recipe development. Provides group/individual counseling and children's services.

Hemochromatosis Research Foundation
P.O. Box 8569
Albany, NY 12208
(518) 489-0972
Margaret A. Krikker, M.D., President

Professional organization interested in hereditary hemochromatosis. Assists patients and their families with diagnosis, treatment, genetic counseling, and support group information. Offers telephone referral service of physicians and treatment centers. Conducts research.

Iron Overload Diseases Association
433 Westwind Drive
North Palm Beach, FL 33408
(407) 840-8512; Fax (407) 842-9881
Roberta Crawford, President

Support organization for hemochromatosis patients and their families. Organizes self-help groups, encourages public education and research, sponsors screening program and patient referral service. Serves as physician research clearinghouse.

National Center for the Study of Wilson's Disease
5447 Palisade Avenue
Bronx, NY 10471
(718) 523-8717; Fax (718) 523-8708
I. Herbert Scheinberg, M.D., President

Research-supporting organization interested in hereditary diseases of metal metabolism, including Wilson's disease and Menkes' disease. Sponsors diagnostic and treatment center for Wilson's disease.

National Gaucher Foundation
19241 Montgomery Village Avenue, Suite E-21
Gaithersburg, MD 20879
(301) 990-3800; Fax (301) 990-4898; (800) 234-6217
Karen A. Cohen, Executive Director

Support organization interested in Gaucher's disease, a common
inherited metabolic disorder. Funds research and clinical programs.
Offers confidential support to persons with the disorder. Provides
information.

National Hypoglycemia Association
P.O. Box 120
Ridgewood, NJ 07451
(201) 670-1189
Lenore L. Cohen, Founder and Director

Support organization for hypoglycemics composed of patients,
health-care professionals, and family members. Offers support
groups, speakers' bureau, seminars, and workshops. Provides physician referrals, evaluations, and consultation services.

National Organization for Albinism and
  Hypopigmentation (NOAH)
1500 Locust Street
Philadelphia, PA 19102
(215) 545-2322; (800) 473-2310
Janice L. Knuth, President

Support organization composed of individuals with albinism (an
inherited metabolic disorder, which can impair vision) or hypopigmentation (which can impair hearing), their families, and health-
care professionals. Promotes public education, offers family and
individual support, and fosters research.

Paget's Foundation for Paget's Disease of Bone and
  Related Disorders
200 Varick Street, Suite 1004
New York, NY 10014-4810
(212) 229-1582; Fax (212) 229-1502; (800) 23-PAGET
Charlene Waldman, Executive Director

Professional/patient/family-support organization serving individuals with Paget's disease. Provides patient education, public education, patient assistance, research advocacy. Offers referral service to medical specialists.

Dr. John W. Tintera Memorial Hypoglycemia Lay Group
149 Spindle Road
Hicksville, NY 11801
(516) 731-3302
Elaine Arnstein, President and Secretary

Parent/patient–support organization for individuals with hypoglycemia. Shares information on the metabolic disorder. Promotes research.

Wilson's Disease Association
P.O. Box 75324
Washington, DC 20013
(703) 636-3014 (Voice/TDD)
Carol A. Terry, President

Support organization for persons interested in Wilson's disease, Menkes' disease, and other disorders of copper metabolism. Sponsors research. Promotes public awareness, early detection, and proper treatment. Offers financial aid to patients in need. Acts as information clearinghouse.

SCLERODERMA

Scleroderma Federation
Peabody Office Building
One Newbury Street
Peabody, MA 01960
(508) 535-6000; Fax (508) 535-6696
Marie A. Coyle, President

Research-supporting and fundraising organization concerned with scleroderma (a connective-tissue disorder). Encourages public education. Provides patients with referrals to specialists and educational materials. Encourages the formation of local support groups. Serves as information clearinghouse.

Scleroderma International Foundation
704 Gardner Center Road
New Castle, PA 16101
(412) 652-3109
Mrs. Arkie Barlet, President

Five-country organization acting as a support network for individuals with scleroderma (a chronic skin condition sometimes affecting the connective tissue, arterial lining, and digestive tract). Supports research and education.

Scleroderma Research Foundation
Box 200
Columbus, NJ 08022
(609) 261-2200; Fax (609) 723-6700; (800) 637-4005
Emanuel A. Coronis, Jr., Chairman

Fundraising and research-supporting organization concerned with scleroderma. Promotes the development of a national patient/family–support network. Fosters early diagnosis and treatment through public/medical education programs.

Scleroderma Support Group
8852 Enloe Avenue
Garden Grove, CA 92644
(714) 892-5297
Clara K. Ihlbrock, President

Support group and research-funding organization for patients with scleroderma.

United Scleroderma Foundation
P.O. Box 399
Watsonville, CA 95077
(408) 728-2202; Fax (408) 728-3328
Diane Williams, Founder and Director

Support organization concerned with scleroderma. Offers workshops and seminars. Maintains support networks. Promotes research.

OTHER

National Organization for Rare Disorders
P.O. Box 8923
New Fairfield, CT 06812-1783
(203) 746-6518; Fax (203) 746-6481; (800) 999-NORD
Abbey S. Meyers, Executive Director

Information and referral clearinghouse providing assistance to individuals with rare disabilities/diseases. Maintains patient support network. Monitors the Orphan Drug Act.

Well Spouse Foundation
P.O. Box 28876
San Diego, CA 92128
(619) 673-9043
Barbara Drucker, President

Support group for relatives/spouses of chronically ill individuals. Provides advocacy services.

Gastrointestinal Disorders

ILEITIS AND COLITIS

Crohn's and Colitis Foundation of America
444 Park Avenue South, Eleventh Floor
New York, NY 10016-7374
(212) 685-3440; Fax (212) 779-4098; (800) 932-2423
Barbara Boyle, Executive Director

Research-funding organization concerned with ileitis (Crohn's disease) and ulcerative colitis. Provides educational brochures to patients, physicians, and the public. Maintains celebrity speakers' bureau. Funds research and workshops.

LIVER DISEASES

American Liver Foundation
1425 Pompton Avenue
Cedar Grove, NJ 07009
(201) 256-2550; Fax (201) 256-3214; (800) 223-0179
Thelma King Thiel, President

Health agency concentrating on liver diseases. Funds research; promotes the prevention and cure of liver diseases. Provides public education, physician referrals, and patient-support groups. Sponsors educational programs for health-care professionals. Coordinates meetings between liver-disease patients and research specialists. Provides legislative advocacy services, provides speakers' bureau, and encourages organ donations. Manages funds raised to assist with liver transplant surgery costs.

METABOLIC DISORDERS

American Celiac Society/Dietary Support Coalition
58 Musano Court
West Orange, NJ 07052
(201) 325-8837
Annette Bentley, Executive Officer

Organization of individuals and health-care professionals interested in the diagnosis and care of gluten-sensitive intestinal disease and gluten-sensitive enteropathy (celiac sprue). Offers information on gluten-free diet and special gluten-free food products. Provides speakers' bureau.

Celiac Sprue Association/U.S.A.
P.O. Box 31700
Omaha, NE 68103-0700
(402) 558-0600
Leon H. Rottmann, President

Support network for individuals and families with celiac sprue (a genetic disorder causing digestive malabsorption of the protein in cereal grains) and dermatitis herpetiformis (a gluten-related skin disorder also involving problems with cereal grain diet). Supports research. Provides information on gluten-free foods and maintaining a gluten-free diet.

Gluten Intolerance Group of North America
P.O. Box 23053
Seattle, WA 98102-0353
(206) 325-6980
Elaine I. Hartsook, Ph.D., Director

Organization composed of 1,500 individuals with celiac sprue (gluten-sensitive enteropathy) and their families, health-care professionals, and smaller celiac sprue organizations. Offers psychological support, patient/public education, and nutritional guidance. Conducts research. Encourages food product labeling (on gluten content) and recipe development. Provides group/individual counseling and children's services.

Hemochromatosis Research Foundation
P.O. Box 8569
Albany, NY 12208
(518) 489-0972
Margaret A. Krikker, M.D., President

Professional organization interested in hereditary hemochromatosis. Assists patients and their families with diagnosis, treatment, genetic counseling, and support-group information. Offers telephone referral service of physicians and treatment centers. Conducts research.

Iron Overload Diseases Association
433 Westwind Drive
North Palm Beach, FL 33408
(407) 840-8512; Fax (407) 842-9881
Roberta Crawford, President

Support organization for hemochromatosis patients and their families. Organizes self-help groups, encourages public education and research, sponsors screening program and patient referral service. Serves as physician research clearinghouse.

National Center for the Study of Wilson's Disease
5447 Palisade Avenue
Bronx, NY 10471
(718) 523-8717; Fax (718) 523-8708
I. Herbert Scheinberg, M.D., President

Research-supporting organization interested in hereditary diseases of metal metabolism, including Wilson's disease and Menkes' disease. Sponsors diagnostic and treatment center for Wilson's disease.

Wilson's Disease Association
P.O. Box 75324
Washington, DC 20013
(703) 636-3014 (Voice/TDD)
Carol A. Terry, President

Support organization for persons interested in Wilson's disease, Menkes' disease, and other disorders of copper metabolism. Sponsors research. Promotes public awareness, early detection, and proper treatment. Offers financial aid to patients in need. Acts as information clearinghouse.

ULCERS

Cure Foundation
VA-Wadsworth, Building 115, Room. 117-B
Wilshire and Sawtelle
Los Angeles, CA 90073
(310) 825-5091

Foundation providing public/medical education on peptic ulcers. Funds research. Supports the Center for Ulcer Research and Education.

National Ulcer Foundation
675 Main Street
Montrose, MA 02176
(617) 665-6210
Blaise F. Alfano, M.D., Executive Secretary

Organization providing education and information to the public regarding peptic ulcers.

OTHER DIGESTIVE DISORDERS

Digestive Disease National Coalition
711 Second Street, NE, Suite 200
Washington, DC 20002
(202) 544-7497; Fax (202) 546-7105
Dale P. Dirks, Representative

Federation of organizations dealing with digestive diseases. Promotes increased public awareness and nutritional education. Advocates federal funding of research efforts.

Gray Panthers
2025 Pennsylvania Avenue, NW, Suite 821
Washington, DC 20006
(202) 466-3132

Intergenerational, national organization fighting to change attitudes and laws on specific issues of importance to Americans of all ages: defense reduction, environment, affordable housing, "isms" of society, health care, "Network" task forces address national issues. Provides publications, newsletter.

National Digestive Diseases Information Clearinghouse
Box NDDIC
9000 Rockville Pike
Bethesda, MD 20892
(301) 468-6344
Elizabeth Singer, Director

National resource center providing information and education on digestive diseases to patients, health-care professionals, and the public. Responds to inquiries, provides referrals, and distributes literature.

Hospice and Homecare

Foundation for Hospice and Home Care
519 C Street, NE
Washington, DC 20002
(202) 547-6586; Fax (202) 546-8968
Bill Halamandaris, CEO

Dedicated to helping people set up quality home care, hospice included, as an alternative to institutional care. It provides certification programs and workshops for home health aides and publishes educational materials.

Hospice Association of America
519 C Street, NE
Washington, DC 20002
(202) 546-4759; Fax (202) 547-3540
Janet E. Neigh, Executive Director

Organization made up of health-care professionals and organizations involved in hospice care. Promotes the use of hospice care for terminally ill individuals. Provides hospice referral service, Medicare reimbursement assistance, and hospice start-up guidance. Holds AIDS workshops. Offers speakers' bureau.

National Association of Home Care
519 C Street, NE, Stanton Park
Washington, DC 20002
(202) 547-7424; Fax (202) 547-3540
Val J. Halamandaris, President

The association represents agencies that provide home care, including home health agencies, hospice programs, and homemaker/home health-aide agencies. Publications of the association available upon request.

National Association of Private Geriatric Care Managers
655 North Alvernon Way, Suite 108
Tucson, AZ 85711
(602) 881-8008; Fax (602) 325-7925
Laury L. Adsit, Executive Director

Promotes quality service and care for elderly citizens. Provides referral service and distributes information to individuals interested in geriatric care centers.

National Citizens Coalition for Nursing Home Reform
1224 M Street, NW, Suite 301
Washington, DC 20005
(202) 393-2018; Fax (202) 393-4122
Cyma R. Heffter, Development Coordinator

Watches over and initiates nursing home reform laws and regulations, with a primary mission of improving the quality of care and life for nursing- and boarding-home residents. Publications and brochures about nursing homes and a list of officials to contact in each state available upon request.

National Hospice Organization
1901 North Moore Street, Suite 901
Arlington, VA 22209
(703) 243-5900; Fax (703) 525-5762; (800) 658-8898
John J. Mahoney, President

Promotes quality care for terminally ill people and provides information about hospices and about local hospice services. List of publications available upon request.

National Institute for Jewish Hospice
8723 Alden Drive, Suite 652
Los Angeles, CA 90048
(213) 854-3036; Fax (619) 322-3817; (800) 446-4448
LeVana Lev, Executive Director

Resource center for assisting terminally ill Jewish people and their families. Offers information on traditional Jewish views on death, dying, and grief. Trains hospice personnel and family members in working with terminally ill individuals.

National Institute on Community-Based Long-Term Care
c/o National Council on the Aging
409 Third Street, SW, Second Floor
Washington, DC 20024
(800) 424-9046; (202) 479-1200

Provides directory of adult day-care centers in the United States. Promotes and enhances adult day-care programs; provides services and activities for disabled older persons on long-term basis.

National League of Nursing (NLN)
350 Hudson Street
New York, NY 10014
(212) 989-9393; Fax (212) 989-3710
Pamela Maraldo, Contact

Works to improve standards of health care. Accredits home health-care agencies, nursing homes, and community health programs to ensure that patients receive quality care. List of accredited home health-care agencies available upon request.

Nursing Home Information Service
c/o National Council of Senior Citizens
1331 F Street, NW
Washington, DC 20004-1171
(202) 347-8800

Publications about long-term care and lifestyles for the aging.

Legal Services for the Elderly

Legal Counsel for the Elderly
601 E Street, NW
Building A, Fourth Floor
Washington, DC 20049
(202) 434-2124; Fax (202) 434-6464
Wayne Moore, Director

Provides direct, free legal services to Washington, DC, residents, age 60 and older, and back-up assistance and training to extend legal services and nursing home advocacy to the elderly. Operates Protective Services Support Project, which offers case consultation, legal advice, legislative support, and an information clearinghouse on issues pertinent to protective services for the elderly.

Legal Services for the Elderly
130 West Forty-second Street, Seventeenth Floor
New York, NY 10036
(212) 595-1340; Fax (212) 719-1939
Jonathan A. Weiss, Executive Director

Lawyers who advise on and litigate cases concerning problems of the elderly. Conducts research, litigation, and educational programs; maintains library.

National Academy of Elder Law Attorneys (NAELA)
655 North Alvernon Way, Suite 108
Tucson, AZ 85711
(602) 881-4005; Fax (602) 325-7925
Laury L. Adsit, Director

Practicing attorneys, law professors, and others interested in providing legal services to the elderly. Promotes technical expertise and education for legal services addressing the needs of the elderly and their families. Provides referral network of practicing members.

National Consumers League
815 Fifteenth Street, NW, Suite 928
Washington, DC 20005
(202) 639-8140
Linda Golodner, Executive Director and President

Protects consumers from fraud in all industries, including health services and health insurance. Contact the league for information and brochures about Medigap insurance and long-term-care services, including hospice, home health care, and ambulatory services.

National Legal Center for the Medically Dependent and Disabled
50 South Meridian Street, Suite 605
Indianapolis, IN 46204
(317) 632-6245; Fax (317) 632-6542
James Bopp, Jr., President

Service organization working to defend the legal rights of indigent or disabled people in order for them to obtain proper medical care.

Provides lawyer referral services. Operates speakers' bureau. Maintains library of bioethical, medical, and legal information. Affiliated with National Legal Aid and Defender Association.

People's Medical Society
462 Walnut Street
Allentown, PA 18102
(800) 624-8773; (215) 770-1670

Nonprofit organization to help consumers obtain their medical rights, as, for instance, in the case of being overcharged by doctor or hospital.

Mental Disorders

GENERAL MENTAL HEALTH

American Mental Health Association
1021 Prince Street
Alexandria, VA 22043
(703) 684-7722; Fax (703) 684-5968; (800) 433-5959
    (information booklet orders only)
John Horner, Chairman

Fundraising organization, which supports research, increases public awareness, provides public education, and fights stigma associated with mental illness.

Hogg Foundation for Mental Health
Box 7998, University Station
University of Texas
Austin, TX 78712
(512) 471-5041
Publications Division

Agency funding programs in Texas. Publishes several books and pamphlets on mental health, including *Mental Health in Nursing Homes, Individual Freedom and the Requirements of Modern Society, Emotional Maturity,* and *Family Violence: The Well Kept Secret.*

National Association for Rural Mental Health

301 East Armour Boulevard, Suite 420
Kansas City, MO 64111
(816) 756-3140
Teresa Cavender, Contact

Fundraising and professional training organization. Works to promote effective mental-health services in rural areas.

National Council of Community Mental Health Centers

12300 Twinbrook Parkway, Suite 320
Rockville, MD 20852
(301) 984-6200; Fax (301) 881-7159
Charles G. Ray, Executive Director

Alliance of mental-health organizations and interested individuals dedicated to improving mental-health services and promoting full insurance coverage for treatment. Offers publications and resource materials.

National Institute of Mental Health

Consumer Information Center
Department 541X
Pueblo, CO 81009

Center distributing the free publication, *A Consumer's Guide to Mental Health Services* (541X), which addresses common questions about mental health and its treatment.

ANXIETY DISORDERS

Anxiety Disorders Association of America

6000 Executive Boulevard, Suite 200
Rockville, MD 20852
(301) 231-9350; Fax (301) 231-7392; (900) 737-3400
  (information line)
Dr. Norman Klombers, Executive Director

Group of 4,000 professionals and family members concerned about anxiety disorders (phobias, panic disorders, obsessive-compulsive disorders, etc.). Supports research; provides public and professional education; fosters local self-help groups; serves as information clearinghouse.

Fly Without Fear
310 Madison Avenue
New York, NY 10017
(212) 697-7666
Carol Gross, Director

For-profit local weekly support group for individuals afraid of airline travel. Conditioning exercises include meetings with ground controllers and safety experts, visits to airports, and "Seminar in the Sky" flights. Also provides lectures to other organizations on fear of flying.

Obsessive-Compulsive Anonymous
P.O. Box 215
New Hyde Park, NY 11040
(516) 741-4901; Fax (212) 768-4679
Roy C., Contact

Self-help group for individuals with obsessive-compulsive disorders. Uses 12-step recovery program; publishes book, *Obsessive-Compulsive Anonymous*.

Obsessive Compulsive Foundation
P.O. Box 9573
New Haven, CT 06535
(203) 772-0565; Fax (203) 498-8476
James W. Broatch, Executive Director

Support organization made up of professionals, individuals with OCD, and family members. Conducts research, disseminates information, offers educational programs, assists with the formation and funding of local support groups.

PASS Group

Panic Attack Sufferers' Support Group
6 Mahogany Drive
Williamsville, NY 14221
(716) 689-4399
Shirley Swede, Program Coordinator

Telephone counseling program for individuals experiencing panic attacks and/or agoraphobia.

Phobia Clinic

White Plains Hospital Center
Davis Avenue at East Post Road
White Plains, NY 10601
(914) 681-1038
Manuel D. Zane, M.D., Director

Model program (local in scope) for treating individuals with phobias through the use of "contextual therapy." Offers intensive course, self-help groups, 8-week clinics, and individual therapy.

TERRAP Programs

Territorial Apprehensiveness Programs
648 Menlo Avenue, No. 5
Menlo Park, CA 94025
(415) 327-1804; Fax (415) 327-1043; (800) 2-PHOBIA
Crucita U. Hardy, M.D., Executive Officer

For-profit organization providing information and counseling on the self-help treatment of anxieties, fears, and phobias, with emphasis on agoraphobia. Conducts research. Trains professionals in the TERRAP Method. Maintains library; produces newsletter for people with phobias ($18/yr.)

AUTISM AND MENTAL RETARDATION

American Association on Mental Retardation

1719 Kalorama Road, NW
Washington, DC 20009
(202) 387-1968; (800) 424-3688
Ms. M. Doreen Croser, Executive Director

Professional organization providing information on the cause, treatment, and prevention of mental retardation. Promotes quality professional services.

Autism Services Center
Pritchard Building
605 Ninth Street, P.O. Box 507
Huntington, WV 25710-0507
(304) 525-8014; Fax (304) 525-8026
Ruth C. Sullivan, Ph.D., Director

Facility concerned with ensuring that appropriate professional training is provided to individuals responsible for the care of autistic
and developmentally disabled individuals. Offers workshops, seminars, studies, and surveys. Maintains library of legal materials related to autism. Keeps roster of autism professionals, educators, and
therapists. Operates several projects for autistic individuals, including Autism Group Home, Apartment Living, Monitored Employment, Case Management Services, and Respite Services. Offers free
packet of information on autism.

National Autism Hotline
The Pritchard Building
605 Ninth Street, P.O. Box 507
Huntington, WV 25710-0507
(304) 525-8014; Fax (304) 525-8026
Ruth C. Sullivan, Ph.D., Director

Service agency for individuals with developmental disabilities such
as autism. Helps families meet the needs of these individuals. Provides supervised apartments, group homes, respite services, job-
coached employment, independent-living services, case management,
and advocacy services.

BRAIN INJURY

Academy of Aphasia
c/o Dr. Victoria A. Fromkin
UCLA
Department of Linguistics
Los Angeles, CA 90024
(310) 206-3206
Dr. Victoria A. Fromkin, Chairperson

Society of medical specialists in the field of aphasia (defect in comprehension and/or use of language due to brain disease/injury). Encourages research and interdisciplinary scientific communication.

American Chronic Pain Association
P.O. Box 850
Rocklin, CA 95677
(916) 632-0922

Nonprofit organization. Local self-help groups provide mutual support for chronic pain sufferers; over 700 chapters. Newsletter and publications available.

National Head Injury Foundation (NHIF)
1776 Massachusetts Avenue, Suite 100
Washington, DC 20036
(202) 296-6443; Fax (202) 296-8850; (800) 444-NHIF
    (information service)
George Zitnay, Ph.D., President and CEO

National association providing supportive services and information to head injury survivors and their families. Serves as information clearinghouse on head injury and its rehabilitation. Maintains support group network; offers public education; fosters research; provides advocacy services; maintains hotline and speakers' bureau.

Phoenix Project
c/o Constance Miller
P.O. Box 84151
Seattle, WA 98124
(206) 329-1371; Fax (206) 623-4251
Constance Miller, Contact

Organization providing information and guidance to head injury survivors. Offers referrals, provides seminars, and maintains speakers' bureau.

DEPRESSION

Depressives Anonymous: Recovery from Depression
329 East Sixty-second Street
New York, NY 10021
(212) 689-2600
Dr. Helen DeRosis, Founder

Self-help organization (3,000 members) for individuals experiencing depression or anxiety. Offers classes, weekly meetings, newsletter, brochures, and pamphlets; supports research.

Foundation for Depression and Manic Depression
7 East Sixty-seventh Street
New York, NY 10021
(212) 772-3400
Ronald R. Fieve, M.D., President

Research and training institution sponsoring clinical drug trial program for patients unresponsive to currently available medications. Conducts cocaine/substance abuse treatment program; has psychodiagnostic laboratory on site.

National Chronic Pain Outreach Association
7979 Old Georgetown Road, Suite 100
Bethesda, MD 20814-2429
(301) 652-4948

Nonprofit. Local support groups hold regular meetings, hear guest speakers, maintain listings of resources, offer emotional support.

Provides information clearinghouse for literature about chronic pain; *Lifeline* magazine, and listings of support groups, and pain centers by state.

National Depressive and Manic Depressive Association
730 North Franklin, Suite 501
Chicago, IL 60610
(312) 642-0049; Fax (312) 642-7243; (800) 82-NDMDA
Susan Dime-Meenan, Executive Director

Support and advocacy organization composed of 30,000 depressive and manic-depressive individuals and their families. Promotes research; sponsors lectures; conducts confidential local meetings. Provides telephone information and support service.

National Foundation for Depressive Illness
P.O. Box 2257
New York, NY 10116
(212) 268-4260; (800) 248-4344
Peter Ross, Executive Director

Organization of professionals and patients interested in affective mood disorders. Provides information. Offers educational programs to professionals and the public; maintains speakers' bureau and referral service.

SCHIZOPHRENIA

American Schizophrenia Association
900 North Federal Highway, Suite 330
Boca Raton, FL 33432
(407) 393-6167
Mary Roddy Haggerty, Executive Director

Organization composed of health-care professionals, patients, and family members. Promotes research into biochemical and genetic causes of schizophrenia; advocates improved treatment. Provides public and professional education; offers referral service for the orthomolecular treatment of mental illness; publishes brochure.

National Institute of Mental Health
Consumer Information Center
Department 546X
Pueblo, CO 81009

Center distributing the free publication, *Schizophrenia: Questions and Answers* (546X), which describes the causes, treatments, and outlook for schizophrenia.

National Institute of Mental Health
Public Inquiries/Aging Branch
Parklawn Building, Room 15C-05
5600 Fishers Lane
Rockville, MD 20857
(301) 443-4513

Publishes mental-health directory of outpatient clinics, psychiatric hospitals, and mental-health professionals in area. Provides information and booklets on mental health, including depression, phobias, substance/alcohol abuse.

National Mental Health Association
1021 Prince Street
Alexandria, VA 22314-2971; (800) 969-6642; (703) 684-7722

Local chapters provide information about mental-health problems, resources, and support services; referrals.

Schizophrenics Anonymous
1209 California Road
Eastchester, NY 10709
(914) 337-2252
Elizabeth A. Plante, Director

Self-help organization sponsored by the American Schizophrenia Association. Offers 12-step recovery program for diagnosed schizophrenics with discussion topics including symptoms/treatment, responsibility, and associated guilt. Provides newsletter and health information.

STRESS-RELATED DISORDERS

American Institute of Stress
124 Park Avenue
Yonkers, NY 10703
(914) 963-1200; Fax (914) 965-6267; (800) 24-RELAX
Paul J. Rosch, M.D., President and Chairman

Information clearinghouse on personal and social consequences of stress. Compiles research data; evaluates stress management programs; and sponsors symposia, workshops, and consulting services.

Institute for the Development of Emotional and Life Skills (IDEALS)
P.O. Box 391
State College, PA 16804
(814) 237-4805
Patricia A. Yoder, Executive Director

Training center for the improvement of emotional and interpersonal skills on both the professional mental-health worker's level and on the ordinary worker/manager's level. Promotes reduced stress in family and business environments.

Institute for Labor and Mental Health
3137 Telegraph Avenue
Oakland, CA 94609
(415) 653-6166
Dr. Richard Epstein, Director

Agency dealing with issues of occupational stress. Identifies causes; promotes communication; assists unions with grievances. Provides counseling; offers legal advocacy services; advises government and businesses on stress reduction.

International Association for Clear Thinking
3939 West Spencer Street
Appleton, WI 54912
(414) 739-8311; (800) 236-8311, Wisconsin only
Shirley Bender, Executive Director

Center providing services to individuals who want to reduce the level of emotional stress in their lives. Teaches Rational Behavior Therapy coping skills. Offers self-help programs, individualized support, seminars, workshops, counseling sessions, support groups, and literature.

Society for Traumatic Stress Studies
435 North Michigan Avenue, Suite 1717
Chicago, IL 60611
(312) 644-0828; Fax (312) 644-8557
Robert Tonai, Executive Officer

Research organization studying the treatment of individuals with traumatic stress disorders. Provides information, seminars, and lawyer referral service.

OTHER MENTAL DISORDERS/EMOTIONAL PROBLEMS

Deaf-Reach
3521 Twelfth Street, NE
Washington, DC 20017
(202) 832-6681; Fax (202) 832-8454; (202) 832-6681 (TDD)
Carole Schauer, Executive Director

Local service provider to deaf persons with mental/emotional problems. Operates group homes for mentally ill deaf persons. Provides referral services, housing placement assistance, personal counseling, day programs, community advocacy activities. Publishes newsletter and brochure.

Emotional Health Anonymous
P.O. Box 63236
Los Angeles, CA 90063-0236
(213) 268-7220
Virginia Fierro, Office Manager

Self-help group for individuals recovering from emotional problems and emotional illnesses. Offers crisis intervention services; sponsors daily meetings in southern California; publishes newsletters and pamphlets.

Emotions Anonymous
P.O. Box 4245
St. Paul, MN 55104
(612) 647-9712; Fax 647-1593
Karen Crawford, Director

Self-help organization serving individuals with emotional illnesses.
Provides literature and information; makes telephone referrals to
local chapters.

Hospitalized Veterans Writing Project
5920 Nall, Room 102
Mission, KS 66202
(913) 432-1214
Sharon Smith, President

Organization encouraging hospitalized U.S. veterans to write for
pleasure and emotional rehabilitation. Conducts writing classes in
hospitals and bestows monetary awards for outstanding pieces of
nonfiction, poetry, fiction, and cartoon.

Huxley Institute for Biosocial Research
900 North Federal Highway, Suite 330
Boca Raton, FL 33432
(407) 393-6167; (800) 847-3802
Mary Roddy Haggerty, Executive Director

Research and training institute concerned with mental-health disorders and treatment/rehabilitation resources. Offers educational services to family members, professionals, community organizations,
and government agencies. Maintains referral center in New York
City and library on orthomolecular treatment of schizophrenia and
other disorders.

National Mental Health Consumer Self-Help
Clearinghouse
311 South Juniper Street, Room 902
Philadelphia, PA 19107
(215) 735-6367
Paolo del Vecchio, Coordinator

Organization providing technical assistance to people attempting to develop self-help projects for mental-health issues. Provides informational referrals, written materials, and consultations.

National Self-Help Clearinghouse
25 West Forty-third Street, Room 620
New York, NY 10036
(212) 642-2944; Fax (212) 719-2488
Frank Riessman, Co-Director

Clearinghouse for information on and referrals to self-help groups. Maintains speakers' bureau and 200-volume library. Supports research and training; offers newsletter and brochures.

Neurotics Anonymous International Liaison
11140 Bainbridge Drive
Little Rock, AR 72212
(501) 221-2809
Grover Boydston, Chairman

Self-help organization with 10,000 members using a 12-step program of recovery from emotional illness. Holds meetings for mentally and emotionally disturbed individuals to exchange experiences and recovery stories. Publishes quarterly newsletter, pamphlets, and books.

Recovery
802 North Dearborn Street
Chicago, IL 60610
(312) 337-5661; Fax (312) 337-5756
Shirley Sachs, Executive Director

Mental-health organization promoting neuropsychiatrist Abraham A. Low's self-help method of controlling temperamental behavior and changing attitudes toward fears and nervous symptoms. Publishes newsletter; has 1,000 community-level groups.

Self Abuse Finally Ends (SAFE)
c/o Karen Conterio
P.O. Box 267810
Chicago, IL 60626
(312) 722-3113; (800) DONTCUT (information line)
Karen Conterio, Contact

Self-help group for self-injuring persons. Maintains speakers' bureau; compiles statistics.

Self-Help Center

1600 Dodge Avenue, Suite S-122
Evanston, IL 60201
(708) 328-0471; Fax (708) 328-0754
Daryl Isenberg, Ph.D., Executive Director

Clearinghouse for information on various types of self-help groups. Conducts workshops, training programs, and research on effectiveness of self-help group approach. Maintains computer database; publishes brochures, pamphlets, workbooks, and directories of existing self-help groups.

CONSUMER ADVOCACY GROUPS

National Alliance for the Mentally Ill

2101 Wilson Boulevard, Suite 302
Arlington, VA 22201
(703) 524-7600; Fax (703) 524-9094
Laurie M. Flynn, Executive Director

Alliance of self-help support groups and political advocacy groups concerned with the quality treatment and legal rights of individuals with severe/chronic mental illnesses. National office serves as information clearinghouse and offers referrals to local groups, which provide emotional/practical support for families and maintain libraries. Provides speakers' bureau; promotes research; publishes newsletter and brochures.

National Association of Psychiatric Survivors

P.O. Box 618
Sioux Falls, SD 57101
(605) 334-4067
Rae Unzicker, Coordinator

Organization with 2,000 members of current and former mental-health patients, family members, and others interested in the rights of mental-health patients. Seeks to end involuntary psychiatric intervention and forced treatments in favor of self-help and peer-support group approaches, and other nonmedical alternatives. Fights social stigma attached to mental illness. Provides referral and advocacy services, speakers' bureau, newsletter, and brochure.

National Mental Health Association (NMHA)
1021 Prince Street
Alexandria, VA 22314-2971
(703) 684-7722; Fax (703) 684-5968; (800) 969-NMHA
John Horner, President

Consumer advocacy organization promoting mental-health research. Assesses quality of care at various mental-health-care facilities. Serves as national clearinghouse for educational materials; conducts public education campaigns.

National Mental Health Consumers' Association
P.O. Box 1166
Madison, WI 53701
Patrick Irick, Chairperson

Consumer advocacy organization composed of mental-health-care professionals, current and former patients, and other interested persons. Actively promotes the creation of local self-help groups.

Project Overcome
50 Fort Street, N, Apartment 224
Minneapolis, MN 55406
(612) 340-0165
Rosalind Artison-Koenning, Executive Director

Consumer advocacy organization made up of current and former mental-health-care patients. Seeks to eliminate social stigma attached to mental illness. Offers speakers' bureau, seminars, lectures, newsletter; maintains library.

Reclamation, Inc.
2502 Waterford
San Antonio, TX 78217
(512) 824-8618
Don H. Culwell, Director

Organization composed of former mental-health patients seeking to remove the stigma associated with mental illness. Provides assistance in living outside the hospital setting (resocialization, employment, and housing). Seeks to improve media coverage and public image of mental-health patients. Provides political advocacy services, maintains library and speakers' bureau; publishes quarterly newsletter.

FACILITIES/TREATMENT PROGRAMS

Adventures in Movement for the Handicapped (AIM)
945 Danbury Road
Dayton, OH 45420
(513) 294-4611; Fax (513) 294-3783
Dr. Jo A. Geiger, Executive Director

Support organization, which developed and promotes the AIM Method of Specialized Movement Education, to improve muscle control and coordination through rhythmic exercises of gross- and fine-motor movements. The program is suitable/adaptable to various handicaps, including visual impairment, hearing impairment, learning disabilities, emotional problems, and orthopedic problems.

Association for Advancement of Blind and Retarded
164-09 Hillside Drive
Jamaica, NY 11432
(718) 523-2222
Christopher Weldon, Executive Director

Organization serving multihandicapped blind and severely retarded adults. Operates intermediate-care facilities, short-term treatment centers, and summer camp. Provides information and referral services.

The Bridge
248 West 108th Street
New York, NY 10025
(212) 663-3000; Fax (212) 663-3181
Murray Itzkowitz, Executive Director

Mental health and rehabilitation facility for chronic mentally/emotionally disabled adults and for homeless mentally disabled adults. Offers community residence housing, rehabilitation programs, vocational training, job placement.

Mental Research Institute (MRI)
555 Middlefield Road
Palo Alto, CA 94301
(415) 321-3055; Fax (415) 321-3785
Judith E. Foddrill, Administrator

Behavioral science-oriented organization, which offers professional training, research, educational programs, and workshops. Operates sliding-scale free clinic for short-term, family-oriented therapy. Provides emergency treatment for family violence. Operates specialized clinical centers for problems such as eating disorders and depression. Maintains speakers bureau and 1,500-volume library.

Occupational Program Consultants Association
c/o Kris Brennan
Lincoln EAP, Inc.
201 North Eighth Street, No. 101
Lincoln, NE 68508
(402) 476-0186
Kris Brennan, President

Consulting agency, which provides employee assistance program services to businesses. Helps businesses put these programs in place, so that employees with substance abuse problems and/or emotional problems can be referred for treatment.

Social/Vocational Rehabilitation Clinic
c/o Post-Graduate Center West
344 West Thirty-sixth Street
New York, NY 10018
(212) 971-3200; Fax (212) 560-6794
Michael Bellotti, Program Director

Psychiatric outpatient clinic providing comprehensive therapeutic program with the goals of reducing inpatient hospital admissions and promoting independent living and social integration. Offers case management services.

NEEDS OF AGING

American Association for International Aging
1133 Twentieth Street, NW, Suite 330
Washington, DC 20036
(202) 833-8893; Fax (202) 833-8762
Helen K. Kerschner, Ph.D., President

Seeks to improve the socioeconomic conditions of older low-income persons in developing countries through self-help, mutual support, and economic development activities. Sponsors international developmental programs for retired Americans.

American Association of Retired Persons (AARP)
601 E Street, NW
Washington, DC 20049
(202) 434-2277
Horace B. Deets, Executive Director

A membership organization dedicated to improving the lives of persons age 50 and over. Services provided by volunteers include a widowed persons' service, driver improvement programs, and health information. Members may participate in group health insurance, a mail-order pharmacy, auto and home insurance, travel services, and investment programs. AARP publishes pamphlets on aging, housing, retirement planning, travel, and support services for caregiving, hospitalization, health, and exercise. AARP also publishes a bimonthly magazine and monthly newspaper. Call or write for membership fee information.

American Dietetic Association
216 West Jackson Boulevard, Suite 800
Chicago, IL 60606
(312) 899-0040; Fax (312) 899-1979
Beverly Bajus, CEO/Executive Director

Professional society for registered dietitians. Provides information about health, food, and nutrition and will provide a list of registered dietitians in your area. Free publications available upon request.

American Guidance Inc.
6231 Leesburg Pike, Suite 305
P.O. Box 448
Falls Church, VA 22044
(800) 736-1460; (703) 533-1464

Publishes *American Guidance for Seniors*, a book about available benefits, entitlements, and assistance including federal and Social Security, Medicare, health insurance, low-income programs, food stamps, Medicaid, veterans' benefits, funerals, and dying.

American National Postal Employees Retirees Association
c/o William Bert Johnson
18900 SchoolCraft
Detroit, MI 48223
William Bert Johnson, President

Postal employees and retirees and immediate family members. Promotes health and welfare of members. Sponsors seminars and competitions, offers specialized education, compiles statistics.

American Senior Citizens Associations
P.O. Box 41
Fayetteville, NC 28302
(919) 323-3641
Ben Sutton, Executive Vice President

Purpose is to promote the physical, emotional, mental, and economic well-being of senior citizens. Belief is that senior citizens have the right to live with competence, security, and dignity. Promotes programs to help senior citizens be active in their communities. Seeks affiliations with state senior-citizen associations.

Asociación Nacional Pro Personas Mayores
3325 Wilshire Boulevard, Suite 800
Los Angeles, CA 90010
(213) 487-1922; Fax (213) 385-3014
Carmela G. Cacayo, President/CEO

Articulates needs of Hispanic and other low-income elderly. Seeks to include the Hispanic elderly in social service programs aimed at older Americans. Administers the Senior Community Service Employment Project, funded by the Department of Labor, which provides employment to more than 1,900 low-income people over 55 years of age in eleven states.

Association of Retired Americans
P.O. Box 610286
Dallas, TX 75261
(800) 662-8040

Senior Americans interested in enhancing their lives through group benefits. Offers program of high-quality, low-cost benefits and services to members including discounts on prescriptions, eyeglasses, and hearing aids; low-interest credit cards, travel discounts, etc. Assists government agencies with development of benefit programs for retired Americans.

Beverly Foundation
70 South Lake Avenue, Suite 750
Pasadena, CA 91101
(818) 792-2292
Carroll Wendland, Ph.D., President

Encourages a fresh perspective on problems and opportunities concerning the elderly. Creates imaginative self-help programs and opportunities for older adults and their communities.

Brethren Homes and Older Adult Ministries
1451 Dundee Avenue
Elgin, IL 60120
(708) 742-5100
Jay A. Gibble, Executive Director

Shares common concerns and programs of service to older adults.

Catholic Golden Age
430 Penn Avenue
Scranton, PA 18503
(717) 342-3294; Fax (717) 961-5779
Joseph P. Leary, President

Purpose is to advance the well-being of older people in the United States through research, education, technical assistance, and training. Focuses primarily on legal rights, guardianship, and alternative protective services, and delivery of legal services. Provides counseling services.

Center for Consumer Healthcare Information
4000 Birch Street, Suite 112
Newport Beach, CA 92660
Correspondence:
P.O. Box 16067
Irvine, CA 92713
(800) 627-2244; (714) 752-2335

Publisher's directory of about 70,000 health-care facilities and support services, including home-care, rehabilitation, psychiatric, and addiction treatment programs; hospices, adult day care, burn and cancer centers; information and support resources section, self-help. Has extensive database; can license the data.

The Center for Social Gerontology
117 North First Street
Ann Arbor, MI 48104
(313) 665-1126
Penelope A. Hommel, Executive Director

The Center for Social Gerontology aims to study and discuss the meaning of a longer life and gerontology, emphasizing religion and spirituality, to provide older persons with motivation to lead self-fulfilling lives, and to emphasize the role of religious faith in the endeavors and activities of older people.

Christian Foundation for Children and Aging
1 Elmwood Avenue
Kansas City, MO 66103-3719
(913) 384-6500; Fax (913) 384-2211
Robert K. Hertzer, President

Seeks to advance the physical, mental, spiritual, and social welfare of the economically disadvantaged, especially children and aging persons in developing countries and the United States. Provides Christian education and guidance to needy persons.

Council on Family Health

225 Park Avenue South, Seventeenth Floor
New York, NY 10003
(212) 598-3617

Organization sponsored by medicine manufacturers. Issues variety
of publications on safe use of medicines, and on health and health
emergencies.

Daughters of the Elderly Bridging the Unknown Together (DEBUT)

c/o Pat Meier
710 Concord Street
Elletsville, IN 47429
(812) 876-5319
Pat Meier, President

Provides nonjudgmental support and education in all areas of caring and coping with the complex process of aging.

Diplomatic and Consular Officers, Retired (DACOR)

1801 F Street, NW
Washington, DC 20006
(202) 682-0500
William B. Cobb, Executive Director

Retired and active members of the Foreign Service and other federal government agencies who have served in officer positions, prin-
cipally concerned with international relations. Operates DACOR
Bacon House Foundation for educational and charitable purposes.

Ebenezer Society

2722 Park Avenue South
Minneapolis, MN 55407
(612) 879-1467; Fax 879-1473
Mark Thomas, President

Lutheran organization providing quality services and facilities for
older people with varying needs. Offers nursing-home care and
medical treatment for low-income elderly. Ebenezer means "stone
of help."

Eldercare Locator

Service of National Association of Area Agencies on Aging;
   (800) 677-1116

Toll-free assistance in identifying community (local) resources for
seniors nationwide including Meals-on-Wheels, transportation, activity centers, legal assistance, and housing.

Elder Craftsmen

135 East Sixty-fifth Street
New York, NY 10021
(212) 861-5260
Barbara B. Stives, Executive Director

Designed to give the elderly an opportunity to make a positive statement through the medium of crafts, while nurturing the American
craft tradition. Provides a nonprofit outlet for crafts, fabricated by
seniors participating in the crafts/works project and sold directly to
the public, or sold on consignment for other senior craftsmen.

Elder Hostel, Inc.

75 Federal Street, Third Floor
Boston, MA 02110
(617) 426-7788
William D. Berkely, President

Offers special, low-cost, short-term, residential academic programs
for adults 60 years of age and older and their (younger) spouses
and companions. Offers a wide range of noncredit liberal arts and
science courses taught by college faculty. Provides financial aid.

Episcopal Society for Ministry on Aging

323 Wyandotte Street
Bethlehem, PA 18015
(215) 868-5400
Joan Lukens, Executive Director

An agency of the Episcopal Church developing and supporting
ministries on aging. Serves the spiritual, psychological, and physical wants and needs of older persons and their families; fosters the
continuing contributions of the elderly to church and society.

Families U.S.A. Foundation
1334 Sixth Street, NW
Washington, DC 20005
(202) 628-3030; Fax (202) 347-2417
Ronald F. Pollack, Executive Director

Develops projects and educational activities designed to help the elderly.

Fund for Assuring an Independent Retirement
100 Indiana Avenue, NW, Suite 813
Washington, DC 20001
(202) 393-4695
Vince R. Sombrotto, President and Chairman

Coalition of organizations whose members are employed by or retired from the federal government. Seeks to protect the wages and benefits of members. Conducts research and political education programs and analyzes legislative proposals for the benefit of member organizations and Congress.

Golden Companions
P.O. Box 754
Pullman, WA 99163
(509) 334-9351
Joanne R. Buteau, President

Seeks to assist members in finding travel companions. Offers travel information and tour discounts. Provides a mail exchange service.

Good Faith
1732 Glenn Street
Cayce, NC 29033
(803) 794-2260
Schyrl B. Amos, Executive Secretary-Treasurer

Raises funds to cover the cost of dental plates for elderly and handicapped persons.

Gray Panthers
1424 Sixteenth Street, NW, Suite 602
Washington, DC 20036
(202) 387-3111

Aims to combat ageism—the discrimination against persons on the
basis of chronological age. Advises and acts as a catalyst for and
organizes local groups of young, middle-aged, and older persons to
work on issues of their choosing.

Hispanic American Geriatric Society
1 Cutts Road
Durham, NH 03824-3102
(603) 868-5757
Dr. Eugene Tillock, President

Provides advocacy for older Hispanic Americans; offers advice,
health-care services, and health-education programs.

Institute of Certified Financial Planners
7600 East Eastman Avenue, Suite 301
Denver, CO 80231
(303) 751-7600; Fax (303) 751-1037
Brent A. Neiser, CPF, Executive Director

National organization of licensed professionals who provide financial planning for long-term care, medical insurance, life insurance,
and taxes. Names of financial planners in your area and free brochure available upon request.

International Senior Citizens Association
1102 South Crenshaw Boulevard
Los Angeles, CA 90019
(213) 857-6434

Provides coordination on the international level to safeguard the
interests and needs of senior citizens, establishes means of communication among older citizens for educational and cultural developments, acts as a catalyst, and presents forums through which older
persons may contribute to world betterment.

Jewish Association for Service for the Aged
40 West Sixty-eighth Street
New York, NY 10023
(212) 724-3200; Fax (212) 769-1218
David J. Stern, Executive Vice President

Social welfare organization whose objective is to provide the services necessary to enable the older adult to remain in the community. Services include case management, information, and referral to appropriate health, welfare, educational, social, recreational, and vacation services, government benefits and entitlements, personal counseling, financial assistance, health and medical services, housing, and long-term care.

Little Brothers—Friends of the Elderly
1658 West Belmont Avenue
Chicago, IL 60657
(312) 477-0106; Fax (312) 883-5271

Seeks to combat the isolation often experienced by elderly people by providing friendship and other social services. Sponsors visitation programs, parties, and summer vacations. Also offers assistance with chores, maintenance, and delivery of hot meals.

Mature Outlook
6001 North Clark Street
Chicago, IL 60660
(800) 336-6330

National organization of seniors over 50 years of age. Provides benefits, services, and information to members. Offers discounts on a variety of services. Publishes magazine and newsletter.

National Alliance of Senior Citizens
1700 Eighteenth Street NW, Suite 401
Washington, DC 20009
(202) 986-0117

National membership organization of seniors. Legislative advocate. Supplemental benefits such as discounts on rental cars, vacations, long-distance telephone calls; mail order prescriptions and dental/vision/hearing program. Publishes *Senior Guardian*, senior citizen membership publication.

National Association of Area Agencies on Aging (NAAAA)
1112 Sixteenth Street, NW, Suite 100
Washington, DC 20024
(202) 296-8130
Jonathan D. Linkous, Executive Director

An umbrella organization, representing more than 650 area agencies, which has been mandated by Congress to help older people gain from social and medical services across the country. Call NAAAA to find the telephone number of your local agency for information and referrals to services.

National Association of Meal Programs
204 E Street, NE
Washington, DC 20002
(202)547-6157; Fax (202) 547-6348
Gail Martin, Executive Director

Professional and volunteer, members of the association deliver meals to the homes of elderly individuals. Referrals to local meal programs.

National Association of Retired Federal Employees
1533 New Hampshire Avenue, NW
Washington, DC 20036
(202) 234-0832
Harry Price, President

Composed of retired U.S. government, civilian, and DC employees, their spouses, persons drawing annuities as survivors of deceased government employees, present employees eligible for optional retirement, and federal employees with at least five years of service. Seeks to serve annuitants and potential annuitants and their survivors under the retirement laws; sponsors and supports beneficial legislation; promotes the general welfare of civil service annuitants and their families. Also interested in preretirement programs, especially in federal and district government agencies, and in the broad field of problems of the aged and aging.

National Conference on Public Employee Retirement Systems

311 Roosevelt Avenue
San Antonio, TX 78210
(512) 534-3262; Fax (512) 534-5877
Carlos Resendez, Executive Secretary

Composed of national, state, and local organizations whose purpose is to promote and safeguard the rights and benefits of public employees in retirement systems. Serves as congressional liaison. Conducts an annual legislative workshop.

National Council on the Aging, Inc. (NCA)

409 Third Street, SW
Washington, DC 20024
(202) 479-1200
Dr. Daniel Thursz, President

National nonprofit organization, which provides information, training, and support for research on aging and related fields for both professionals and volunteers. Subgroups within the NCA include the National Institute of Adult Daycare, the National Institute of Senior Centers, and the National Institute of Senior Housing. NCA publishes information and help guides for caregivers.

National Council on Child Abuse and Family Violence

1155 Connecticut Avenue, NW, Suite 300
Washington, DC 20036
(202) 424-6695; Fax (202) 914-3616; (800) 222-2000
Alan Davis, President

To support community-based prevention and treatment programs providing assistance to children, women, and the elderly who are victims of abuse and violence.

National Council of Senior Citizens (NCSC)

1331 F Street, NW
Washington, DC 20024-1171
(202) 347-8800
Lawrence T. Smedley, Executive Director

NCSC is a national social-activist association of councils, clubs, and community groups working toward bettering the lives of older people. NCSC provides information about federal housing programs, job programs under the Older American Act, Medicare, and long-term-care insurance. Call or write for membership fee information.

National Geriatrics Society
1200 West Crooked Lake Place
Eustis, FL 32736-6433
Dr. J. Eckhardt, Executive Officer

Public, voluntary, and proprietary institutions providing long-term care and treatment for the chronically ill aged. Promotes maintenance of proper operational standards and qualified administration of facilities caring for the aged.

National Health Information Center and Communication Technology—Office of Disease Prevention and Health Promotion (ODPHP)
U.S. Public Health Service
11426-28 Rockville Pike
Rockville, MD 20852
Correspondence: P.O. Box 1133
Washington, DC 20013-1133
(800) 336-4797; (301) 565-4167

Database of organizations including federal and federally-sponsored offices and programs providing health information and assistance. Assists consumers and health-care workers by referring them to appropriate health-information sources. Issues publications regarding health promotion and disease prevention, information about treatment, and names of support groups for various diseases and conditions. Publications include *Healthfinders*, pamphlet about free health information; *Healthy People 2000*, resource list; and others concerning dieting and smoking.

National Indian Council on Aging
6400 Uptown Boulevard, NE
City Centre, Suite 510-W
Albuquerque, NM 87110
(505) 888-3302

Seeks to bring about improved, comprehensive services to the Indian and Alaskan native elderly. Acts as focal point for needs of older Indians, disseminates information on Indian aging programs, provides technical assistance and training to tribal organizations in the development of their programs. Publishes newsletter for older American Indians.

National Interfaith Coalition of Aging (NICA)
409 Third Street, SW
Washington, DC 20024
(202) 479-6689
John F. Evans, Program Manager

NICA is a division of the National Council on the Aging. Its members represent people of all religious faiths. Members work together to plan assistance and support research for religious groups that service the needs of the elderly.

National Resource Network
3631 Fairmount
Dallas, TX 75219
(214) 528-9080
Beverly Redfearn, President

Banks, savings and loan associations, and other institutions united to help individuals with basic financial planning, especially when there is a change in lifestyle (marriage, divorce, retirement), and to help families of deceased persons in gathering information concerning claim procedures for life insurance, profit-sharing plans, Social Security, teachers' and veterans' benefits, and other financial resources.

National Senior Sports Association
10560 Main Street
Fairfax, VA 22030
(703) 385-7540; Fax (703) 591-4169
Lloyd Wright, President & Executive Director

Helps older Americans improve and maintain physical and emotional well-being through organized sports and recreation. Conducts regional tournaments in golf and bowling. Conducts programs and informational services.

Older Women's League (OWL)
666 Eleventh Street, NW, Suite 700
Washington, DC 20001
(202) 783-6686; Fax (202) 638-2356
Joan A. Kuriansky, Executive Director

OWL is dedicated to educating the public about the issues and problems of older women, including caring for parents and spouses. OWL offers mutual aid and support services, with focus on single or widowed older women.

Opening Door
Route 2, Box 1805
Woodford, VA 22580
(804) 633-6752
William A. Duke, Jr., President

Acts as a clearinghouse and consultant to the travel and lodging industry for disabled travelers. Sponsors seminars on disability etiquette and the effect of the Americans with Disabilities Act on public accommodations. Bestows awards.

PRIDE Foundation—Promote Real Independence for the Disabled and Elderly
Box 1293, 391 Long Hill Road
Groton, CT 06340
(203) 445-1448
Evelyn S. Kennedy, Executive Director

Provides rehabilitation assistance for the handicapped and elderly in the areas of home management, independent dressing, and personal grooming. Designs and develops special garments to help the handicapped feel more comfortable and dress independently, designs assistance devices for use in the kitchen, bedroom, and bathroom. Provides discussion leaders for community outreach and assistance to health agencies, social service groups, and volunteer organizations.

Private Care Association
242 West Valley Avenue, Suite 103
Homewood, AL 35209
(205) 945-1669
Marc Catalono, President

To acquaint the public with the existence of reputable agencies providing sitters and companions primarily for the elderly; to establish standards of care for older Americans. Conducts educational programs, maintains placement services, compiles statistics.

Retired Persons Services (Pharmacy)
500 Montgomery Street
Alexandria, VA 22314-1563
(703) 684-0244; Fax (703) 684-0246
John R. McHugh, President

Provides non- and prescription drugs and other health-care items through mail service for members of American Associations of Retired Persons in California, Connecticut, District of Columbia, Florida, Indiana, Montana, Nevada, Oregon, Pennsylvania, Texas, and Virginia.

Retired Senior Volunteer Program
1100 Vermont Avenue, NW
Washington, DC 20525
(202) 606-4851
Suzanne Fahy, Contact

Brings persons of retirement age more fully into community life through volunteer services, which vary according to their preference and community needs. Projects are planned, organized, and operated at the local level.

Senior Action in a Gay Environment
208 West Thirteenth Street
New York, NY 10011
(212) 741-2247; Fax (212) 366-1947
Arlene Kochman, Executive Director

Dedicated to meeting the needs of older gays and lesbians and ending the isolation that has kept them separate from each other, and from the larger community. SAGE provides information and referral services in legal matters, personal visits, social activities, and long-term-care facilities and referral to social service agencies. Provides in-service training for agency members and institutions serving older gays. Sponsors AIDS Service Program for the Elderly.

Senior Companion Program
Washington Urban League
2900 Newton Street, NE
Washington, DC 20018
(202) 529-8701
Constance M. Burns, Assistant Director

Offers volunteer opportunities for low-income persons age 60 and over to establish one-to-one relationships with other older persons, particularly the frail elderly in their homes, in an effort to delay or prevent institutionalization. Provides services to the elderly in institutions in an attempt to render them capable of returning to community life.

Senior Gleaners, Inc.
3185 Longview Drive
North Highlands, CA 95660
(916) 971-1530
Frank Swiger, President

Retired senior citizens who salvage edible but often unsalable foods. The gleaners collect what farmers cannot harvest or cannot sell after the harvest, not only for themselves but also to distribute to charitable organizations. Farmers who donate their unsalable produce receive a federal tax deduction.

Senior PAC (Political Action)
c/o Robert Samuel
1000 Vermont Avenue, NW, Suite 400
Washington, DC 20005
Robert Samuel, Director

A political action committee dedicated to representing older and retired Americans. Works to strengthen and defend Social Security and Medicare programs.

September Days Club
2200 Sutherland Avenue
Knoxville, TN 37919
(404) 728-4000; Fax (404) 728-4460
Jamie Rosenberg, Director

A nonprofit discount travel organization for people 50 and older, created by Days Inn of America, Inc.

Vietnamese Senior Citizens Association
c/o Fairmont Gardens, Apartment 201
4129 Wadsworth Court
Annadale, VA 22003
(703) 354-8431
Chu Ngoc Lien, President

Offers social and cultural assistance and fellowship to members. Seeks to preserve and develop Vietnamese culture, tradition, and customs. Sponsors community events and maintains a cemetery for members.

Nursing Homes and Special Housing for the Elderly

American Association of Homes for the Aging
901 E Street, NW, Suite 500
Washington, DC 20004-2037
(202) 783-2242; Fax (202) 223-5920
Sheldon R. Goldberg, President

Provides a unified means of identifying and solving problems in order to protect and advance the interests of the residents served. Believes that long-term care should be geared to individual needs and provided in a spectrum ranging from nursing care to independent living and community-based care.

American Health Care Association
1201 L Street, NW
Washington, DC 20005
(205) 842-4444

Federation of state associations of licensed nursing homes. Provides referrals to state organizations and publishes consumers' guide to selecting a nursing home.

B'nai B'rith Senior Citizens Housing Committee
1640 Rhode Island Avenue, NW
Washington, DC 20036
(202) 857-6581; Fax (202) 857-0980
Mark D. Olshan, Ph.D., Director

Provides housing facilities in six countries for elderly and handi-capped people with low incomes. Operates B'nai B'rith Senior Citizens Housing Network, comprising 21 apartment buildings and serving 4,000 senior citizens.

Concerned Relatives of Nursing Home Patients
P.O. Box 18820
Cleveland Heights, OH 44118
(216) 321-0403
Mary A. Mendelson, Executive Director

Seeks to achieve dignity and comfort for all nursing-home patients whether they are private pay, Medicare, or Medicaid patients. Monitors quality of care in nursing homes and legislation affecting patients' lives. Acts as advocacy group for patients' rights, and rep-resents patients' interests before legislative bodies.

Foundation Aiding the Elderly
P.O. Box 254849
Sacramento, CA 96865-4849
(916) 481-8558
Carole Herman, President

Seeks to promote and monitor federal legislation and nursing-home industry activities affecting nursing-home residents. Provides infor-mation to the public on what the group identifies as poor quality and industry nonaccountability regarding noncompliance with federal nursing-home regulations.

National Center on Rural Aging

c/o National Council on the Aging
409 Third Street, SW, Second Floor
Washington, DC 20024
(800) 424-9046; (202) 479-1200

Planners and providers of services for the aging and others interested in issues related to older persons living in rural areas. Develop policies related to their needs and interests.

National Resource Center for Rural Elderly

University of Missouri—Kansas City
5100 Rockville Road
Kansas City, MO 64110
(816) 235-1024

Information about housing programs and services for the elderly in rural America; publications.

Nursing Home Information Service

c/o National Council of Senior Citizens
1331 F Street, NW
Washington, DC 20004-1171
(202) 342-8800; Fax (202) 629-9505
Lawrence T. Smedley, Coordinator

National Senior Citizens Research and Education Center project. Provides information on nursing-home standards and regulations, alternative community and health services, criteria for choosing a nursing home, and guidelines for obtaining Medigap insurance (insurance covering medical expenses after Medicare's percentage is paid).

Project SHARE (Senior Housing At a Reduced Expense)

336 Fulton Avenue
Hempstead, NY 11550
(516) 292-1300
Salvatore Ambrosino, Executive Director

Promotes the availability of housing at reduced cost to senior citizens in house-sharing arrangements in Nassau County, New York.

Organ Transplants

American Transplant Association
P.O. Box 225978
Dallas, TX 75222
(214) 467-4714
Linn Roberts, Contact

Referral network for transplant patients and their families. Provides financial assistance to patients for care and emergency transportation. Educates the public to increase awareness of organ/tissue donation programs.

International Society for Heart and Lung Transplantation
435 North Michigan Avenue, Suite 1717
Chicago, IL 60611
(312) 644-0828; Fax (312) 644-8557
James B. Gantenberg, Executive Director

Organization of health-care professionals interested in artificial hearts, heart transplantation, and heart-lung transplantation. Supports research and professional communication. Works to increase public awareness and government agency recognition of medical developments.

United Network of Organ Sharing
1100 Boulders Parkway, Suite 500
P.O. Box 13770
Richmond, VA 23225
(804) 330-8500; Fax (804) 330-8517; (800) 24-DONOR
Gene A. Pierce, Executive Director

Clearinghouse for organs used in U.S. transplant operations. Operates the Organ Center, which matches donated organs with recipients and arranges for transport of organs.

Professional Caregivers

NURSES, OCCUPATIONAL AND PHYSICAL THERAPISTS, PSYCHIATRY

American Academy of Orthopedic Surgeons
6300 North River Road
Rosemont, IL 60018-4226
(708) 823-7186; Fax (708) 823-8125
Thomas C. Nelson, Executive Director

A professional organization made up of doctors who specialize in injuries and diseases of the musculoskeletal system. Publishes free brochures on arthroscopy; joint replacement; common foot problems; neck, back, and shoulder pains; sprains and strains. Send self-addressed envelope and request for information about a particular topic.

American Academy of Physical Medicine and Rehabilitation
122 South Michigan Avenue, Suite 1300
Chicago, IL 60603-6107
(312) 922-9366; Fax (312) 922-6754
Ronald A. Heinrichs, Executive Director

A professional organization of psychiatrists specializing in physical rehabilitation. List of specialists in your area available upon request.

American Association for Geriatric Psychiatry
P.O. Box 376-A
Greenbelt, MD 20768
(301) 220-0952
Alice Conde, Executive Director

Provides brief articles on psychiatric topics and case reports pertaining to elderly patients.

American Dental Association
211 East Chicago Avenue
Chicago, IL 60611
(312) 440-2860

Provides information on free and low-cost services for older people
through state dental associations.

American Geriatrics Society
770 Lexington Avenue, Suite 300
New York, NY 10021
(212) 308-1414; Fax (212) 832-8646
Linda Hiddemen Barondess, Executive Vice President

Professional society of physicians and other health-care professionals interested in the problems of the aged. Encourages and promotes
the study of geriatrics and stresses the importance of medical research in the field of aging.

American Nurses Association
600 Maryland Avenue, SW, Suite 100 West
Washington, DC 20024-2571
(202) 554-4444; Fax (202) 554-2262; (800) 274-4ANA
Barbara K. Redman, Contact

A professional society representing the nation's registered nurses.
The ANA sets standards for nurses and educates the public and
Congress about the nursing profession. Publications are available
upon request.

American Occupational Therapy Association, Inc.
P.O. Box 1725
1383 Piccard Drive
Rockville, MD 20849-1725
(301) 948-9626; Fax (301) 948-5529
Jeanette Bair, Executive Director

A professional organization for therapists who help disabled people
restore their ability to perform daily living skills such as cooking,
eating, bathing, dressing, employment, and other activities. Brochures
about occupational therapy and a list of state associations are available upon request.

American Physical Therapy Association
1111 North Fairfax Street
Alexandria, VA 22314
(703) 684-2782
William D. Coughlan, CEO

A professional organization of physical therapists who help patients recover from injury, stroke, or other illness by strengthening muscles and improving coordination. Brochures about physical therapy and listings of stroke rehabilitation facilities are available upon request.

American Podiatric Medical Association
9312 Old Georgetown Road
Bethesda, MD 20814
(301) 571-9200; Fax (301) 530-2752
Frank J. Malouff, Executive Director

Professional organization composed of doctors who specialize in the diagnosis and treatment of foot injuries and disease by medical or surgical means. Publishes free brochures on diabetes, arthritis, bunions, heel pain, Medicare benefits, and finding a local podiatrist.

American Red Cross
431 Eighteenth Street, NW
Washington, DC 20006
(202) 737-8300
Elizabeth Dole, President

Many of its 2,700 chapters nationwide offer safety and health programs in first aid, CPR aquatics, back injury, prevention, stress management, and health for people over 50 years of age. Many chapters train nurse assistants who work in long-term-care facilities.

American Society for Geriatric Dentistry
211 East Chicago Avenue
Chicago, IL 60611
(312) 440-2661
Paul Van Ostenberg, D.D.S., Executive Director

Devoted to the maintenance and improvement of the oral health of the elderly. Promotes the continuing education of the practitioner of geriatric dentistry and other professionals involved with health care for the elderly.

Center for Understanding Aging
200 Executive Boulevard, Suite 201
P.O. Box 246
Southington, CT 06489
(203) 621-2079; Fax (203) 621-2989
Dr. Donna P. Couper, Executive Director

Professionals in gerontology, education, health care, and other fields interested in developing intergenerational programming. Seeks to dispel myths about aging and old age.

National Association of Activity Professionals
1225 I Street, NW, Suite 300
Washington, DC 20005
(202) 289-0722; Fax 842-0621
Charles F. Price, Executive Director

Objectives are to promote quality health care and services for the elderly and/or handicapped persons; to assist in the delivery of activity services; fosters research and the production of relevant literature.

National Association of Boards of Examiners for Nursing Home Administrators
808 Seventeenth Street, NW, Suite 200
Washington, DC 20006
(202) 223-9750
Jerome A. Miller, Executive Director

Produces exam to test the competence of nursing-home administrators, operates continuing review service, disseminates information on nursing-home administration.

National Association of State Retirement Administrators

P.O. Box 66794
Baton Rouge, LA 70896-6794
(504) 928-0821; Fax (504) 338-1844
Bert D. Hunsaker, Administrative Officer

Administrators of statewide public employee retirement systems. Encourages nationwide review of pension and retirement programs; sponsors conferences; provides technical information services to members.

National Foundation of Dentistry for Handicapped

1800 Glenarm Place, Suite 500
Denver, CO 80202
(303) 298-9650

Provides referrals to dentists who make house calls for shut-ins in Colorado, Illinois, and New Jersey.

National Institute of Senior Housing

c/o National Council on the Aging
409 Third Street, NW, Second Floor
Washington, DC 20024
(202) 479-6682; Fax (202) 479-0735
Betty Ransom, Program Director

Goals are to organize and maintain a national response to the growing need for affordable, decent housing and living arrangements for older adults. Promotes the development of community-based housing options for senior citizens.

National Rehabilitation Information Center

8455 Colesville Road, Suite 935
Silver Spring, MD 20910-3319
(301) 588-9284; Fax (301) 587-1967; (800) 346-2742
Mark Odum, Director

Organization set up by the U.S. Department of Education to provide information about disabilities and rehabilitation. Call toll-free

number for resource, research, and referral services, and for a copy
of its free quarterly newsletter.

Pharmaceutical Manufacturers' Association

1100 Fifteenth Street, NW, Suite 900
Washington, DC 20005
(202) 835-3400

Represents the prescription-drug industry. Consumer information
available upon request.

Society of Geriatric Ophthalmology

73 Second Street
South Orange, NJ 07079
(201) 763-1381
John Norris, President

Works to disseminate information regarding the problems of geriatric patients and to stimulate research. Provides speakers and programs dealing with the needs of the elderly.

Special Constituency Section for Aging and Long-Term Care Services

c/o American Hospital Association
1 North Franklin
Chicago, IL 60606
(312) 422-3302
Susanne R. Sonik, Director

Promotes recognition, growth, and support of aging and long-term
care services developed by institutional membership with the AHA
structure through representation, advocacy, technical assistance, and
information.

Pulmonary Diseases

ASTHMA

National Jewish Center for Immunology and Respiratory Medicine
1400 Jackson Street
Denver, CO 80266
(303) 388-4461; (800) 222-LUNG
Leonard Perlmutter, President

A teaching and research center providing clinical care for patients with respiratory diseases. The toll-free number offers information about these diseases and their treatment, and names of doctors who have completed their training program at the center.

BLACK LUNG DISEASE

National Coalition of Black Lung and Respiratory Disease Clinics
P.O. Box 209
Jacksboro, TN 37757
(615) 562-1156
Glenna Michaels, Chairperson

Coalition (120 members) of federally-funded black lung clinics, allied health organizations, and individuals. Promotes federally-funded pulmonary rehabilitation to treat miners diagnosed with black lung disease.

CYSTIC FIBROSIS

Cystic Fibrosis Foundation
6931 Arlington Road, Suite 200
Bethesda, MD 20814
(301) 951-4422; Fax (301) 951-6378; (800) FIGHT CF
Robert K. Dresing, President and CEO

Foundation sponsoring more than 120 centers for cystic fibrosis patients nationwide. Provides referrals to local facilities. Disseminates information on the congenital disease. Provides a money-saving pharmacy service.

National Jewish Center for Immunology and Respiratory Medicine
1400 Jackson Street
Denver, CO 80266
(303) 388-4461; (800) 222-LUNG
Leonard Perlmutter, President

A teaching and research center providing clinical care for patients with respiratory diseases. The toll-free number offers information about these diseases and their treatment, and names of doctors who have completed their training program at the center.

EMPHYSEMA

Emphysema Anonymous, Inc.
P.O. Box 3224
Seminole, FL 34642
(813) 391-9977
William E. Jaeckle, Executive Director

Support organization concerned with emphysema. Offers education and assistance to patients, and provides nonmedical counseling to patients and their families.

National Jewish Center for Immunology and Respiratory Medicine
1400 Jackson Street
Denver, CO 80266
(303) 388-4461; (800) 222-LUNG
Leonard Perlmutter, President

A teaching and research center providing clinical care for patients with respiratory diseases. The toll-free number offers information about these diseases and their treatment, and names of doctors who have completed their training program at the center.

LUNG CANCER

American Lung Association
1740 Broadway
New York, NY 10019-4374
(212) 315-8700; Fax (212) 265-5642
John R. Garrison, Managing Director

A voluntary organization, which funds research and conducts educational programs about lung diseases, including influenza, pneumonia, emphysema, chronic bronchitis, and lung cancer. Smoking-cessation programs are also provided. A list of free publications is available upon request.

Spirit and Breath Association
8210 Elmwood Avenue, Suite 209
Skokie, IL 60077
(708) 673-1384
Morton Liebling, Founder and Director

Support organization for lung cancer patients and their families. Provides moral and physical support. Encourages information exchange. Supports physical and psychological rehabilitation. Offers volunteer visitation program to hospitalized patients. Maintains speakers' bureau.

OTHER PULMONARY DISEASES

National Association for Ventilator Dependent Individuals
3601 Poplar Street
P.O. Box 3666
Erie, PA 16508
(814) 455-6171
Daniel W. Dubowski, President

Support group for respiratory patients requiring long- or short-term ventilator use. Educates health-care service personnel. Works to increase public awareness. Distributes information on resources, services, and education.

National Jewish Center for Immunology and Respiratory Medicine
1400 Jackson Street
Denver, CO 80266
(303) 388-4461; (800) 222-LUNG
Leonard Perlmutter, President

A teaching and research center providing clinical care for patients with respiratory diseases. The toll-free number offers information about these diseases and their treatment, and names of doctors who have completed their training program at the center.

Respiratory Health Association
301 Sicomac Avenue
Wyckoff, NJ 07481
(201) 848-5875; Fax (201) 848-5793
Fran W. Holcomb, Executive Director

Professional organization of pulmonary physicians and other health-care professionals working to improve respiratory health through Better Breathing classes (teaching exercises, breathing techniques, nutrition, daily living skills, and proper use of medications), swimming classes for asthmatics, smoking-cessation programs, and activities for people with chronic lung disease. Offers counseling, support groups, seminars, and school education programs. Provides vacation cruises for individuals needing supplementary oxygen therapy.

Well Spouse Foundation
P.O. Box 28876
San Diego, CA 92128
(619) 673-9043
Barbara Drucker, President

Support group for relatives/spouses of chronically ill individuals. Provides advocacy services.

Skin Diseases

ALOPECIA

National Alopecia Areata Foundation
P.O. Box 150760
San Rafael, CA 94915-0760
(415) 456-4644; Fax (415) 456-4274
Vicki Kalabokes, Executive Director

Support organization serving individuals with alopecia areata (disease resulting in partial scalp hair loss), alopecia totalis (total scalp hair loss), alopecia universalis (complete loss of body hair). Promotes increased public awareness. Funds research. Provides up-to-date medical information and practical/emotional support.

EPIDERMOLYSIS BULLOSA

Dystrophic Epidermolysis Bullosa Research Association of America
141 Fifth Avenue, Suite 7-S
New York, NY 10010
(212) 995-2220
Miram Feder, Executive Director

Support organization for individuals with epidermolysis bullosa (an inherited skin disorder involving blister formation) and their families. Supports research. Offers practical advice, guidance, and assistance to victims experiencing physical and emotional suffering. Provides public/medical education. Advocates federally-funded biomedical research of EB. Provides children's services.

ICHTHYOSIS

FIRST—Foundation for Ichthyosis and Related Skin Types
P.O. Box 20921
Raleigh, NC 27619-0921
(919) 782-5728; (800) 545-3286
Ellen Rowe, President

Patient/professional support organization for individuals with ichthyosis (a rare hereditary skin disease). Serves as communication network for families. Offers educational programs/materials on the medical, social, and psychological aspects of ichthyosis.

PSEUDOFOLLICULITIS BARBAE

PFB Project
c/o Robert B. Fitzpatrick
4801 Massachusetts Avenue, NW, Suite 400
Washington, DC 20016
(202) 364-8710
Robert B. Fitzpatrick, Co-Founder

Advocacy organization for pseudofolliculitis barbae (PFB), an incurable skin condition in black men that causes a bump-like rash on the face, which is aggravated by shaving. The organization's members believe that employers who force men with this disorder to shave (rather than grow beards) are guilty of racial discrimination. The project provides legal advocacy services to victims of such discrimination.

PSORIASIS

National Psoriasis Foundation
6443 Southeast Beaverton Highway, Suite 210
Portland, OR 97221
(503) 297-1545; Fax (503) 292-9341
Gail M. Zimmerman, Executive Director

Patient/professional organization concerned with psoriasis. Funds university research projects. Sponsors pen-pal programs for psoriasis victims. Disseminates information to schools, libraries, the media, and Congress in order to increase awareness and encourage federal funding for research. Pharmaceutical company representatives (as members of the foundation) distribute samples of new nonprescription products for psoriasis. Funds postdoctoral research fellowships.

Psoriasis Research Association
107 Vista del Grande
San Carlos, CA 94070
(415) 593-1394
Diane Bradley Mullins, Executive Secretary

Patient/professional organization supporting efforts to find a cause and cure for psoriasis. Maintains library and compiles medical statistics and patient data. Supports research grants to institutions and individuals.

Psoriasis Research Institute
600 Town and Country Village
Palo Alto, CA 94301
(415) 326-1848; Fax (415) 326-1262
Eugene M. Farber, M.D., President

Center creating and conducting research projects for the study, treatment, and cure of psoriasis. Provides advanced therapeutic programs and treatment at the Psoriasis Medical Center. Provides patient counseling and biofeedback. Offers monthly self-help workshop for psoriasis patients.

SCLERODERMA

Scleroderma Federation
Peabody Office Building
1 Newbury Street
Peabody, MA 01960
(508) 535-6000; Fax (508) 535-6696
Marie A. Coyle, President

Research-supporting and fundraising organization concerned with scleroderma (a connective tissue disorder). Encourages public education. Provides patients with referrals to specialists and educational materials. Encourages the formation of local support groups. Serves as information clearinghouse.

Scleroderma International Foundation
704 Gardner Center Road
New Castle, PA 16101
(412) 652-3109
Mrs. Arkie Barlet, President

Five-country organization acting as a support network for individuals with scleroderma (a chronic skin condition sometimes affecting the connective tissue, arterial lining, and digestive tract). Supports research and education.

Scleroderma Research Foundation
Box 200
Columbus, NJ 08022
(609) 261-2200; Fax (609) 723-6700; (800) 637-4005
Emanuel A. Coronis, Jr., Chairman

Fundraising and research-supporting organization concerned with scleroderma. Promotes the development of a national patient/family support network. Fosters early diagnosis and treatment through public/medical education programs.

Scleroderma Support Group
8852 Enloe Avenue
Garden Grove, CA 92644
(714) 892-5297
Clara K. Ihlbrock, President

Support group and research-funding organization for patients with scleroderma.

United Scleroderma Foundation
P.O. Box 399
Watsonville, CA 95077
(408) 728-2202; Fax (408) 728-3328
Diane Williams, Founder and Director

Support organization concerned with scleroderma. Offers workshops and seminars; maintains support networks; promotes research.

SKIN CANCER

Skin Cancer Foundation
245 Fifth Avenue, Suite 2402
New York, NY 10016
(212) 725-5176; Fax (212) 725-5751
Perry Robins, President

Foundation concerned with the prevention and early detection of skin cancer. Funds research and sponsors medical symposia. Provides public education programs. Assesses sunscreen products for effectiveness as skin-damage prevention agents.

VITILIGO

National Vitiligo Foundation
P.O. Box 6337
Tyler, TX 75711
(903) 534-8075; Fax (903) 534-8075
Allen C. Locklin, President

Physician/patient support organization offering information and counseling related to vitiligo (a skin disease that destroys pigment cells). Raises funds for research. Promotes increased awareness of the disease.

OTHER SKIN DISEASES

Celiac Sprue Association/U.S.A.
P.O. Box 31700
Omaha, NE 68103-0700
(402) 558-0600
Leon H. Rottmann, President

Support network for individuals and families with celiac sprue (a genetic disorder causing digestive malabsorption of the protein in cereal grains) and dermatitis herpetiformis (a gluten-related skin disorder also involving problems with cereal grain diet). Supports research. Provides information on gluten-free foods and maintaining a gluten-free diet.

National Arthritis and Musculoskeletal and Skin Disease Information Clearinghouse
9000 Rockville Pike
P.O. Box AMS
Bethesda, MD 20892-2903
(301) 495-4484; Fax (301) 587-4352

Provides information about federal programs related to rheumatic and musculoskeletal diseases and skin diseases. Free publications available.

Women's Health

BREAST CANCER

Breast Cancer Advisory Center
P.O. Box 224
Kensington, MD 20895
Fax (301) 949-1132
Rose Kushner, Executive Director

Information clearinghouse on breast cancer. Provides referral service. Features library, lectures, and informative materials.

Susan J. Komen Breast Cancer Foundation
5005 LBJ, Suite 370
Dallas, TX 75244
(214) 450-1777; Fax (214) 450-1710; (800) IM-AWARE
Patrick McDonough, Executive Director

Organization promoting early detection, research, and treatment of breast cancer. Provides political advocacy services in seeking insurance coverage for breast cancer examination. Offers education and speakers' bureau. Promotes self-examination.

National Alliance of Breast Cancer Organizations
1180 Avenue of the Americas, Second Floor
New York, NY 10036
(212) 719-0154; Fax (212) 768-8828
Amy Langer, Administrative Director

Resource center for information about breast cancer, breast diseases, detection, care, and research. Offers health policy advocacy services and advice on political legislation. Provides educational materials, as well as information on support groups, breast-care centers, and hospital programs.

Reach to Recovery
c/o American Cancer Society
1599 Clifton Road, NE
Atlanta, GA 30329
(404) 320-3333
Jerilynn Jones, Contact

Peer-support program for women with breast cancer. Offers short-term visitation by volunteers (at physician's request) to discuss physical, emotional, and cosmetic needs and to provide preoperative and postoperative support and information to the patient and her family.

Society for the Study of Breast Disease
Sammons Tower
3409 Worth
Dallas, TX 75246
(214) 821-2962; Fax (214) 827-7032
Gerorg N. Peters, M.D., Secretary

Association of health-care professionals involved in the study of breast diseases. Provides information on diagnosis and treatment developments to physicians and other health-care professionals. Promotes research. Encourages professional discussion.

Y-Me National Organization for Breast Cancer Information and Support

c/o Sharon Green
18220 Harwood Avenue
Homewood, IL 60430
(708) 799-8338; Fax (708) 799-5937; (800) 221-2141 weekdays;
   (708) 799-8228, 24-hour hotline
Sharon Green, Executive Director

Peer-support organization for women with breast cancer. Offers information, counseling, referral service, hotline, and library.

ENDOMETRIOSIS

American College of Obstetricians and Gynecologists

409 Twelfth Street, SW
Washington, DC 20024
(800) 673-8444; (202) 863-2518/19

Provides referrals and offers publications regarding menopause, estrogen use, and osteoporosis. Ask for resource center.

Endometriosis Association

8585 North Seventy-sixth Place
Milwaukee, WI 53223
(414) 355-2200; (800) 992-ENDO, in United States; (800) 426-
   2END, in Canada
Mary Lou Ballweg, Executive Director

Support organization of and for women with endometriosis (a disorder of the endometrial tissue). Provides information on treatment and research. Offers self-help support and meetings. Provides public education and speakers' bureau. Offers crisis counseling.

HYSTERECTOMY

Hysterectomy Educational Resources and Services Foundation (HERS)
422 Bryn Mawr Avenue
Bala-Cynwyd, PA 19004
(215) 667-7757
Nora W. Coffey, President

Organization offering information to women to help them make educated decisions about hysterectomy. Maintains communication network to allow one-on-one sharing between women who have had hysterectomies and women who plan to have them. Provides legal referrals and physician referrals (for second opinions). Offers speakers' bureau.

INTERSTITIAL CYSTITIS

Interstitial Cystitis Association
P.O. Box 1553
Madison Square Station
New York, NY 10159
(212) 979-6057
Dr. Vicki Ratner, President

Support organization for women with interstitial cystitis (an inflammation of the urinary bladder wall). Seeks increased public/medical awareness of the severity of IC. Funds related research.

OSTEOPOROSIS

National Osteoporosis Foundation (NOF)
1150 Seventeenth Street, Suite 500
Washington, DC 20037
(202) 223-2226; Fax (202) 223-2237
Sandra C. Raymond, Executive Director

NOF is dedicated to reducing the widespread prevalence of osteoporosis. A list of free publications is available upon request. Membership entitles you to the quarterly newsletter, *The Osteoporosis Report*, containing information on diagnosis, prevention, treatment, and support groups.

OTHER WOMEN'S HEALTH ASSOCIATIONS

National Black Women's Health Project
1237 Ralph David Albernathy Boulevard, SW
Atlanta, GA 30310
(404) 758-9590; Fax (404) 752-6756; (800) ASK-BWHP
Cynthia Newbille, Director

Activist organization encouraging black women to reduce prevalent health-care problems (including hypertension, obesity, breast and cervical cancers, diabetes, kidney disease, arteriosclerosis, and teenage pregnancy) through mutual and self-help efforts. Emphasizes need for health information, access to services, communication with health-care providers, awareness of health-care resources and self-help approaches, and benefits of mutual support.

National Women's Health Resource Center
2440 M Street, NW, Suite 201
Washington, DC 20037
(202) 293-6045; Fax (202) 293-7256
Yvonne Hiott, Program Coordinator

Organization promoting women's understanding of and participation in their own health care. Education/research interests focus on diseases unique to or prevalent among women. Provides health issue advocacy services. Develops models for clinical service.

8

Private Foundation Funding

The listings in this section are probably the easiest and most accessible funding sources for the average individual seeking a grant. Until now, this information has not been made readily available to the general public. And yet thousands of foundations give away millions of dollars to individuals to help them pay for medical treatment for major, long-term, and chronic illnesses.

Do you just walk up, hold out your hand, and expect someone to put money in it? Of course not. Getting grant money takes time, effort, and thought on your part. You are going to have to find out who is giving away money. You are going to have to fill out applications. You may meet with frustration or rejection somewhere down the road. The odds, however, are in your favor that you will qualify for some sort of funding.

The information in this section is organized by state. Wherever possible, each listing includes a description of what the foundation funds, any restrictions (e.g., you must reside in a particular town or city), the total amount of money awarded annually, the range of monies given, the average size of the award, information on how to apply, deadline date(s), and name(s) of contact person(s).

Private Foundation Funding, Geographical Restrictions

ALABAMA

Kate Kinloch Middleton Fund
P.O. Drawer 2527
Mobile, AL 36622
(205) 438-9597
Application Address:
409 First Alabama Bank Building
Mobile, AL 36602

Description: Grants or low-interest loans to help defray the costs of unexpected serious illness.
Restrictions: Limited to residents of Mobile County, Alabama.
$ Given: In FY '91, $131,569 for 80 grants was awarded to individuals; range, $39–$4,604.
Assets: $2,026,453
Contact: Joan Sapp, Trustee
Initial approach: Interview

CALIFORNIA

William Babcock Memorial Endowment
305 San Anselmo Avenue, Suite 219
San Anselmo, CA 94960
(415) 453-0901

Description: Grants and loans to persons burdened with exceptional medical expenses exceeding insurance coverage and falling outside the purview of other community agencies.
Restrictions: Limited to persons who are residents of Marin County, California.
$ Given: In FY '92, $432,086 for 491 grants was awarded to individuals; average range, $100–$1,000.
Assets: $4,965,046
Contact: Alelia Gillin, Executive Director
Initial approach: Call for application guidelines
Application information: Application form required
Deadlines: None

Albert B. Cutter Memorial Fund
c/o Bank of America
P.O. Box 712
Riverside, CA 92506
(714) 781-1464

Description: Limited grants to persons in extreme circumstances who are not eligible for other sources of aid.
Restrictions: Applicants must have been permanent residents of Riverside, California, for at least one year, and must have been referred by a local agency.
$ Given: In 1991, grants awarded to individuals totaled $21,264.
Contact: Trust Department
Initial approach: Applications are accepted from local agencies; individuals are referred by these agencies.
Application information: Application form required; interview or presentation recommended.
Deadlines: None

Danish Cheer Committee, Inc.
1557 Lakewood Way
Upland, CA 91786

Description: Grants to needy or destitute elderly persons.
Restrictions: Limited to elderly who reside in Upland, California.
$ Given: In FY '90, total given to individuals was $13,942.
Assets: $198,251
Initial approach: Letter
Application information: Application form required
Deadlines: None

Hattie Givens Testamentary Trust
1017 West Eighteenth Street
Merced, CA 95340
(209) 722-7429
Application Address:
1810 M Street
Mercer, CA 95340

Description: Support limited to health care, including money for individuals to receive medical assistance. Funds also available for family services, hospices, the handicapped, and secondary education.
Restrictions: Limited to California.
$ Given: $9,000 for 3 grants; average range, $600–$5,000.
Assets: $1 million
Contact: The trustees

Initial approach: Letter
Application information: Application form required

The Marguerite Home Association
555 Capitol Mall, Suite 200
Sacramento, CA 95814

Description: Financial assistance to needy elderly women.
Restrictions: Limited to Sacramento, California.
$ Given: In FY '91, $52,150 for 284 grants was awarded to individuals.
Assets: $1,016,712
Initial approach: Contributes only to preselected individuals
Application information: Applications are not accepted

New Horizons Foundations
700 South Flower Street, Suite 1222
Los Angeles, CA 90017-4160
(213) 626-4481

Description: Financial assistance to Christian Scientists who are over 65
   years of age.
Restrictions: Limited to residents of Los Angeles County, California.
$ Given: In FY '92, $16,127 for 8 grants was awarded to individuals;
   range, $300–$6,000.
Assets: $426,354
Contact: G. Grant Gifford, President
Initial approach: Letter or telephone call
Application information: Application form and interview required
Deadline: None

John Pervical and Mary C. Jefferson Endowment Fund
114 East De La Guerra, No. 7
Santa Barbara, CA 93101
(805) 963-8822

Description: Relief assistance for medical, dental, and living expenses.
Restrictions: Limited to residents of Santa Barbara County, California.
$ Given: In FY '91, $80,919 for 38 grants was awarded to individuals;
   range, $374–$7,100.
Assets: $3,053,789
Contact: Patricia M. Brouard, Trustee
Initial approach: Letter
Application information: Application form required

Virginia Scatena Memorial Fund for San Francisco School Teachers
c/o Bank of America
P.O. Box 37121
San Francisco, CA 94137

Description: Financial assistance to retired San Francisco school teachers who are needy, sick, or disabled.
Restrictions: Limited to retired teachers of the San Francisco Public School Department.
$ Given: In FY '90, $9,000 for 4 grants was awarded to individuals; range, $1,800–$2,700.
Assets: $126,467
Contact: Susan Morales
Initial approach: Letter
Application information: Application form required
Deadlines: None; applications reviewed semiannually by advisory committee.

COLORADO

Presbyterian/St. Lukes Community Foundation
55 Madison, Suite 655
Denver, CO 80206
(303) 322-3515; Fax: (303) 322-4576

Description: Health-care support for organ transplant and cancer patients, the elderly, and women.
Restrictions: Limited to the Rocky Mountain region.
$ Given: $200,000 for 4 grants; range, $7,000–$96,000.
Assets: $6.5 million
Contact: Nancy H. Shanks, Ph.D., Executive Director
Initial approach: Letter
Application information: Not required

CONNECTICUT

Blue Horizon Health & Welfare Trust
c/o Reid & Reige
Lakeville, CT 06039
(203) 435-9251

Application Address:
17 Cobble Road
Salisbury, CT 06068

Description: Financial assistance for medical costs.
Restrictions: Limited to residents of Connecticut.
$ Given: $200,199 for 4 grants was awarded to individuals; range,
    $7,320–$96,876.
Assets: $161,707
Contact: Frances M. Wagner, Trustee
Initial approach: Letter
Deadlines: None

Bridgeport Ladies Charitable Trust

c/o Citytrust
951 Main Street
Bridgeport, CT 06604

Description: Support available for health and home care for the
    handicapped, the aged, and children.
Restrictions: Funding primarily in the greater Bridgeport, Connecticut,
    area.
$ Given: $36,000 for 100 grants; range, $100–$1,000.
Assets: $550,000
Contact: Mrs. Jeffrey S. Lockhart, President
Initial approach: Must be referred from Emily Woodside Service or
    other community agencies
Application information: Not required
Deadlines: None

Marion Isabelle Coe Fund

c/o Bank of Boston
P.O. Box 2210
Waterbury, CT 06722

Description: Relief assistance to adults for general living and medical
    expenses. Grants provide continuing assistance to needy individuals
    to enable them to remain in their own homes. Awards paid in
    monthly installments and are renewed annually.
Restrictions: Limited to residents of Goshen, Litchfield, Morris, and
    Warren, Connecticut.
$ Given: Monthly awards range from $45–$140.
Contact: Mrs. Speers
Initial approach: Letter
Deadlines: None

The de Kay Foundation
c/o Manufacturers Hanover Trust Company
270 Park Avenue
New York, NY 10017
(212) 270-6000

Description: Grants to elderly individuals in financial need, particularly
to those who are sick or disabled or who lack proper care.
Restrictions: Limited to residents of New York, New Jersey, and
Connecticut.
$ Given: In FY '91, $193,260 for 79 grants was awarded to individuals;
range, $20–$7,000.
Assets: $20,058,211
Contact: Peter McSparran
Initial approach: Letter
Application information: Application form required
Deadlines: None

The Westport-Weston Foundation
c/o The Westport Bank & Trust Company
P.O. Box 5177
Westport, CT 06881
(203) 222-6988

Description: Grants for medical and basic living expenses.
Restrictions: Limited to residents of Westport and Weston, Connecticut.
$ Given: Grants range from $42–$350.
Contact: Susanne M. Allen, Trust Officer
Initial approach: Letter

Widow's Society
c/o Connecticut National Bank
777 Main Street
Hartford, CT 06115
Application Address:
20 Bayberry Lane
Avon, CT 06001
(203) 678-9660

Description: Financial assistance to needy women.
Restrictions: Limited to residents of Connecticut.
$ Given: In FY '91, $128,554 for 182 grants was awarded to individu-
als; average range, $35–$4,800.
Assets: $2,488,171
Contact: Dorothy Johnson, President

Initial approach: Letter
Application information: Applications are usually referred through social service agencies, but individuals may also submit letters.

Woman's Seamen's Friend Society of Connecticut
74 Forbes Avenue
New Haven, CT 06512
(203) 467-3887

Description: Financial assistance for sick and disabled seamen and their families.
Restrictions: Limited to residents of Connecticut.
$ Given: In FY '90, total given to individuals was $40,125.
Assets: $2,879,391
Contact: M. Courtwright
Initial approach: Letter

DELAWARE

Delaware Foundation-Quigly Trust
300 Delaware Avenue
Wilmington, DE 19801
Application Address:
P.O. Box 1669
Wilmington, DE 19899

Description: Support for medical care including medication.
Restrictions: Must be a resident of the state of Delaware.
$ Given: $10,000 for 14 grants was awarded to individuals; range, $60–$1,900.
Assets: $221,000
Contact: Delaware Foundation
Initial approach: Letter
Application information: Application form required
Deadlines: None

FLORIDA

Gore Family Memorial Foundation
c/o Sun Bank
P.O. Box 14728
Fort Lauderdale, FL 33302

Application Address:
4747 North Ocean Drive, No. 204
Fort Lauderdale, FL 33302

Description: Support for the handicapped for equipment, medical expenses, housing, and transportation costs. Grants for short-term or one-time assistance.
Restrictions: Limited to Broward County, Florida, and the surrounding areas.
$ Given: $323,589 for 401 grants was awarded to individuals.
Assets: $16,608,444
Initial approach: Letter
Application information: Application form required
Deadlines: None

Hope Foundation
2335 Tamiami Trail, North, Suite 510
Naples, FL 33940

Description: Grants for cancer, mental health, and social services.
$ Given: $50,000 for total given (breakdown to individuals not specified).
Assets: $1.1 million
Contact: Mr. Philip M. Francoeur, Trustee
Initial approach: Letter
Deadlines: None

The Ryan Foundation
1511 West Broadway
Oviedo, FL 32765
(407) 365-8390

Description: Emergency assistance for basic necessities including essential medical care.
Restrictions: Limited to needy local area residents of Florida.
$ Given: $62,203 for 77 grants to individuals; average range, $13–$39,704.
Contact: Jean Beede
Initial approach: Letter or telephone
Application information: Application form required
Deadlines: None

Roy M. Speer Foundation
1803 U.S. Highway 19
Holiday, FL 34691-5536

Description: Grants to individuals in financial difficulty as a result of medical problems.
Restrictions: Limited to residents of Florida.
$ Given: In FY '89, 2 grants were awarded to individuals; average range, $250–$1,500.
Initial approach: Letter
Application information: Write for guidelines
Deadlines: None

Winter Park Community Trust Fund
c/o Barnett Banks Trust Company, N.A.
P.O. Box 1000
Winter Park, FL 32790
Application Address:
2823 Amber Gate Road
Winter Park, FL 32789

Description: Grants for needy residents of Orange and Seminole Counties, Florida.
Restrictions: See above.
$ Given: In FY '91, $14,800 for 12 grants was awarded to individuals; range, $400–$1,950.
Assets: $2,295,814
Initial approach: Letter, including name, address, birth date, marital status, and Social Security number.

GEORGIA

Clark and Ruby Baker Foundation
c/o Bank South N.A.
Personal Trust Department
P.O. Box 4956 (MC 45)
Atlanta, GA 30302-9824
(404) 529-4627

Description: Grants primarily to retired Methodist ministers for pensions and medical assistance.
Restrictions: Limited to Georgia residents.
$ Given: $23,028 for 13 grants to individuals.
Assets: $2,071,277
Contact: Richard L. Watton, Trust Officer
Initial approach: Letter or telephone
Application information: Interview required
Deadlines: None

Thomas C. Burke Foundation
182 Riley Avenue, Suite B
Macon, GA 31204-2345
(912) 477-1931

Description: Support for individuals with diseases, primarily cancer.
Restrictions: Must be a resident of the state of Georgia, primarily in
    Bibb County.
$ Given: $131,858 in grants awarded to individuals.
Assets: $3.7 million
Contact: Carolyn P. Griggers
Initial approach: Telephone or in person
Application information: Not required; must be referred by a physician.
Deadlines: None

Savannah Widow's Society
P.O. Box 30156
Savannah, GA 31410
(912) 232-6312

Description: Grants for single women, 55 or older. Also, aid for
    seriously disabled or handicapped persons who already have medical
    coverage, but are in need of additional monies to cover health care in
    a reasonably comfortable manner.
Restrictions: Limited to Chatham County, Georgia.
$ Given: In FY '90, $99,931 for 104 grants was awarded to individuals;
    range, $10–$8,400.
Assets: $1,296,719
Contact: Becky Traxler, President
Initial approach: Letter
Application information: Formal application required

HAWAII

The Hawaii Community Foundation
222 Merchant Street
Honolulu, HI 96813
(808) 537-6333

Description:
Program: Winifred D. Robertson Fund One-time assistance to adult
    residents of Oahu, Hawaii.
Program: Alice M. G. Soper Fund One-time grants to adults, aged 50 or
    older, in financial need due to illness or disability.

Program: Gwenfried Allen Fund Financial assistance for the elderly and
  mentally ill.
Restrictions: Limited to residents of Hawaii (for all programs).
$ Given: In 1991, $117,500 for 125 grants was awarded to individuals;
  range, $250–$1,500.
Assets: $140,141,937
Initial approach: Telephone
Application information: Call for guidelines; application form required.
Deadlines: None

The May Templeton Hopper Foundation
1412 Whitney Street
Honolulu, HI 96822
(808) 944-2807

Description: Assistance to cover costs of medication, rent, day care, and
  other services.
Restrictions: Limited to those 62 years or older who have lived in
  Hawaii at least 5 years.
$ Given: $130,131 for 74 grants to individuals; average range, $240–
  $9,600.
Assets: $10,469,609
Contact: Diana H. Lord, President
Initial approach: Telephone
Application information: Application form required
Deadlines: The fifth working day of the month to be considered that
  month

ILLINOIS

Swiss Benevolent Society of Chicago
P.O. Box 2137
Chicago, IL 60690

Description: Grants to elderly and other individuals of Swiss descent or
  nationality in cases of need or emergency.
Restrictions: Limited to Chicago area residents of Swiss descent or
  nationality.
$ Given: $54,567 of 41 grants awarded to individuals.
Assets: $1,336,680
Initial approach: Letter
Application information: Application form required; write for guide-
  lines.
Deadlines: None

INDIANA

Mosette Levin Trust
c/o First Citizens Bank, N.A. Trust Department
P.O. Box 1125
Michigan City, IN 46360
(800) 873-7001
Application Address:
c/o First Citizens Bank
515 Franklin Square
Michigan City, IN 46360
(219) 874-9301

Description: Support for medical assistance to individuals with cancer.
Restrictions: Limited to residents of LaPorte County, Indiana.
$ Given: $25,728 for 29 grants; range, $40–$4105.
Assets: $489,477
Contact: Tina Mesean
Initial approach: Letter
Application information: Application form and interview required
Deadlines: None

Frank L. and Laura L. Smock Foundation
c/o Lincoln National Bank and Trust Company
P.O. Box 2363
Fort Wayne, IN 46801-0960
(219) 461-6451

Description: Medical assistance and nursing care to the ill, needy, disabled, blind, and aged.
Restrictions: Limited to individuals of the Presbyterian faith throughout Indiana.
$ Given: $130,820 for 28 grants; range, $3–$30,189.
Assets: $417,491
Contact: Alice Kopfer, Assistant Vice President

KANSAS

Charlotte Hill Charitable Trust
P.O. Box 754
Winfield, KS 67156
(316) 221-4600

Description: Grants to single women over age 60 with limited income and assets.
Restrictions: Limited to residents of the Arkansas City and Winfield, Kansas, areas.
$ Given: In FY '91, $24,275 for 27 grants was awarded to individuals; range, $70–$2,589.
Assets: $35,097
Contact: Kay Roberts, Trustee
Initial approach: Letter
Application information: Application form required
Deadlines: None

MAINE

Camden Home for Senior Citizens
66 Washington Street
Camden, ME 04843
(207) 236-2087
Application Address:
Belfast Road
Camden, ME 04843
(207) 236-2014

Description: Grants for medical care and medicine.
Restrictions: Limited to residents of Camden, Rockport, Lincolnville, and Hope, Maine.
$ Given: In FY '91, $45,948 for 257 grants was awarded to individuals; range, $50–$350.
Assets: $1,021,609
Contact: Charles Lowe, President
Initial approach: Letter or telephone
Application information: Write or call for guidelines
Deadlines: None

Lena P. Frederick Trust Fund
c/o Key Trust Company
P.O. Box 1054
Augusta, ME 04330
(207) 623-5625

Description: Grants for medical assistance.
Restrictions: Limited to residents of Belfast, Maine.
$ Given: In FY '91, $13,683 was awarded to individuals.

Assets: $312,932
Initial approach: Letter or telephone
Application information: Application form required
Deadlines: None

Anita Card Montgomery Foundation
20 Mechanic Street
Camden, ME 04843-1707

Description: Grants to needy individuals, including funding for medical
 and dental expenses.
Restrictions: Limited to residents of Camden, Rockport, Lincolnville,
 and Hope, Maine.
$ Given: In FY '91, $9,207 for 19 grants was awarded to individuals;
 range, $50–$1,297.
Assets: $8,424
Contact: Julia Libby, President
Initial approach: Letter
Application information: Write for guidelines
Deadlines: None

Portland Female Charitable Society
20 Noyes Street
Portland, ME 04103
Application Address:
142 Pleasant Street, No. 761
Portland, ME 04101

Description: Financial aid for medical and dental expenses.
Restrictions: Limited to residents of Portland, Maine.
$ Given: In FY '91, $10,297 for 89 grants was awarded; range, $15–
 $950.
Assets: $145,638
Contact: Janet Matty, Vice President
Initial approach: Letter
Application information: Write for information; applications are usually
 presented by health-care professionals or social workers; interviews
 required.
Deadlines: None

Herbert Wadsworth Trust
c/o Fleet Bank of Maine
1 East Avenue
Rochester, NY 14638

Description: Financial assistance for citizens of Winthrop, Maine, who are hospitalized in a well-regulated and recognized facility outside the town of Winthrop.
Restrictions: Limited to citizens of Winthrop, Maine.
$ Given: In FY '91, $10,503 for 4 grants was awarded to individuals; average range, $156–$2,100.
Assets: $152,201
Initial approach: Letter
Application information: Write for guidelines
Deadlines: None

MARYLAND

The Eaton Fund, Inc.
c/o Mercantile-Safe Deposit & Trust Company
766 Old Hammod Ferry Road
Linthicum, MD 21090
Application Address:
2 Hopkins Plaza
Baltimore, MD 21201
(410) 237-5321

Description: Relief assistance for women over 60 years of age.
Restrictions: Limited to residents of Baltimore, Maryland.
$ Given: In FY '91, $18,325 for 9 grants was awarded to individuals; range, $525–$3,000.
Assets: $108,746
Contact: Scott Murphy
Initial approach: Letter
Application information: Application form required

Steeplechase Fund
400 Fair Hill Drive
Elkton, MD 21921

Description: Assistance to injured jockeys, their widows, and families for medical and other expenses.
Restrictions: See above.
$ Given: Grants to individuals totaling $9,369; range, $167–$4,200.
Contact: Charles Colgan
Initial approach: Letter
Application information: Include information on medical expenses and occurrence of injury

Anna Emory Warfield Memorial Fund, Inc.

c/o Mercantile Bank & Trust
2 Hopkins Plaza
Baltimore, MD 21201
(410) 547-0612

Description: Relief assistance to elderly women in the Baltimore, Maryland, area.
Restrictions: Limited to women in the Baltimore, Maryland, area.
$ Given: In 1992, $162,500 for 45 grants was awarded to individuals; range, $325–$4,225.
Assets: $3,914,627
Contact: Thelma K. O'Neal, Secretary
Initial approach: Letter
Application information: Write to request application guidelines; formal application required.
Deadlines: None

MASSACHUSETTS

Association for the Relief of Aged Women of New Bedford

27 South Sixth Street
New Bedford, MA 02740

Description: Relief aid to needy, aged women.
Restrictions: Limited to residents of New Bedford, Massachusetts.
$ Given: In FY '91, $328,004 for 19 grants was awarded to individuals; range, $693–$34,677.
Assets: $7,343,290
Initial approach: Letter
Application information: Write for guidelines

Howland Fund for Aged Women

c/o Child and Family Service
1061 Pleasant Street
New Bedford, MA 02740

Description: Relief assistance to poor, aged women.
Restrictions: Limited to the aged women of New Bedford, Massachusetts.
$ Given: In FY '91, $12,900 for 13 grants was awarded to individuals; range, $300–$1,200.
Assets: $261,351

Contact: Sally Ainsworth, President of Trustees
Initial approach: By trustees
Application information: Formal application required
Deadlines: None

Charlotte M. Robbins Trust

c/o State Street Bank & Trust Company
P.O. Box 351, M-11
Boston, MA 02101
(617) 654-3360
Application Address:
c/o State Street Bank
225 Franklin Street
Boston, MA 02110

Description: Financial assistance to aged couples and aged women.
Restrictions: Limited to aged residents of the towns of Groton, Ayer, Shirley, and Littleton, Massachusetts.
$ Given: In 1991, total given was $24,764.
Assets: $308,010
Contact: Cheryl D. Curtin, Vice President
Initial approach: Letter
Application information: Write letter to application address stating income, expenses, assets, and reason money is needed.

Salem Female Charitable Society

c/o Fiduciary Trust Company
175 Federal Street
Boston, MA 02110
Application Address:
33 Warren Street
Salem, MA 01970

Description: Financial aid to needy women of the Salem, Massachusetts, area.
Restrictions: Original grant limited to residents of the Salem, Massachusetts, area; recipients may, however, relocate without forfeiting grant.
$ Given: In FY '91, $21,050 for 17 grants was awarded to individuals; range, $50–$1,800.
Assets: $490,080
Contact: Mrs. Roseanne Dennis, Treasurer
Initial approach: Letter
Application information: Write for guidelines
Deadlines: None

Urann Foundation

P.O. Box 1788
Brockton, MA 02403
(508) 588-7744

Description: Medical assistance grants for Massachusetts families engaged in cranberry farming and processing; grants intended to assist in payment of hospital and medical bills.
Restrictions: Limited to families located in Massachusetts.
$ Given: In 1991, $49,433 for 31 grants was awarded; two medical assistance grants totaling $2,533 were awarded.
Assets: $2,325,982
Contact: Robert C. LeBoeuf, Administrator
Initial approach: Phone or letter
Application information: Formal application required
Deadlines: None

MICHIGAN

Pardee Cancer Treatment Fund of Bay County

213 Center Avenue
Bay City, MI 48708
Application Address:
400 South Trumbull
Bay City, MI 48708
(517) 894-5332

Description: Financial assistance for persons with cancer to help pay medical bills.
Restrictions: Limited to residents of Bay County, Michigan.
$ Given: In FY '91, $29,425 for 22 grants was awarded to individuals.
Assets: $32,224
Contact: Patricia White, Manager
Initial approach: Letter
Application information: Application form and interview required
Deadlines: None

MINNESOTA

Charles D. Gilfillan Memorial, Inc.

W-555 First National Bank Building
St. Paul, MN 55101

Application Address:
3537 Edward Street, NE
Minneapolis, MN 55418
(612) 788-9010

Description: Financial assistance for medical, surgical, and dental costs
for the financially distressed.
Restrictions: Limited to Minnesota residents, with preference given to
small rural communities.
$ Given: In 1991, $39,771 for 79 grants was awarded to individuals;
range, $34–$3,000.
Assets: $64,611
Contact: Ms. Leah Slye, Secretary
Initial approach: Letter
Application information: Formal application required
Deadlines: None

Fanny S. Gilfillan Memorial, Inc.
c/o Lawrence Harder
Route 4
Redwood Falls, MN 56283
Application Address:
Redwood County Welfare Department
Box 27
Redwood Falls, MN 56283
(507) 637-5741

Description: Financial assistance to needy individuals of Redwood
County, Minnesota, including hospitalization bills.
Restrictions: See above.
$ Given: In FY '90, $51,063 for 29 grants was awarded to individuals;
range, $60–$4,505.
Assets: $847,426
Initial approach: Letter
Application information: Application form required; interviews required.
Deadlines: None

Hanna R. Kristianson Trust
P.O. Box 1011
Albert Lea, MN 56007
Application Address:
Clarks Grove, MN 56016
(507) 256-4415

Description: Financial aid to needy individuals over 50 years of age.
Restrictions: Limited to residents of Freeborn County, Minnesota, who
    are over 50 years of age.
$ Given: In 1989, grants to individuals were $8,333.
Assets: $135,531
Contact: Richard S. Haug, Trustee
Initial approach: Letter or telephone
Application information: Call or write for guidelines
Deadlines: None

The Saint Paul Foundation
1120 Norwest Center
St. Paul, MN 55101
(612) 224-5463

Description: Relief assistance grants.
Restrictions: Limited to residents of St. Paul and Minneapolis, Minne-
    sota, and to employees of 3M Company.
$ Given: In 1991, grants to individuals were $243,980.
Assets: $183,314,845
Contact: Paul A. Verret, President
Initial approach: Letter or telephone
Application information: Write or call for guidelines

MISSOURI

The Leader Foundation
7711 Carondelet Avenue, Tenth Floor
St. Louis, MO 63105
(314) 725-7300

Description: Funding for pensions, family services, and health organiza-
    tions.
Restrictions: Intended primarily for residents of Saint Louis, Missouri.
$ Given: $ 76,308 for 23 grants to individuals; range, $600–$6,000.
Contact: Edwin G. Shifrin, Vice President
Initial approach: Letter
Application information: Write for guidelines
Deadlines: None

NEW HAMPSHIRE

Abbie M. Griffin Hospital Fund
111 Concord Street
Nashua, NH 03060

Description: Support for payment of hospital bills.
Restrictions: Limited to residents of Merrimack and Hillsborough
   Counties, New Hampshire.
$ Given: $10,001 for 7 grants; range, $273–$4,161.
Assets: $273,925
Contact: S. Robert Winer, Trustee
Initial approach: Letter
Application information: Application form required
Deadlines: None

NEW JERSEY

The de Kay Foundation
c/o Manufacturers Hanover Trust Company
270 Park Avenue
New York, NY 10017
(212) 270-6000

Description: Grants to elderly individuals in financial need, particularly
   to those who are sick or disabled or who lack proper care.
Restrictions: Limited to residents of New York, New Jersey, and
   Connecticut.
$ Given: In FY '91, $193,260 for 79 grants was awarded to individuals;
   range, $250–$7,000.
Assets: $20,058,211
Contact: Peter McSparran
Initial approach: Letter
Application information: Application form required
Deadlines: None

Otto Sussman Trust
P.O. Box 1374
Trainsmeadow Station
Flushing, NY 11370-9998

Description: Financial assistance for medical bills and care-giving
   expenses to individuals with serious or terminal illness.

Restrictions: Limited to residents of New York, New Jersey, Oklahoma, and Pennsylvania.
$ Given: In FY '90, $183,387 for 112 grants was awarded to individuals.
Assets: $3,193,877
Contact: Edward S. Miller, Trustee
Initial approach: Letter
Application information: Write letter requesting application form and guidelines; explain circumstances of need; formal application required.
Deadlines: None

NEW YORK

Benedict Family Charitable Foundation, Inc.
82 Wall Street
New York, NY 10005

Description: Grants to needy individuals.
Restrictions: Limited to residents of New York.
$ Given: In 1990, total given was $16,349 (grants to individuals unspecified).
Assets: $244,981
Contact: Alfred Benedict, President
Initial approach: Letter

The James Gordon Bennett Memorial Corporation
c/o New York Daily News
220 East Forty-second Street
New York, NY 10017

Description: Grants to journalists who have been employees of a daily New York City newspaper for 10 years or more. Acceptance based on need. Funds to be used for "the physical needs of persons . . . who, by reason of old age, accident, or bodily infirmity or through lack of means, are unable to care for themselves."
Restrictions: Priority given to journalists who have worked in the borough of Manhattan.
$ Given: Grants range from $150–$6,000.
Assets: $3,697,471
Contact: Denise Houseman
Initial approach: Letter

Application information: Write for guidelines and program information; application form required.
Deadlines: None

The Clark Foundation
30 Wall Street
New York, NY 10005
(212) 269-1833

Description: Financial aid for medical and hospital care to needy individuals in upstate New York and New York City.
Restrictions: See above.
$ Given: In FY '92, $65,166 for 11 grants was awarded to individuals; average range, $1,360–$17,710.
Assets: $264,654,849
Contact: Joseph H. Cruikshank, Secretary
Initial approach: Letter
Application information: Write for guidelines
Deadlines: None

Josiah H. Danforth Memorial Fund
8 Fremont Street
Gloversville, NY 12078

Description: Financial aid for medical care.
Restrictions: Limited to residents of Fulton County, New York.
$ Given: In FY '91, $25,309 for 112 grants was awarded to individuals; range, $22–$500.
Assets: $430,904
Initial approach: Letter
Application information: Write for guidelines; application form required.
Deadlines: None

The de Kay Foundation
c/o Manufacturers Hanover Trust Company
270 Park Avenue
New York, NY 10020
(212) 270-6000

Description: Grants to elderly individuals in financial need, particularly to those who are sick or disabled or who lack proper care.
Restrictions: Limited to residents of New York, New Jersey, and Connecticut.
$ Given: In FY '91, $193,260 for 79 grants was awarded to individuals; range, $250–$7,000.

Assets: $20,058,211
Contact: Peter McSparran
Initial approach: Letter
Application information: Application form required
Deadlines: None

The Dubose and Dorothy Heyward Memorial Fund
c/o The Bank of New York
48 Wall Street, 4-M
New York, NY 10015
(212) 495-1177

Description: Support for treatment and cancer research as well as arts organizations.
$ Given: $2 million in total given (breakdown to individuals not specified).
Contact: Katherine W. Floyd
Initial approach: Letter
Application information: Write for guidelines
Deadlines: None

Mary W. MacKinnon Fund
c/o Wilber National Bank Trust Department
245 Main Street
Oneonta, NY 13820-2502
(607) 432-1700

Description: Funding for medical, hospital, nursing home, and rehabilitative care for elderly and indigent of Sidney, New York.
Restrictions: See above.
$ Given: Grants totaling $85,884 were awarded to individuals.
Assets: $1,362,058
Contact: Trust Department
Initial approach: Applications must be submitted through a physician or hospital
Deadlines: None

The Ostberg Foundation, Inc.
44 East Twenty-third Street
New York, NY 10010
(212) 677-1700

Description: Limited aid for the ill and elderly.
Restrictions: Limited to residents of New York City.

$ Given: In FY '91, $68,501 for 44 grants was awarded to individuals; range, $100–$4,559.
Assets: $928,559
Contact: Joseph Kattan
Initial approach: Telephone
Application information: Formal application required
Deadlines: None

Otto Sussman Trust
P.O. Box 1374
Trainsmeadow Station
Flushing, NY 11370-9998

Description: Financial assistance for medical bills and care-giving expenses to individuals with serious or terminal illness.
Restrictions: Limited to residents of New York, New Jersey, Oklahoma, and Pennsylvania.
$ Given: In FY '90, $183,387 for 112 grants was awarded to individuals.
Assets: $3,193,877
Contact: Edward S. Miller, Trustee
Initial approach: Letter
Application information: Write letter requesting application form and guidelines; explain circumstances of need; application form required.
Deadlines: None

Vanderlinden Charitable Trust
c/o Leonard Rachmilowitz
26 Mill Street
Rhinebeck, NY 12572
(914) 876-3021

Description: Grants for financially distressed residents of upstate New York; funds may be used to meet a variety of needs, including medical bills.
Restrictions: Limited to upstate New York.
$ Given: In FY '89, $23,260 for 101 grants was awarded to individuals; range, $4–$540.
Contact: Leonard Rachmilowitz
Initial approach: Letter or telephone
Application information: Write or call for guidelines
Deadlines: None

OHIO

Christian Business Cares Foundation
P.O. Box 1862
Akron, OH 44309
(216) 762-8825

Description: One-time only support in times of life-threatening emergencies.
Restrictions: Funding primarily in northeastern Ohio.
$ Given: $40,320 for 99 grants; average range, $37–$5,711.
Assets: $16,616
Contact: Don Wetzel, Treasurer
Initial approach: Letter
Application information: Application form required
Deadlines: None

Columbus Female Benevolent Society
228 South Drexel Avenue
Columbus, OH 43209

Description: Direct aid to pensioned widows.
Restrictions: Limited to widows who are residents of Franklin County, Ohio.
$ Given: In 1991, $38,373 for an unspecified number of grants was awarded to individuals.
Assets: $106,577
Initial approach: Recipients are referred by people in the community who are familiar with their circumstances
Application information: No direct applications accepted

The S. N. Ford and Ada Ford Fund
c/o Society Bank & Trust
P.O. Box 10099
Toledo, OH 43699-0099
(419) 525-7665

Description: Grants for hospitalization and care for the aged and incurably ill.
Restrictions: Limited to residents of Richland County, Ohio.
$ Given: Grants range from $8–$16,120.
Contact: Nick Gesouras, Regional Trust Officer
Initial approach: Letter
Application information: Write for guidelines and annual report

Virginia Gay Fund
751 Grandon Avenue
Columbus, OH 43209

Description: Relief assistance for elderly women who have been school
   teachers for a minimum of 20 years and are over the age of 55.
Restrictions: Limited to Ohio.
$ Given: In FY '91, $61,570 for 25 grants was awarded to individuals;
   range, $400–$6,000.
Assets: $1,698,427
Contact: Board of Trustees
Initial approach: Letter
Application information: Application form required

Grace A. Gossens Testamentary Trust
One Seagate, Twenty-fourth Floor
P.O. Box 10032
Toledo, OH 10032
Application Address:
416 West Wayne
Maumee, OH 43537
(419) 893-8603

Description: Relief assistance to elderly women who reside in rest
   homes.
Restrictions: Limited to the Maumee, Ohio, area.
$ Given: In 1991, $5,500 for 1 grant was awarded.
Assets: $270,734
Contact: Alice J. Servais, Trustee
Initial approach: Written application stating applicants' financial needs
Deadlines: None

Paul Motry Memorial Fund
c/o Dean S. Lucal
P.O. Box 357
Sandusky, OH 44870-0357

Description: Funding for health services and hospitals.
Restrictions: Limited to residents of Erie and western Ottawa Counties,
   Ohio.
$ Given: $57,800 for 132 grants to individuals; range, $11–$10,000.
Assets: $547,430
Initial approach: Letter
Application information: Application for assistance must include
   doctor's letter

Virginia Wright Mothers Guild, Inc.
426 Clinton Street
Columbus, OH 43202-2741

Description: Grants to aged women in need.
Restrictions: Strictly limited to female residents of Columbus, Ohio.
$ Given: $7,485 for 9 grants to individuals; range, $540–$915.
Assets: $80,161
Contact: M. Courtwright
Initial approach: Letter
Application information: Write for guidelines

OKLAHOMA

Otto Sussman Trust
P.O. Box 1374
Trainsmeadow Station
Flushing, NY 11370-9998

Description: Financial assistance for medical bills and care-giving
    expenses to individuals with serious or terminal illnesses.
Restrictions: Limited to residents of New York, New Jersey, Oklahoma,
    and Pennsylvania.
$ Given: In FY '90, $183,387 for 112 grants was awarded to individu-
    als.
Assets: $3,193,877
Contact: Edward S. Miller, Trustee
Initial approach: Letter
Application information: Write letter requesting required application
    form; explain circumstances of need.
Deadlines: None

OREGON

**The Elizabeth Church Clarke Testamentary Trust/Fund
    Foundation**
U.S. National Bank of Oregon
P.O. Box 3168
Portland, OR 97208

Application Address:
Scottish Rite Temple
709 Southwest Fifteenth Avenue
Portland, OR 97205
(503) 228-9405

Description: Grants for medical aid. Payment may be made directly to
the individuals or to the physicians and hospitals providing services.
Restrictions: Limited to residents of Oregon.
$ Given: In 1990, total given was $68,441.
Assets: $1.5 million
Contact: Walter L. Peters, Executive Secretary
Initial approach: Letter
Application information: Include all details on need and amount of
request
Deadlines: None

Louis G. and Elizabeth L. Clarke Endowment Fund
Scottish Rite Temple
709 Southwest Fifteenth Avenue
Portland, OR 97205
(503) 228-9405

Description: Grants to needy Masons or their immediate families who
require hospitalization in the Portland, Oregon, metropolitan area
(Multomah, Clackamus, and Washington Counties).
Restrictions: Limited to Masons and their immediate families.
$ Given: In FY '91, an unspecified number of grants totaling $72,099
were awarded to individuals.
Assets: $1,091,429
Contact: G. L. Selmyhr, Executive Secretary
Initial approach: Letter
Application information: Write for guidelines

Blanche Fischer Foundation
1550 Security Pacific Building
1001 Southwest Fifth Avenue, Suite 1550
Portland, OR 97204
(503) 323-9111

Description: Financial aid for physically handicapped individuals.
Restrictions: Limited to residents of Oregon.
$ Given: In 1991, $42,724 for 132 grants was awarded to individuals;
range, $20–$2,500.

Assets: $1,174,757
Contact: William K. Shepard, President
Initial approach: Letter
Application information: Write for application guidelines; application
    form required.
Deadlines: None

Sophia Byers McComas Foundation
c/o U.S. National Bank of Oregon
P.O. Box 3168
Portland, OR 97208
(503) 275-6564

Description: Grants to elderly and indigent residents of Oregon who are
    not receiving assistance.
Restrictions: Limited to residents of Oregon.
$ Given: In FY '91, an unspecified number of grants totaling $69,525
    were awarded to individuals.
Assets: $1,330,230
Contact: Frank E. Staich, Vice President
Initial approach: Individuals may not directly apply
Application information: Applicants are recommended to the trustees by
    various church groups, service agencies, etc.

Scottish Rite Oregon Consistory Almoner Fund, Inc.
709 Southwest Fifteenth Avenue
Portland, OR 97205
(503) 228-9405

Description: Assistance to financially distressed Masons and their
    families to help meet medical expenses.
Restrictions: Limited to Masons and their wives, widows, and children
    who are residents of the state of Oregon.
$ Given: In FY '91, an unspecified number of grants totaling $14,526
    were awarded to individuals.
Assets: $308,073
Contact: Walter Peters, Executive Director
Initial approach: Letter
Application information: Write for guidelines
Deadlines: None

PENNSYLVANIA

Margaret Baker Memorial Trust Fund
c/o Mellon Bank (East) N.A.
P.O. Box 7236
Philadelphia, PA 19101-7236
Application Address:
P.O. Box 663
Phoenixville, PA 19460

Description: Financial aid to widows and single women over age 30.
Restrictions: Limited to the Phoenixville, Pennsylvania, area.
$ Given: $15,546 for 6 grants to individuals.
Assets: $296,664
Contact: L. Darlington Lessig, Treasurer
Initial approach: Letter
Application information: Include applicant's age, income, infirmity (if
    any), and other supportive material, plus the name of a person who
    can verify the request.
Deadlines: Applications accepted throughout the year; awards usually
    made in July and November.

Female Association of Philadelphia
c/o Provident National Bank
1632 Chestnut Street
Philadelphia, PA 19103
(215) 525-6234

Description: Relief assistance to women who earn an annual income of
    less than $10,000 and are over the age of 60.
Restrictions: Limited to residents of Philadelphia, Pennsylvania.
$ Given: In FY '91, $98,550 for 298 grants was awarded to individuals.
Assets: $1,978,080
Initial approach: Letter

French Benevolent Society of Philadelphia
1301 Medical Arts Building
1601 Walnut Street
Philadelphia, PA 19102
(215) 563-3276

Description: Aid to persons born in France, or born to French parents,
    who are in need due to age, illness, or misfortune.
Restrictions: Limited to French residents of Philadelphia, Pennsylvania.

$ **Given:** In 1991, an unspecified number of grants totaling $38,924 were awarded to individuals.

Assets: $81,785

Initial approach: Call the office on Wednesdays or Thursdays

Application information: Formal application required

Deadlines: None

Addison H. Gibson Foundation

Six PPG Place, Suite 860
Pittsburgh, PA 15222
(412) 261-1611

Description: Funds to cover hospital and medical costs for individuals with "correctable physical difficulties."

Restrictions: Limited to residents of western Pennsylvania (with emphasis on Allegheny County).

$ **Given:** Grants range from $159–$12,056.

Assets: $17,869,335

Contact: Rebecca Wallace Sapiente, Director

Initial approach: Applicants must be referred by a medical professional

Application information: Application forms required. Medical professional must provide name, age, sex, and address of person for whom funding is sought; describe the nature of recommended assistance; and provide the name of patient's primary physician. Grants are made directly to the medical professionals/institutions providing services.

Deadlines: None

William B. Lake Foundation

c/o Fidelity Bank, N.A.
Broad and Walnut Streets
Philadelphia, PA 19109
(215) 985-8712
Application Address:
c/o Sophia O'Lessker, Social Worker
Fox Craft Square, Apt. 185
Jenkintown, PA 19046

Description: Money for the treatment and support of individuals with respiratory tract diseases.

Restrictions: Must be a resident of Philadelphia or surrounding area.

$ **Given:** In 1991 an unspecified number of grants totaling $30,000 were awarded to individuals.

Assets: $614,562

Contact: Sophia O'Lessker, Social Worker

Initial approach: Letter including complete details and documentation
Application information: None
Deadlines: May 1 and November 1

Lottie Sleeper Hill and Josiah Sleeper Fund
c/o Fidelity Bank
Broad and Walnut Streets
Philadelphia, PA 19109
(215) 985-8712

Description: Support to individuals for health care.
$ Given: $35,000 for 56 grants to individuals; range, $20–$3,400.
Assets: $440,000
Contact: Sister Mary Margaret, Secretary/Treasurer
Initial approach: Letter
Application information: Write for guidelines
Deadlines: None

Otto Sussman Trust
P.O. Box 1374
Trainsmeadow Station
Flushing, NY 11370

Description: Financial assistance for medical bills and care-giving
  expenses to individuals with serious or terminal illness.
Restrictions: Limited to residents of New York, New Jersey, Oklahoma,
  and Pennsylvania.
$ Given: In FY '90, $183,387 for 112 grants was awarded to individu-
  als.
Assets: $3,193,877
Contact: Edward S. Miller, Trustee
Initial approach: Letter
Application information: Request required application form and
  guidelines; explain circumstances of need.
Deadlines: None

RHODE ISLAND

Bristol Home for Aged Women
20 Harborview Avenue
Bristol, RI 02809-1710
(401) 253-7260

Description: Financial aid for elderly, needy women.
Restrictions: Limited to residents of Bristol, Rhode Island.
$ Given: In FY '91, an unspecified number of grants totaling $60,700 were awarded to individuals.
Assets: $1,090,949
Contact: Mrs. Alfred E. Newton, Treasurer
Initial approach: Letter
Application information: Include cost and description of service needed
Deadlines: None

Robert B. Cranston/Theophilus T. Pitman Fund

18 Market Square
Newport, RI 02840
(401) 847-4260

Description: Grants to the aged, temporarily indigent, and indigent people of Newport County, Rhode Island. Funds for medical assistance, food, utilities, clothing, and housing.
Restrictions: Limited to residents of Newport County, Rhode Island.
$ Given: In FY '90, an unspecified number of grants totaling $67,454 were awarded to individuals.
Assets: $1,188,489
Contact: The Reverend D. C. Hambly, Jr., Administrator
Application information: Interview or reference from a local welfare agency required.
Deadlines: None

Inez Sprague Trust

c/o Rhode Island Hospital Trust
1 Hospital Trust Plaza
Providence, RI 02903
(401) 278-8880

Description: Financial assistance and medical expenses for needy individuals.
Restrictions: Limited to residents of Rhode Island.
$ Given: In FY '90, $28,371 was awarded to individuals.
Assets: $513,186
Contact: Trustee
Initial approach: Letter
Application information: Write for guidelines
Deadlines: None

Townsend Aid for the Aged
c/o Fleet National Bank
100 Westminster Street
Providence, RI 02903

Description: Financial assistance for needy, elderly individuals.
Restrictions: Limited to residents of Newport, Rhode Island.
$ Given: In FY '90, an unspecified number of grants totaling $76,575
    were awarded to individuals.
Assets: $1,477,264
Initial approach: Letter
Application information: Applications not accepted

SOUTH CAROLINA

Graham Memorial Fund
P.O. Box 533
Bennettsville, SC 29512
Application Address:
308 West Main Street
Bennettsville, SC 29512
(803) 479-6804

Description: Grants for medical assistance and general welfare.
Restrictions: Limited to residents of Bennettsville, South Carolina.
$ Given: $9,367 for 36 grants awarded to individuals; range, $60–$257.
Assets: $142,006
Contact: Chairman
Initial approach: Letter
Application information: Application form required
Deadlines: June 1

TEXAS

H. C. Davis Fund
P.O. Box 2239
San Antonio, TX 78298

Description: Grants to assist Masons living in the 39th District of
    Texas.

Restrictions: See above.
$ Given: In FY '91, $25,885 for 9 grants was awarded to individuals; range, $750–$6,000.
Assets: $353,924
Initial approach: Letter
Application information: Application form required; write for guidelines.
Deadlines: None

Pardee Cancer Treatment Association of Greater Brazosport
127-C Circle Way
Lake Jackson, TX 77566

Description: Support for treatment of cancer.
Restrictions: Must be resident of southern Brazoria County, Texas.
$ Given: In FY '90, $206,930 for 137 grants was awarded to individuals.
Assets: $192,679
Contact: Ms. Shirley Funk
Initial approach: Letter
Application information: Application form required
Deadlines: None

UTAH

Dialysis Research Foundation
c/o Bonneville Dialysis Association
5575 South 500 East
Ogden, UT 84405

Description: Support for dialysis treatment research and to individuals with renal disease on dialysis.
Restrictions: Limited to renal disease.
$ Given: $54,000 for grants to individuals.
Assets: $317,000
Initial approach: Letter of proposal
Deadlines: None

VIRGINIA

A. C. Needles Trust Fund Hospital Care
c/o Dominion Trust Company
P.O. Box 13327
Roanoke, VA 24040

Description: Grants for hospital care to financially distressed individuals.
Restrictions: Limited to individuals in the Roanoke, Virginia, area.
$ Given: In 1990, $48,518 for 14 grants was awarded to individuals; range, $598–$7,000.
Assets: $828,216
Initial approach: Letter
Application information: Write for guidelines

WASHINGTON

G. M. L. Foundation, Inc.
c/o Gordon Cook
P.O. Box 916
Port Angeles, WA 98362

Description: Grants to individuals who need medical help.
Restrictions: Limited to residents of Clallam County, Washington.
$ Given: In 1990, $14,966 for grants was awarded to individuals.
Assets: $473,000
Contact: Graham Ralston, Secretary
Initial approach: Letter
Application information: Write for guidelines

Laurendeau Foundation for Cancer Care
2700 Iron Street
Bellingham, WA 98225
(206) 671-7854

Description: Grants to individuals for outpatient care.
Restrictions: Limited to residents of Bellingham, Washington.
$ Given: In 1990, an unspecified number of grants totaling $18,416 were awarded to individuals.
Assets: $129,876
Initial approach: Letter
Application information: Application form required

Carrie Welch Trust
P.O. Box 244
Walla Walla, WA 99362

Description: Financial assistance to needy and/or worthy senior citizens.
Restrictions: Limited to individuals in Washington State, with preference
to residents of Walla Walla.
$ Given: In FY '91, $13,270 for 12 grants was awarded to individuals;
range, $125–$2,031.
Assets: $1,258,098
Initial approach: Letter
Application information: Application form required

George T. Welch Testamentary Fund
c/o Baker-Boyer National Bank
P.O. Box 1796
Walla Walla, WA 99362
(509) 525-2000

Description: Medical assistance for financially distressed individuals.
Restrictions: Limited to residents of Walla Walla County, Washington.
$ Given: In FY '91, $142,401 for 111 grants was awarded to individu-
als.
Assets: $3,230,013
Contact: Dennis D. Gisi, Trust Officer
Initial approach: Letter
Application information: Application form required
Deadlines: February 20, May 20, August 20, and November 20

Whatcom Foundation, Inc.
Bellingham National Bank Building
Room 423
Bellingham, WA 98225
(206) 733-9511

Description: Grants to needy individuals for basic life needs and medical
care.
Restrictions: Limited to residents of Whatcom County, Washington.
$ Given: In FY '91, grants totaling $10,307 were awarded to individu-
als.
Assets: $66,177
Contact: Linda Lopez
Initial approach: Letter or telephone
Application information: Formal application required
Deadlines: Applications are due by noon each Wednesday and are
reviewed each following Monday throughout the year

WEST VIRGINIA

Good Shepard Foundation, Inc.
Route 4, Box 349
Kinston, NC 28501-9317
(919) 569-3241

Description: Financial assistance for medical care.
Restrictions: Limited to residents of Trent Township, West Virginia.
$ Given: In FY 91, $17,000 for 6 grants was awarded to individuals;
    range, $2,000–$3,500.
Assets: $11,955
Contact: Sue White, Secretary-Treasurer
Initial approach: Letter
Application information: Application form required
Deadlines: None

WISCONSIN

Island Memorial Medical Fund, Inc.
c/o Richard Purinon
Main Road
Washington Island, WI 54246

Description: Support for medical care.
Restrictions: Grants paid directly to provider of services.
$ Given: $20,000 for 5 grants; average range, $600–$8,800.
Assets: $64,000
Initial approach: Letter
Application information: Application form required
Deadlines: Contact foundation for schedule

Margaret Wiegand Trust
c/o Bank One Wisconsin Trust Company, N.A.
P.O. Box 1308
Milwaukee, WI 53201

Description: Money for blind individuals, including medical care,
    education, and other support services.
Restrictions: Must be a resident of the Waukesha County, Wisconsin,
    area.
$ Given: In FY '91, $7,230 for 11 grants was awarded to individuals;
    range, $155–$1,500.

Assets: $116,721
Contact: Ms. Judith Holland, Trust Officer
Initial approach: Letter
Application information: Application form required
Deadlines: None

Private Foundation Funding, No Geographical Restrictions

Charles and Elsa Bendheim Foundation
1 Parker Plaza
Fort Lee, NJ 07024

Description: Grants to individuals for charitable purposes, including aid to the sick and destitute.
Restrictions: Applicants must be Jewish and in need of financial assistance.
$ Given: In 1989, total given was $171,880.
Initial approach: Letter
Application information: Write for guidelines

Broadcasters Foundation, Inc.
320 West Fifty-seventh Street
New York, NY 10019
(212) 586-2000

Description: Grants to needy members of the broadcast industry and their families.
Restrictions: See above.
$ Given: In 1990, $14,400 for 7 grants was awarded to individuals; range, $1,800–$2,400.
Assets: $317,451
Initial approach: Letter
Application information: Application form required
Deadlines: None

Lottie Sleeper Hill and Josiah Sleeper Fund
c/o Fidelity Bank
Broad and Walnut Streets
Philadelphia, PA 19108
(215) 985-8712

Description: Funding for health services.
$ Given: 56 grants to individuals totaling $30,112; average range, $16–$3,380.
Application information: Write for guidelines

The Hugel Foundation
824 Gravier Street
New Orleans, LA 70112

Description: Grants for health care and Catholic giving.
$ Given: 1 individual grant totaling $3,500.
Application information: Write for guidelines

Island Memorial Medical Fund, Inc.
c/o Richard Purinon
Main Road
Washington Island, WI 54246

Description: Financial assistance to help cover medical expenses for needy individuals. Funds paid directly to physicians or treatment facilities.
$ Given: Grants range from $630–$8,760.
Contact: Richard Purinon
Initial approach: Letter
Application information: Write foundation for application guidelines and current deadline information
Deadlines: Varies

Max Mainzer Memorial Foundation, Inc.
570 Seventh Avenue, Third Floor
New York, NY 10018
(212) 921-3865

Description: Grants to financially distressed members of the American Jewish KC Fraternity or their widows.
Restrictions: See above.
$ Given: In FY '91, $34,287 for 15 grants was awarded to individuals; range, $52–$3,750.
Assets: $233,781
Initial approach: Letter
Application information: Contact foundation for guidelines
Deadlines: None

NFL Alumni Foundation Fund
c/o Sigmund M. Hyman
P.O. Box 248
Stevenson, MD 21153-0248
(301) 486-5454

Description: Financial assistance to disabled former National Football League alumni (prior to 1959), including grants for death benefits and medical expenses.
Restrictions: See above.
$ Given: $49,335 for 10 grants awarded to individuals; eligible persons may receive grants to supplement their total annual income by up to $12,000 with a $250/month maximum.
Assets: $32,950
Contact: Sigmund M. Hyman
Initial approach: Letter
Application information: Write for guidelines
Deadlines: None

Katherine C. Pierce Trust
c/o State Street Bank & Trust Company
P.O. Box 351
Boston, MA 02101
(617) 654-3357

Description: Financial assistance for needy women.
Restrictions: See above.
$ Given: In 1991, $44,200 for 13 grants was awarded to individuals; average range, $500–$5,000.
Assets: $889,945
Contact: Robert W. Seymour, Trust Officer
Initial approach: Letter
Application information: Include personal history, needs, and financial condition.
Deadlines: None

Corporate Employee Grants Arranged by State, According to Corporate Location

ALABAMA

The William H. and Kate F. Stockham Foundation, Inc.
c/o Stockham Valves & Fittings, Inc.
4000 North Tenth Avenue
P.O. Box 10326
Birmingham, AL 35202
Application Address:
c/o Kathyrn W. Miree
AmSouth Bank Trust Department
P.O. Box 11426
Birmingham, AL 35202
(205) 326-5387

Description: Need-based grants.
Restrictions: Strictly limited to Stockham Valves & Fittings, Inc.,
    employees, former employees, and their dependents.
$ Given: In 1990, $57,293 for 29 grants was awarded to individuals.
Assets: $3,466,793
Contact: Herbert Stockham, Chairman
Initial approach: Letter
Application address: Write for guidelines
Deadlines: None

CALIFORNIA

A. P. Giannini Foundation for Employees
c/o Bank of America Trust Department
P.O. Box 37121
San Francisco, CA 94137
(415) 622-4915

Description: Relief grants to help cover medical bills and other emer-
    gency expenses.
Restrictions: Limited to Bank of America employees and their families,
    and to employees of Bank of America subsidiaries.

$ Given: In 1991, $72,835 for 13 grants was awarded to individuals; range, $520–$27,604.
Assets: $738,604
Contact: Trust Department
Initial approach: Letter
Application information: Include reason for grant request, amount requested, and assessment of applicant's financial status.
Deadlines: None

Clorinda Giannini Memorial Benefit Fund
c/o Bank of America Trust Department
P.O. Box 37121
San Francisco, CA 94137
(415) 241-7511

Description: Emergency assistance grants for illness, accident disability, surgery, medical and nursing care, hospitalization, financial difficulties, and loss of income.
Restrictions: Limited to Bank of America employees.
$ Given: In FY '91, $48,681 for 21 grants was awarded to individuals; average range, $610–$4,264.
Assets: $1.3 million
Contact: Susan Morales, Assistant Vice President
Initial approach: Letter
Application information: Application form required
Deadlines: None

George S. Ladd Memorial Fund
c/o V. M. Edwards
633 Folsom Street, Room 420
San Francisco, CA 94107
(800) 248-6130

Description: Financial assistance grants, including funding for medical treatment.
Restrictions: Limited to elderly and retired employees of Pacific Bell, Nevada Bell, and Pacific Northwest Bell.
$ Given: In 1991, $54,251 for 21 grants was awarded to individuals; range, $40–$7,933.
Assets: $565,290
Initial approach: Letter
Application information: Write for guidelines

Mate Foundation
c/o I. Magnin Administration Center
P.O. Box 7651
San Francisco, CA 94120-7651
(415) 362-2100

Description: Support for individuals for medical and personal emergencies.

Restrictions: Limited to present or former employees of I. Magnin Company.

$ Given: In 1991, an unspecified number of grants totaling $37,805 were awarded to individuals.

Assets: $691,336

Initial approach: Letter

Application information: Write for guidelines

Deadlines: None

Pfaffinger Foundation
Times Mirror Square
Los Angeles, CA 90053
(213) 237-5743

Description: Need-based grants.

Restrictions: Limited to employees and former employees of The Times Mirror Company.

$ Given: In 1991, an unspecified number of grants totaling $2.1 million were awarded to individuals; average range, $500–$40,553.

Assets: $52,888,596

Contact: James C. Kelly, President

Initial approach: Letter

Application information: Application form required

Deadlines: None

Notification: Final notification usually in one week after application is received.

Winnett Foundation
c/o Bullocks Executive Offices
800 South Hope Street
Los Angeles, CA 90017-4684
(213) 612-5000

Description: Need-based grants.

Restrictions: Limited to employees and former employees of Bullock's Department Store.

$ Given: In FY '91, $46,584 for 15 grants was awarded to individuals; range, $850–$6,040.

Assets: $653,889
Contact: Cara Green
Initial approach: Letter

ILLINOIS

The Clara Abbott Foundation
1 Abbott Park Road
Abbott Park, IL 60064-3500
(312) 937-1091

Description: Relief grants, loans, and aid to the aged.
Restrictions: Limited to employees, retirees, and families of employees of Abbott Laboratories.
$ Given: In 1991, $3,653,000 for 1,600 grants was awarded to individuals.
Assets: $158,000,000
Contact: David C. Jeffries, Executive Director
Initial approach: Letter or telephone
Application information: Write or call for guidelines
Deadlines: None

MASSACHUSETTS

Charles F. Bacon Trust
c/o Bank of New England, N.A.
28 State Street
Boston, MA 02109
(617) 573-6416

Description: Assistance grants.
Restrictions: Limited to former employees of Conrad and Chandler Company who have retired or resigned due to illness.
$ Given: In 1990, $17,000 for 4 grants was awarded to individuals; range, $2,000–$6,000.
Assets: $2,117,071
Contact: Kerry Herlihy, Senior Trust Officer
Initial approach: Letter
Application information: Application form required
Deadlines: December 31

Henry Hornblower Fund, Inc.
Box 2365
Boston, MA 02107
(617) 589-3286

Description: Need-based grants.
Restrictions: Limited to current and former employees of Hornblower
    & Weeks.
$ Given: In 1990, $4,000 for 2 grants was awarded to individuals;
    range, $1,000–$3,000.
Assets: $2,631,713
Contact: Nathan N. Withington, President
Initial approach: Letter
Application information: Write for guidelines
Deadlines: None

Sexton Can Company Employees Aid Fund
125 Cambridge Park Drive
Cambridge, MA 02149

Description: Support for individuals for medical expenses.
Restrictions: Limited to present or former employees of Sexton Can
    Company or their dependents.
$ Given: $3,800 for 2 grants; range, $800–$3,000.
Initial approach: Letter or telephone
Application information: Write for guidelines

MINNESOTA

CENEX Foundation
5500 Cenex Drive
Inver Grove Heights, MN 55075
(612) 451-5105

Description: Financial assistance grants.
Restrictions: Limited to former employees of CENEX and its affiliates.
$ Given: In 1990 $80,745 for 34 grants was awarded to individuals;
    average range, $500–$10,000.
Assets: $3,122,866
Contact: Mary Kaste, Manager
Initial approach: Letter
Application information: Application form required
Deadlines: None

MISSOURI

Butler Manufacturing Company Foundation
Penn Valley Park
P.O. Box 419917
BMA Tower
Kansas City, MO 64141-0197
(816) 968-3208

Description: Hardship grants to aid individuals in emergency financial distress due to serious illness, fire, or natural disaster.
Restrictions: Limited to Butler Manufacturing Company employees, retirees, and their dependents.
$ Given: In 1991, $3,672 for 3 grants was awarded to individuals; range, $1,000–$1,500.
Assets: $4,252,202
Contact: Barbara Lee Fay, Foundation Administrator
Initial approach: Letter
Application information: Write for application guidelines and program information; interviews required.
Deadlines: None

Hall Family Foundations
c/o Charitable and Crown Investment
Department 323
P.O. Box 419580
Kansas City, MO 64141-6580
(816) 274-8516

Description: Grants for emergency relief assistance.
Restrictions: Strictly limited to employees of Hallmark.
$ Given: In 1990, $273,082 for 147 grants was awarded to individuals.
Assets: $407,362,996
Contact: Margaret H. Pence, Director/Program Officer
Initial approach: Letter
Application information: Write or call for guidelines

Kansas City Life Employees Welfare Fund
3520 Broadway
Kansas City, MO 64111-2565
(816) 753-7000

Description: Medical assistance grants.
Restrictions: Limited to Kansas City Life employees and their spouses and/or dependents.
$ Given: In 1990, $1,600 for 2 grants was awarded to individuals.
Assets: $7,051
Contact: Dennis M. Gaffney
Initial approach: Letter
Application information: Write for guidelines
Deadlines: None

David May Employees Trust Fund
c/o The May Department Stores Company
Attention Tax Department
Sixth and Olive Streets
St. Louis, MO 63101

Description: Need-based grants.
Restrictions: Limited to employees and former employees of the May Department Store Company.
$ Given: In 1990, $11,000 for 4 grants was awarded to individuals; range, $500–$5,000.
Assets: $123,755
Contact: Tax Department
Initial approach: Letter
Application information: Write for guidelines

Edward F. Swinney Foundation
c/o Boatmen's First National Bank of Kansas City
P.O. Box 419038
Kansas City, MO 64183
(816) 234-7481

Description: Need-based grants.
Restrictions: Limited to employees of Boatmen's First National Bank of Kansas.
$ Given: $33,439 for 129 grants awarded to individuals; average range, $32–$2,000.
Assets: $764,437
Contact: David P. Ross, Trust Officer
Initial approach: Letter
Application information: Application form required
Deadlines: None

NEVADA

George S. Ladd Memorial Fund
c/o V. M. Edwards
633 Folsom Street, Room 420
San Francisco, CA 94107
(800) 248-0130

Description: Financial assistance grants, including funding for medical treatment.
Restrictions: Limited to elderly and retired employees of Pacific Bell, Nevada Bell, and Pacific Northwest Bell.
$ Given: In 1991, $54,251 for 21 grants was awarded to individuals; range, $40–$7,933.
Assets: $565,290
Initial approach: Letter
Application information: Write for guidelines

NEW JERSEY

Ittleson-Beaumont Fund
(formerly Ittleson Beneficial Fund)
c/o The C.I.T. Group Holdings, Inc.
135 West Fiftieth Street
New York, NY 10020
(212) 408-6000
Application Address:
650 C.I.T Drive
Livingston, NJ 07039

Description: Need-based grants to provide supplemental income to individuals demonstrating continuing financial hardship.
Restrictions: Intended primarily, but not exclusively, for current and former employees of C.I.T. Financial Corporation and its affiliates, as well as for the families of employees.
$ Given: In 1990, $37,885 for 17 grants was awarded to individuals; range, $224–$3,600.
Assets: $1,618,949
Contact: William M. Hopf, Controller
Initial approach: Letter
Application information: Submit application letter stating reason for request and providing details of applicant's financial status.
Deadlines: None

NEW YORK

The Ernst & Young Foundation
(formerly the Ernst & Whinney Foundation)
277 Park Avenue
New York, NY 10171

Description: Financial assistance grants to employees and their families.
Restrictions: Limited to Ernst & Young employees and their families.
$ Given: 1 relief grant for $2,400 was awarded.
Contact: Bruce J. Mantia, Administrator
Initial approach: Letter
Application information: Write for guidelines

Hegeman Memorial Trust Fund
1 Madison Avenue
Area 23VW
New York, NY 10010
(212) 578-3493

Description: Grants for health and welfare.
Restrictions: Limited to employees, active and retired, and their New
    York dependents, including dependents of deceased employees, of
    Metropolitan Life Insurance Company.
$ Given: In 1990, $68,700 for 15 grants was awarded to individuals;
    range, $750-$9,500.
Assets: $742,724
Contact: Evelyn D. Ilari, Employee Advisory Services
Initial approach: Letter
Application information: Initial approach by letter including financial
    statement to demonstrate need
Deadlines: None

Ittleson-Beaumont Fund
(formerly Ittleson Beneficial Fund)
c/o The C.I.T. Group Holdings, Inc.
135 West Fiftieth Street
New York, NY 10020
(212) 408-6000
Application Address:
650 C.I.T. Drive
Livingston, NJ 07039

Description: Need-based grants to provide supplemental income to
    individuals demonstrating continuing financial hardship.

Restrictions: Intended primarily, but not exclusively, for current and
  former employees of C.I.T. Financial Corporation and its affiliates, as
  well as for the families of employees.
$ Given: In 1990, $37,885 for 17 grants was awarded to individuals;
  range, $224–$3,600.
Assets: $1,618,949
Contact: William M. Hopf, Controller
Initial approach: Letter
Application information: Submit application letter stating reason for
  request and providing details of applicant's financial status
Deadlines: None

OHIO

National Machinery Foundation, Inc.
Greenfield Street
P.O. Box 747
Tiffin, OH 44883
(419) 447-5211

Description: Need-based grants .
Restrictions: Limited to former employees of National Machinery and
  to other financially distressed individuals in Seneca County, Ohio.
$ Given: In 1990, an unspecified number of grants totaling $113,906
  were awarded to individuals.
Assets: $8,823,613
Contact: D.B. Bero, Administrator
Initial approach: Letter
Application information: Write for guidelines

Richman Brothers Foundation
Box 657
Chagrin Falls, OH 44022
(216) 247-5426

Description: Relief assistance grants.
Restrictions: Limited to employees, pensioners, widows, and children of
  employees of the Richman Brothers Company.
$ Given: Grants range from $100–$1,995.
Contact: Richard R. Moore, President
Initial approach: Letter
Application information: Write for guidelines; application form required.
Deadlines: November 15

OREGON

George S. Ladd Memorial Fund
c/o V. M. Edwards
633 Folsom Street, Room 420
San Francisco, CA 94107
(800) 248-0130

Description: Financial assistance grants, including funding for medical treatment.
Restrictions: Limited to elderly and retired employees of Pacific Bell, Nevada Bell, and Pacific Northwest Bell.
$ Given: In 1991, $54,251 for 21 grants was awarded to individuals; range, $40–$7,933.
Assets: $565,290
Initial approach: Letter
Application information: Write for guidelines

PENNSYLVANIA

Vang Memorial Foundation
P.O. Box 11727
Pittsburgh, PA 15228
(412) 563-0261

Description: Grants-in-aid assistance.
Restrictions: Limited to past, present, and future employees of George Vang, Inc., and related companies, and their dependents.
$ Given: In 1991, $40,589 for 17 grants was awarded to individuals; range, $628–$6,182.
Contact: E. J. Hosko, Treasurer
Initial approach: Letter
Application information: Submit introductory letter, including name, address, and telephone number of applicant and specify type of grant requested and basis of need.
Deadlines: None

TEXAS

Amon G. Carter Star Telegram Employees Fund
P.O. Box 17480
Fort Worth, TX 76102
(817) 332-3535

Description: Medical/hardship assistance and pension supplements.
Restrictions: Limited to employees of the Fort Worth Star-Telegram,
  KXAS-TV, and WBAP Radio.
$ Given: $232,408 for 59 grants awarded; average range, $500–$8,218.
Assets: $14,970,638
Contact: Nenetta Tatum, President
Initial approach: Letter
Application information: Write for guidelines
Deadlines: None

WASHINGTON

George S. Ladd Memorial Fund
c/o V. M. Edwards
633 Folsom Street, Room 420
San Francisco, CA 94107
(800) 248-0130

Description: Financial assistance grants, including funding for medical
  treatment.
Restrictions: Limited to elderly and retired employees of Pacific Bell,
  Nevada Bell, and Pacific Northwest Bell.
$ Given: In 1991, $54,251 for 21 grants was awarded to individuals;
  range, $40–$7,933.
Assets: $565,290
Initial approach: Letter
Application information: Write for guidelines

Companies with Employees Nationwide and Abroad

The Correspondents' Fund
c/o Roseman & Cohen
575 Madison Avenue
New York, NY 10022-2511
Application Address:
c/o The New York Times
229 West 43rd Street
New York, NY 10036

Description: Emergency grants.
Restrictions: Limited to individuals who have worked in the U.S. press,
  television, radio, news, film, and other U.S. organizations within or
  outside the United States; to individuals who have worked in the
  foreign press or other foreign news organizations; and to their
  dependents.
$ Given: Grants range from $2,500–$3,000.
Contact: James L. Greenfield, President
Initial approach: Letter
Application information: Submit an introductory letter including details
  of the circumstances for which aid is requested.
Deadlines: None

9

Area Agencies on Aging

The 670 Area Agencies on Aging are an invaluable clearinghouse of information on programs for the elderly. An Area Agency on Aging (AAA) is a public or private nonprofit agency designated by the state to address the needs and concerns of all older Americans at the local level. Nearly every community throughout the United States either has or is served by their own Area Agency on Aging office. The AAAs are mandated by the federal government to set up and administer programs for nonmedical services within communities: home-delivered meals, illness prevention programs, adult day care, free transportation to doctors' offices, shopping and housekeeping help, and social activities are among the many programs available. The AAAs also perform the important function of steering elderly people and their families to companies that manage and provide professional home-care services including nurses, home-health aides, and physiotherapists. Some AAAs provide financial-planning assistance or will advise where to find it.

Many of the agencies offer a service they call "case management," or service coordination. A social worker visits the older person's home to conduct an assessment and find out what help is needed and how it can be organized. Usually this extremely valuable service is free of charge. If case management is not offered by the AAA in your area, the agency may have information about private case-management services.

Though the quality of help provided by agencies varies from place to place, any office should be able to provide you with some information on the following services, whether government-funded, for-profit, or volunteer-run:

1. Adult day care
2. Case management
3. Friendly visiting services
4. Home health aides
5. Homemaker and chores services
6. Housing services
7. Legal assistance
8. Meals programs
9. Mental-health services
10. Nursing-home and adult-home placement
11. Ombudsman services (investigating complaints)
12. Respite care (for caregivers)
13. Senior citizen centers
14. Shopping assistance
15. Telephone reassurance programs
16. Transportation
17. Visiting nurses

I have listed the state AAA offices for all 50 states, the District of Columbia, and Puerto Rico, as well as the regional AAA offices within each state. The reader should check the regional listings first to see if any of those offices serve his or her geographic area. The names of the regional AAAs reflect the geographic area they serve, that is, Alabama and Tombigbee Area Agency of Aging, Central Alabama Aging Consortium, Jefferson County Office of Senior Citizens. If you are unable to determine which of the regional AAA agencies serves your area, call the State Agency to obtain that information.

Alabama

STATE AGENCY

Commission on Aging
770 Washington Avenue, Suite 470
RSA Plaza
Montgomery, AL 36130
(205) 242-5743
Within state: (800) 243-5463
Contact: Oscar D. Tucker

REGIONAL AGENCIES

Alabama and Tombigbee Area Agency on Aging
12 Water Street
Courthouse Annex, Suite 200
Camden, AL 36726
(800) 762-6329
Contact: Janice M. Armstrong

Central Alabama Aging Consortium
818 South Perry Street
Montgomery, AL 36104
(205) 240-4666
Contact: Martha Pippin

East Alabama Commission Area Agency on Aging
P.O. Box 2186
Anniston, AL 36202
(800) 239-6741
Contact: Bill Cooper

Jefferson County Office of Senior Citizens
2601 Highland Avenue South
Birmingham, AL 35205
(205) 325-1416
Contact: Barbara Bonfield

Lee-Russell Council of Governments Area Agency on Aging
2207 Hamilton Road
P.O. Box 2186
Opelika, AL 36801-2186
(205) 749-5264
Contact: Tracey W. Williams

Middle Alabama Area Agency on Aging
P.O. Box 1270
Community Service Building, Room 138
Columbiana, AL 35051
Blount County: (205) 625-5025
Chilton County: (205) 755-7817
Shelby County: (205) 669-3828

St. Clair County: (205) 472-2914
Walker County: (205) 622-3197
Contact: Frances McCullough

NARCOG Area Agency on Aging
402 Lee Street, NE
P.O. Box C
Decatur, AL 35602
Lawrence County: (205) 974-2490
Cullman County: (205) 734-1241
Morgan County: (205) 351-4600
Contact: Norris Turney

Northwest Alabama Council of Local Governments/Area Agency on Aging
438 Southwest Hamilton Street
P.O. Box L
Russellville, AL 35653
(205) 332-9173
Contact: James Coman

South Central Alabama Development Commission/ Area Agency on Aging
5900 Carmichael Place
Montgomery, AL 36117
(205) 244-6903
Contact: Sylvia Alexander

Southern Alabama Regional Council on Aging
202 North Oates Street
Dothan, AL 36302
(205) 793-6843
Within state: (800) 239-3507
Contact: William Glover

Southern Alabama Regional Planning Commission/Area Agency on Aging
651 Church Street
P.O. Box 1665
Mobile, AL 36633-1665
(205) 433-6541
Contact: Joan States

TARGOG Area Agency on Aging
115 Washington Street
Huntsville, AL 35801
(205) 533-3330
Contact: Nancy Robertson

West Alabama Planning and Development Council Area Agency on Aging
7601 Robert Cardinal Road
Tuscaloosa, AL 35406
Bibb and Greene Counties: (205) 345-5545
Fayette County: (205) 932-3218
Hale County: (205) 371-6318
Pickens County: (205) 367-2200
Lamar County: (205) 695-9573
Tuscaloosa County: (205) 758-3393
Contact: Rodney Gann

Alaska

STATE AGENCY

Older Alaskans Commission
333 Willoughby Avenue
Department of Administration
P.O. Box 110209
Juneau, AK 99811-0209
(907) 465-3250
Contact: Connie J. Sipe

Arizona

STATE AGENCY

Aging and Adult Administration
Department of Economic Security
1789 West Jefferson, 2SW, 950A
Phoenix, AZ 85007
(602) 881-1794
Within state: (800) 362-3474
Contact: Richard Littler

REGIONAL AGENCIES

Area Agency on Aging, Region I, Inc.
1336 East Thomas Road, Suite 108
Phoenix, AZ 85014
(602) 264-4357
Contact: Mary Lynn Kasunic

Northern Arizona Council of Governments/Area Agency on Aging
119 East Aspen
Flagstaff, AZ 86001-5296
(602) 774-1894
Contact: James Quast

Pima Council on Aging
2919 East Broadway
Tucson, AZ 85716
(602) 795-5800
Contact: Marian Lupu

SEAGO/Area Agency on Aging
118 Arizona Street
Bisbee, AZ 85603
(602) 432-5301
Contact: Kathleen Heard

Pinal/Gila Council for Senior Citizens
408 North Sacaton Street, Suite G
Casa Grande, AZ 85222
(602) 836-2758
Contact: Olivia Guerrero

WACOG/Area Agency on Aging
1100 South Maple Avenue
Yuma, AZ 85364
(602) 782-1886
Contact: Elisa Davis

Arkansas

STATE AGENCY

Division of Aging and Adult Services
Arkansas Department of Human Services
Seventh and Main Streets
P.O. Box 1437, Slot 1412
Little Rock, AR 72201
(501) 682-8150
Contact: Herb Sanderson

REGIONAL AGENCIES

Area Agency on Aging of Northwest Arkansas
910 B Northvale Shopping Center
P.O. Box 1795
Harrison, AR 72601
(800) 432-9721
Contact: Phil Peters

Area Agency on Aging of Southeast Arkansas
709 East Eighth Avenue
P.O. Box 8569
Pine Bluff, AR 71611
(800) 264-3260
Contact: Betty Bradshaw Sanders

Area Agency on Aging of
  Southwest Arkansas Inc.
600 Columbia 11 East
P.O. Box 1863
Magnolia, AR 71753
Within state: (800) 272-2127
Contact: David Sneed

Area Agency on Aging of West
  Central Arkansas
905 West Grand
Hot Springs, AR 71913
(800) 467-2170
Contact: Darrell Smith

Area Agency on Aging of
  Western Arkansas, Inc.
P.O. Box 1724
Fort Smith, AR 72902
Crawford County: (501) 474-5378
Sebastian County: (501) 996-
  6581; (501) 782-7341
Franklin County: (501) 667-4873
Polk County: (501) 394-5459
Logan County: (501) 963-3475
Scott County: (501) 637-3538
Contact: Jim Medley

Central Arkansas Area Agency
  on Aging, Inc.
700 Riverfront Drive

P.O. Box 5988
North Little Rock, AR 72119
Within state: (800) 482-6359
Contact: Elaine Eubank

East Arkansas Area Agency on
  Aging, Inc.
311 South Main
P.O. Box 5035
Jonesboro, AR 72403
Within state: (800) 467-3278
Contact: Ed Doman

White River Area Agency on
  Aging
3998 Harrison Street
P.O. Box 2637
Batesville, AR 72503
Cleburne County: (501) 362-2413
Fulton County: (501) 895-3760
Independence County: (501) 793-
  4433
Izard County: (501) 368-4420
Van Buren County: (501) 745-
  2244
White County: (501) 268-2587
Woodruff County: (501) 731-5053
Sharp County: (501) 368-4420
Stone County: (501) 368-4420
Jackson County: (501) 523-2842
Contact: Ed Haas

California

STATE AGENCY

Department of Aging
1600 K Street
Sacramento, CA 95814
(916) 322-3888
Contact: Robert P. Martinez

REGIONAL AGENCIES

Almeda County Department on Aging
1234 East Fourteenth Street, Suite 207
San Leandro, CA 94577
(510) 667-3067
Contact: Linda Kretz

Area 1 Agency on Aging
3300 Glenwood Street
Eureka, CA 95501
Humboldt County: (707) 443-9747
Del Norte County: (707) 464-7876
Contact: Patricia A. Berg

Area 4 Area Agency on Aging
0862 Ardeb Way, Suite 101
Sacramento, CA 95825
Nevada County: (916) 272-3505
Placer County: (916) 889-4114
Sacramento County: (916) 442-4995
Sierra County: (916) 993-4770
Sutter and Yuba Counties: (916) 674-2450
Yolo County (Woodland Center): (916) 662-0698
Yolo County (Davis Center): (916) 757-5696
Contact: Deanna Lea

Area 12 Area Agency on Aging
56 North Washington Street
Sonora, CA 95370
Alpine County: (916) 694-2312
Amador County: (209) 223-0442
Calaveras County: (209) 754-1888
Mariposa County: (209) 966-5315
Tuolumne County: (209) 533-2622
Contact: David Yarbrough

Area Agency on Aging— California State University
Second and Normal Streets
Chico, CA 95929
Within state: (800) 822-0109
Contact: Paul Martinsen

Area Agency on Aging— County of Orange
1300 South Grand, Building B
Santa Ana, CA 92705
(714) 567-7500
Contact: Peggy Wetherspoon

Area Agency on Aging— Planning and Service Area 2
228 Butte Street
P.O. Box 1400
Yreka, CA 96097
Lassen County: (916) 257-2133
Modloc County: (916) 233-4438
Shasta County: (916) 241-4841
Siskivou County: (916) 842-4455
Trinity County: (916) 623-2324
Contact: Dennis Dudley

Central Coast Commission for Senior Citizens
208 West Main Street
Santa Maria, CA 93454-5027
Santa Barbara County: (805) 928-5818
San Luis Obispo County: (805) 544-6163
Contact: Joyce Lippman

City of Los Angeles Department of Aging
600 South Spring, Suite 900
Los Angeles, CA 90014
(213) 722-7807
Within state: (800) 634-6516
Contact: Faye Washington

Commission on the Aging
25 Van Ness Avenue, Suite 650
San Francisco, CA 94102
(415) 626-1033
Contact: David Ishida

Contra Costa County Office on Aging
40 Douglas Drive
Martinez, CA 94553-4068
East Contra Costa County: (510) 427-8681
Central Contra Costa County: (510) 646-6550
West Contra Costa County: (510) 374-3943
Contact: Robert Sessler

Council on Aging of Santa Clara County, Inc.
2115 The Almeda
San Jose, CA 95126
(408) 345-4532
Contact: Stephen M. Schmoll

Department of Aging
Children's and Community Services
102 South San Joaquin Street
P.O. Box 201056
Stockton, CA 95201
(209) 948-1200
Contact: Charlotte H. Williams

El Dorado County Area Agency on Aging
937 Spring Street
Placerville, CA 95667
(916) 621-6150
Contact: Doug Nowka

Fresno—Madera Area Agency on Aging
2220 Tulare, Suite 1200
Fresno, CA 93721
Within state: (800) 287-8722
Contact: Jo Johnson

Imperial County Area Agency on Aging
1331 South Clark Road, Building 11
El Centro, CA 92243
(619) 353-2260
Contact: Floyd Willis

Inyo—Mono Area Agency on Aging
119 MacIver Street B and C
P.O. Box 1799
Bishop, CA 93515
Inyo and Mono Counties: (619) 873-6364
North Mono County: (619) 495-2323
Contact: Charles Broten

Kern County Office on Aging
1415 Truxton Avenue
Bakersfield, CA 93301
Kern County: (805) 861-2218
Mojave, Rosamond, Ridgecrest, California City, Baron, Johannesburg, Ino, and Kern Counties: (619) 375-7322
Contact: Eddy Laine

Kings—Tulare Area Agency on Aging
1920 West Princeton, Suite A
Visalia, CA 93277
Kings County: (209) 582-3211 x2825
Tulare County (within state): (800) 321-2462
Contact: John Davis

Los Angeles County Area Agency on Aging
3175 West Sixth Street, Suite 400
Los Angeles, CA 90020
(213) 738-4004
Contact: Lynn Bayer

Marin County Area Agency on Aging—Division of Aging
10 North San Pedro Road, Suite 1012
San Rafael, CA 94903
(415) 456-9062
Contact: Ellen R. Caulfield

Merced County Area Agency for Aging Programs
851 West Twenty-third Street
Merced, CA 95340
(209) 385-7550
Within state: (800) 834-1122
Contact: Dennis K. Tatum

North Coast Opportunities, Inc./Area Agency on Aging
413A North State Street
Ukiah, CA 95482
(707) 462-1954
Contact: Roberta Green

Office for Aging and Community Services
Monterey County Department of Social Services
1000 South Main Street, Suite 202
Salinas, CA 93901
(408) 755-8490
Contact: Marie Glavin

Riverside County Office on Aging
2023 Chicago Avenue, Suite B4
Riverside, CA 92507
(909) 275-8940
Contact: George Telisman

San Bernardino County Office on Aging
686 East Mill Street
San Bernardino, CA 92415
Baker, Barstow, Daggett, Helendale, Hinkley, Kelso, Mountain Pass, Trona, Yermo, Newberry Springs, and Red Mountain: (619) 256-2191
Big River, Havasu, Needles, and Parker Dam: (619) 665-8558
Grand Terrace and Rialto: (714)829-8515
Alta Loma, Chino, Etiwanda, Guasti, Montclair, Mt. Baldy, Ontario, Upland, and Rancho Cucamonga: (714) 986-3821
Bryn Mawr, Loma Linda, Mentone, and Tedlands: (714)793-7707
San Bernadino and Highland: (714)387-2423
Adelanto, Apple Valley, Baldy Mesa, El Mirage, Helendale, Hesperia, Oak Hills, Lucerne Valley, Oro Grande, Phelan, Pinion Hills, Summit Valley, Victorville, and Wrightwood: (619) 245-6509
Yucaipa: (714)797-1177
Amboy, Cadiz, Joshua Tree, Landers, Morongo Valley, Pioneertown, Wonder Valley, Twentynine Palms, and Yucca Valley: (619) 228-5456
Contact: Paul Roy

San Diego County Area Agency on Aging
9335 Hazard Way, Suite 100
San Diego, CA 92123
(619) 560-2500
Contact: Daniel L. Laver

**San Mateo County Area
Agency on Aging**
225 West Thirty-seventh Avenue
P.O. Box 5892
San Mateo, CA 94403
(415) 573-3900
Contact: Charlene Silva

Seniors Council
234 Santa Cruz Avenue
Aptos, CA 95003
San Benito County: (408) 637-
6700
Watsonville, Freedom, and La
Selva Beach Counties: (408)
728-1751
Santa Cruz County: (408) 462-
1433
Contact: Jennifer Davis

**Solano—Napa Agency on
Aging, Inc.**
1814 Capitol Street
Callejo, CA 94590
Benicia and Vallejo: (707) 643-
1797
Fairfield, Cordelia, Suisun, Travis,
and Green Valley: (707) 425-
2922
Vacaville, Elmira, Dixon, and
Allendale: (707) 446-4242

Rio Vista: (707) 374-5706
Napa, Yountville, and American
Canyon: (707) 252-6222
St. Helena, Calistoga, Angwin,
Lake Berryessa, and Pope
Valley: (707) 963-3922
Contact: June Cichowicz

**Sonoma County Area Agency
on Aging**
940 Hopper Avenue
Santa Rosa, CA 95403
(707) 525-0143
Contact: Robin Schaef

**Stanislaus County Area Agency
on Aging**
948 Eleventh Street, Suite LL3
Modesto, CA 95354
(209) 577-4068
Contact: Lynda Griswold

**Ventura County Area Agency
on Aging**
505 Poll Street, Third Floor,
#L4450
Ventura, CA 93001
(805) 652-7500
Contact: Colleen House

Colorado

STATE AGENCY

Aging and Adult Services
Department of Social Services
1575 Sherman Street, Fourth Floor
Denver, CO 80203-1714
(303) 866-3851
Contact: Rita Barreras

REGIONAL AGENCIES

Boulder County Aging Services Division
P.O. Box 471
Boulder, CO 80306
(303) 441-3570

Denver Regional Council of Governments
2480 West Twenty-sixth Avenue, Suite 200B
Denver, CO 80211
(303) 455-1000
Contact: Molly Snyder

East Central Colorado Area Agency on Aging
128 Colorado Avenue
Stratton, CO 80836
(800) 825-0208
Contact: Terry Baylie

Huerfano—Las Animas Area Agency on Aging
200 East First Street
Room 201, Courthouse
Trinidad, CO 81082
(719) 846-4401
Contact: Walter Degurse

Larimer County Office on Aging
1525 Blue Spruce
Ft. Collins, CO 80524
(303) 498-6800
Contact: Shelley McGraw

Lower Arkansas Valley Area Agency on Aging
Otero County Courthouse
Third and Colorado
P.O. Box 494
La Junta, CO 81050
(719) 384-8166
Contact: Lynn Graves

Northeastern Colorado Area Agency on Aging
231 Main Street, Suite 211
Fort Morgan, CO 80701
(303) 867-9409
Contact: Sandra K. Baker

Northwest Colorado Area Agency on Aging
202 Railroad Avenue
P.O. Box 351
Rifle, CO 81650
(303) 625-1723
Contact: Dave Norman

Pikes Peak Area Agency on Aging
15 South Seventh Street
Colorado Springs, CO 80905
(719) 471-2096
Contact: Jeremy J. Huffman

Pueblo Area Agency on Aging
1120 Court Street, Suite 101
Pueblo, CO 81003
(719) 544-9999
Contact: Fran McClave

Region 10 Area Agency on Aging
301 North Cascade
P.O. Box 849
Montrose, CO 81402
(303) 249-2436
Contact: Stan Broome

San Juan Basin Area Agency on Aging
3801 North Main Street
Durango, CO 81301
Montezuma County: (303) 565-4166
Archuleta County: (303) 264-2167
La Plata, Delores, and San Juan Counties: (303) 259-1967
Contact: Charles Speno

Skyline Six Area Agency on Aging
249 Warren
Box 2308
Silverthorne, CO 80498
Eagle County: (303) 328-8815
Grand County: (303) 468-0295
Jackson County: (303) 723-4262
Pitkin County: (303) 920-5432
Routt County: (303) 879-0633
Summit County: (303) 668-5486
Contact: Linda Venturoni

South Central Colorado Seniors, Inc.
512 Ross
P.O. Box 420
Alamosa, CO 81101
(719) 589-4511
Contact: Bill Baker

Upper Arkansas Area Agency on Aging
7405 Highway 50 West, #102
Salida, CO 81201
(719) 539-3341
Contact: Bonnie McEnulty

Weld County Area Agency on Aging
1551 North Seventeenth Avenue
P.O. Box 1805
Greeley, CO 80632
(303) 353-3816
Contact: Linda E. Piper

Connecticut

STATE AGENCY

Connecticut Department on Aging
175 Main Street
Hartford, CT 06106
Within state: (203) 522-4636
Out of state: (203) 566-7772
Contact: Edith Prague

REGIONAL AGENCIES

Eastern Connecticut Area Agency on Aging
401 West Thames Street
Norwich, CT 06360
(203) 887-3561
Contact: Adele Tousignant

North Central Area Agency on Aging
999 Asylum Avenue, Suite 500
Hartford, CT 06105
(203) 724-6443
Contact: Cassandra Johnson

Southwestern Connecticut Area Agency on Aging
25 Van Zant Street, Suite 15-8
Norwalk, CT 06855
(203) 853-7189
Contact: Edith Serke

South Central Connecticut Area Agency on Aging
201 Noble Street
West Haven, CT 06516
(203) 933-5431
Contact: Carla Hayes

Western Connecticut Area Agency on Aging, Inc.
20 East Main Street, Suite 324
Waterbury, CT 06702
(203) 757-5449
Contact: Christina Fishbein

District of Columbia

REGIONAL AGENCY

D.C. Office on Aging
1424 K Street, NW, Second Floor
Washington, DC 20005
(202) 724-5626
Contact: Sammy A. Gawad

Delaware

STATE AGENCY

Division of Aging
Department of Health and Social Services
1901 North DuPont Highway
New Castle, DE 19720
(800) 223-9074
Contact: Eleanor Cain

Florida

STATE AGENCY

Program of Aging and Adult Services
Department of Elder Affairs
Building 1, Room 317
1317 Winewood Boulevard
Tallahassee, FL 32399-0700
(904) 922-5297
Contact: Bentley Lipscomb

REGIONAL AGENCIES

Alliance for Aging, Inc.
9500 South Dadeland Boulevard,
 Suite 400
Miami, FL 33156
Dade County: (305) 358-6060
Monroe County: (800) 273-2044
Contact: John L. Stokesberry

**Area Agency on Aging of
 Broward County, Inc.**
5345 Northwest Thirty-fifth
 Avenue
Ft. Lauderdale, FL 33309
(305) 484-4357
Contact: Edith Lederberg

Area Agency on Aging for North Florida
2639 North Monroe Street, Suite 145B
Tallahassee, FL 32303
Bay County: (904) 769-3468
Calhoun County: (904) 674-4163
Franklin County: (904) 697-3760
Gadsen County: (904) 627-2223
Gulf County: (904) 229-8466
Holmes County: (904) 547-2345
Jackson County: (904) 482-5028
Jefferson County: (904) 997-3418
Leon County: (904) 575-9694
Liberty County: (904) 643-5613
Madison County: (904) 973-2006
Taylor County: (904) 584-4924
Wakulla County: (904) 926-7145
Washington County: (904) 769-6216
Contact: Jim Drake

Area Agency on Aging of Palm Beach/Treasure Coast Inc.
8895 North Military Trail, #301C
Palm Beach Gardens, FL 33410
Indian River County: (407) 569-0764
Martin County: (407) 283-2242
Okeechobee County: (813) 763-9444
Palm Beach County: (407) 930-5040
St. Lucie County: (407) 465-5220
Contact: Laura Landwirth

Area Agency on Aging of South Central Florida
1400 Jackson Street
Fort Myers, FL 33901
Charlotte County: (813) 637-2288
Collier County: (813) 774-8443
DeSoto County: (813) 494-5965
Hendry County: (813) 983-7088

Glades County: (813) 946-1821
Lee County: (813) 433-3900
Sarasota County: (813) 955-2122
Contact: Lincoln E. Tumey

E.C.F.R.P.C. Area Agency on Aging
1011 Wymore Road, Suite 105
Winter Park, FL 32789
Brevard County: (407) 631-2747
Orange County: (407) 648-4357
Osceola County: (407) 847-4357
Seminole County: (407) 831-4357
Contact: Judith G. Thames

Mid-Florida Area Agency on Aging
5700 Southwest Thirty-fourth Street, Suite 222
Gainesville, FL 32608
Alachua County: (904) 336-3822
Bradford County: (904) 964-3837
Citrus County: (904) 746-1844
Columbia County: (904) 752-8235
Dixie County: (904) 498-7910
Gilchrist County: (904) 463-7681
Hamilton County: (904) 792-2136
Hernando County: (904) 796-0485
Lafayette County: (904) 294-1172
Lake County: (904) 326-5304
Levy County: (904) 493-1290
Marion County: (904) 629-7407
Putnam County: (904) 328-2121
Sumter County: (904) 793-5234
Suwannee County: (904) 364-5673
Union County: (904) 496-2922
Contact: Dean R. LaFrentz

Northeast Florida Area Agency on Aging, Inc.
2257 Riverside Avenue

P.O. Box 43187
Jacksonville, FL 32203
Baker County: (904) 259-2223
Clay County: (904) 284-5977
Duval County: (904) 798-9503
Flagler County: (904) 437-7300
Nassau County: (904) 261-0701
St. Johns County: (904) 824-1648
Volusia County: (904) 253-4700
Contact: Elizabeth Lee

Northwest Florida Area Agency on Aging
6706 North Ninth Avenue,
  Building A, Suite 1
Pensacola, FL 32504-7398
Escambia County: (904) 432-1475
Okaloosa County: (904) 833-9165
Santa Rosa County: (904) 939-0477
Walton County: (904) 892-8168
Contact: Dorothy Peoples

Tampa Bay Regional Planning Council Area Agency on Aging

9455 Koger Boulevard
Hendry Building
St. Petersburg, FL 33702
East Pasco County: (904) 567-1111
Pinellas County: (813) 531-4664
West Pasco County: (813) 848-5555
Central Pasco County: (813) 228-8686
Contact: Sally D. Gronda

West Central Florida Area Agency on Aging
1419 West Waters Avenue, Suite 114
Tampa, FL 33604
Highlands County: (813) 465-1199
Hillsborough County: (813) 653-7709
Hardee County: (813) 773-6880
Manatee County: (813) 749-7127
Polk County: (800) 533-0741
Contact: Maureen Kelly

Georgia

STATE AGENCY

Office of Aging
878 Peachtree Street, NE, Room 632
Atlanta, GA 30309
(404) 894-5333
Contact: Judy Hagebak

REGIONAL AGENCIES

Atlamaha Georgia Southern Regional Development Center—Area Agency on Aging
P.O. Box 459
Baxley, GA 31513
Appling County: (912) 367-6127
Bulloch County: (912) 489-1604
Candler County: (912) 685-2580
Jeff Davis County: (912) 375-3603
Evans Area County: (912) 739-1705
Tattnall County: (912) 557-6032
Toombs County: (912) 537-0453
Wayne County: (912) 427-7798
Contact: Gail H. Thompson

Atlanta Tercional Commission, Aging Services Division
3715 Northside Parkway
200 Northcreek, Suite 300
Atlanta, GA 30327
Clauton County: (404) 361-9179
Cobb County: (404) 528-5364
DeKalb County: (404) 377-9901
Douglas County: (404) 489-3100
Fayette County: (404) 461-0813
Fulton County: (404) 522-9913
Gwinnett County: (404) 822-8850
Henry County: (404) 954-2033
Rockdale County: (404) 922-4633
Contact: Cheryll Schramm

Central Savannah River Area Regional Area Agency on Aging
2123 Wrightsboro Road
P.O. Box 2800
Augusta, GA 30914-2800
(404) 733-5800
Contact: Jeanette G. Cummings

Chattahoochee—Flint Area Agency on Aging
P.O. Box 1600
Franklin, GA 30217
(706) 884-2651
Contact: Robert C. Buchanan

Coastal Area Agency on Aging
Coastal Georgia Regional Development
P.O. Box 1917
Brunswick, GA 31521
(912) 264-7363
Contact: Deborah Wilkinson

Coosa Valley Regional Development Center—Area Agency on Aging
P.O. Box 1793
Rome, GA 30163-1001
(706) 295-6485
Contact: Pattie S. Pearson

Georgia Mountains Area Agency on Aging
Georgia Mountains Regional Development Center
P.O. Box 1720
Gainesville, GA 30503
(800) 845-5465
Contact: Pat Viles Freeman

Heart of Georgia Area Agency on Aging
118 South Second Avenue
P.O. Box 503
McCrae, GA 31055
Bleckley County: (912) 934-3223
Dodge County: (912) 374-7255
Dodge County: (912) 275-1721
Pulaski County: (912) 783-1074

Wilcox County: (912) 365-2352
Telfair County: (912) 868-5938
Treutlen County: (912) 529-6300
Wheeler County: (912) 568-7811
Contact: Robert F. Williams

Lower Chattahoochee Regional Development Center—Area Agency on Aging
930 Second Avenue
Columbus, GA 31902-1908
(706) 324-4221
Contact: Katie Howard

McIntosh Trail Area Agency on Aging
408 Thomaston Street
P.O. Drawer A
Barnesville, GA 30204
(404) 227-1904
Contact: Danita Crawford

Middle Flint Regional Development Center—Area Agency on Aging
203 East College Street
P.O. Box 6
Ellaville, GA 31806
(912) 924-1739
Contact: Mickey Holloway

Middle Georgia Regional Development Center—Area Agency on Aging
600 Grand Building
Macon, GA 31201
(912) 751-6160
Contact: Sylvia Haslem

Northeast Georgia Area Agency on Aging
305 Research Drive
Athens, GA 30610
Clarke County: (706) 549-4850

Barrow County: (706) 307-3025
Elbert County: (706) 283-2033
Greene County: (706) 453-7463
Jackson County: (706) 367-5101
Madison County: (706) 783-3128
Oconee County: (706) 769-3979
Oglethorpe County: (706) 743-8848
Walton County: (404) 267-6589
Morgan County: (706) 342-1614
Aging Connection (within state): (800) 924-5085
Aging Connection: (706) 353-1313
Contact: Gayle Keeling

North Georgia Regional Development Center
503 West Waugh Street
Dalton, GA 30720
(706) 272-2300
Contact: Kathy Morrow

Oconee Regional Development Center—Area Agency on Aging
3014 Heritage Road
P.O. Box 707
Milledgeville, GA 31061
Baldwin and Wilkinson Counties: (912) 453-4276
Hancock County: (404) 444-7532
Jasper County: (404) 468-6168
Johnson County: (912) 864-3255
Washington County: (912) 552-0321
Putnam County: (404) 485-9784
Contact: Melinda Edwards

South Georgia Council on Aging
111 North Ashley Street
Valdosta, GA 31601
(912) 241-9108
Contact: Marie Hill

Southeast Georgia Regional Development Center—Area Agency on Aging
3395 Harris Road
Waycross, GA 31501
(912) 285-6097
Contact: Pat Albritton

Sowega Council on Aging, Inc./ Area Agency on Aging
309 Pine Street
Albany, GA 31701
(912) 432-1124
Contact: Kay H. Hind

Hawaii

STATE AGENCY

Executive Office on Aging
Office of the Governor
335 Merchant Street, Suite 241
Honolulu, HI 96813
Within state: (800) 468-4644
Contact: Jeanette Takamura

REGIONAL AGENCIES

Elderly Affairs Division
715 South King Street, #500
Honolulu, HI 96819-3017
(808) 523-4545
Contact: Lynette B. Kurren

Hawaii County Office of Aging
101 Aupuni Street, Suite 342
Hilo, HI 96720
(808) 961-3418
Contact: Jane Testa

Maui County Office on Aging
Department of Human Concerns
2065 Main Street, Suite 109-110
Wailuku, HI 96793
Hana: (808) 243-7774
Lanai: (808) 565-6282
Maui: (808) 243-7774
Molokai: (808) 553-5241
Contact: Roy S. Fusato

Office of Elderly Affairs
4193 Hardy Street
Lihue, HI 96766-1392
(808) 245-4737
Contact: Eleanor J. Lloyd

Idaho

STATE AGENCY

Office on Aging
Room 108, Statehouse
Boise, ID 83720
(208) 334-3833
Contact: Ken Wilkes

REGIONAL AGENCIES

Area Agency on Aging—North Idaho College
1221 Ironwood Drive, Suite 102
Coeur d'Alene, ID 83814
(208) 667-3179
Contact: Debra Gordon

Area II Agency on Aging
1448 G Street, Suite C
Lewiston, ID 83501
(208) 743-5580
(800) 877-3206
Contact: La Fawn Oliver

College of Southern Idaho
P.O. Box 1238
Twin Falls, ID 83303-1238
(208) 737-2065
Contact: Richard F. Boyd

Eastern Idaho Special Services Agency
357 Constitution Way
P.O. Box 51098
Idaho Falls, ID 83405-1098
(208) 522-5391
Contact: Fran Schofield

Ida-Ore Planning and Development Association
25 West Idaho
P.O. Box 311
Weiser, ID 83672
Ada County: (208) 345-7777
Canyon County: (208) 459-1334
Adams, Boise, Gem, Payette, Owyhee, Valley, and Washington Counties: (208) 365-4461
Elmore County: (208) 365-4562
Contact: Elwin E. Grout

Southeast Idaho Council of Governments Area Agency on Aging
1651 Alvin Ricken Drive
Pocatello, ID 83201
(800) 526-8129
Contact: Sister A. M. Greving

Illinois

STATE AGENCY

Illinois Department on Aging
421 Capital Avenue
Springfield, IL 62701
Within state: (800) 252-8966
Contact: Maralee I. Lindley

REGIONAL AGENCIES

Central Illinois Area Agency on Aging
700 Hamilton Boulevard
Peoria, IL 61603
(309) 674-2071
Contact: Barbara Miller

Chicago Department on Aging
510 North Pestigo Court, 3A
Chicago, IL 60611
(312) 744-4106
Contact: Donald R. Smith

East Central Illinois Area Agency on Aging
1003 Maple Hill Road
Bloomington, IL 61704
Champaign County: (217) 384-3749
Clark and Cumberland Counties: (800) 626-7701
Charleston County: (217) 348-8410
Coles County: (217) 234-3311
DeWitt County: (217) 935-9411
Douglas County: (217) 234-4044
Edgar County: (217) 465-8143
Ford County: (217) 379-2523
Iroquois County: (815) 432-5785
Livingston County: (815) 844-3201
Macon County and Decatur: (800) 772-1273
McLean County: (309) 827-4005
Moultrie and Shelby Counties: (217) 728-8521
Piatt County: (217) 762-9934
Vermilion County: (217) 443-2999
Contact: Phyllis A. Pinkerton

Egyptian Area Agency on Aging
RR #2, Box 359-E
Carterville, IL 62918
Alexander County: (618) 734-1050
Franklin County: (618) 937-3511
Gallatin County: (618) 272-7570
Hardin County: (618) 287-2501
Jackson County: (618) 457-4151
Johnson County: (618) 658-8140
Massac County: (618) 524-9755
Perry County: (618) 542-2566
Pope County: (618) 683-7741

Pulaski County: (618) 745-6149
Saline County: (618) 252-7940
Union County: (618) 833-6734
Williamson County: (618) 988-1585
Contact: John M. Smith

Midland Area Agency on Aging
Shawnee Road
P.O. Box 1420
Centralia, IL 62801
Clay County: (618) 662-7304
Fayette County: (618) 283-4122
Effingham County: (217) 347-5569
Marion County: (618) 533-4300
Jefferson County: (618) 242-3505
Contact: Deborah Kuiken

Northeastern Illinois Area Agency on Aging
P.O. Box 809
Kankakee, IL 60901-0809
McHenry County: (800) 339-3200
Kane and Kendall Counties: (800) 942-1724
Kankakee County: (815) 932-1921
Grundy County: (815) 634-2254
DuPage County: (800) 640-3683
Lake County: (800) 942-3930
Will County: (800) 892-1412
Contact: Charles D. Johnson

Northwestern Illinois Area Agency on Aging
638 Hollister Avenue
Rockford, IL 61108
(815) 226-4901
Contact: Janet B. Ellis

Project LIFE Area Agency on Aging
2815 West Washington Street, Suite 220

Springfield, IL 62702
Within state: (800) 252-2918
Contact: Dorothy Kimball

Southeastern Illinois Area Agency on Aging
35 West Main Street
Albion, IL 62806
Within state: (800) 635-8544
Contact: Harold Morris

Southwestern Illinois Area Agency on Aging
331 Salem Place, Suite 170
Fairview Heights, IL 62208
Bond County: (618) 664-1465
Clinton County: (618) 594-2321
Madison County (Southern): (618) 656-0300
Hammel, Alhambra, Leef, and Northern Madison Counties: (618) 465-3298
St. Clair County (except St. Louis): (618) 234-4410
St. Clair County (East St. Louis): (618) 845-5757
Washington County: (618) 243-6533
Monroe County: (618) 939-8880
Randolph County (except Sparta): (618) 826-5108
Randolph County (Sparta area): (618) 443-4020
Contact: Paul G. Walthers

Suburban Area Agency on Aging
1146 Westgate, Suite LL112
Oak Park, IL 60301-1054
Bremen, Thorton, and Rich: (708) 596-2222
Stickney: (708) 424-9200
Calumet: (708) 597-8608

Palos, Lemont, Orland, and Worth: (708) 422-6722
Thorton: (708) 596-6690
Bloom: (708) 754-9400
Lyons, Riverside, and La Grandge: (708) 354-1323
Berwyn and Cicero: (708) 863-3552
Oak Park and River Forest: (708) 383-8060
Proviso: (708) 547-5600
Elk Grove and Schaumburg: (708) 885-1631
Maine: (708) 297-2510
Leyden: (708) 455-3929
Norwood Park: (708) 456-7979
New Trier and Northfield: (708) 446-8750
Evanston and Niles: (708) 328-2404
Barrington, Hannover, Palatine, and Wheeling: (708) 253-5500
Contact: Jonathan Lavin

Western Illinois Area Agency on Aging
729 Thirty-fourth Avenue
Rock Island, IL 61201
Bureau County: (815) 879-3981

Henderson County: (309) 627-2981
Henry County: (309) 853-8831
Knox County: (309) 342-1152
LaSalle County (except cities below): (815) 224-2720
Earlsville, Leland, Serena, Sheridan, Mendota, and Troy Grove: (815) 539-7700
McDonough County: (309) 837-5733
Mercer County: (309) 582-5492
Putnam County: (815) 339-2711
Rock Island County: (309) 788-6335
Warren County: (309) 734-8074
Contact: Greta Brooks

West Central Illinois Area Agency on Aging
1125 Hampshire Street
Quincy, IL 62301
Calhoun County: (618) 576-9331
Adams and Hancock Counties: (800) 252-9027
Brown County: (217) 773-3241
Pike County: (217) 285-4969
Schuyler County: (217) 322-6430
Contact: Lynn Niewohner

Indiana

STATE AGENCY

Aging/In-Home Services
Division of Aging and Rehabilitative Services
402 West Washington Street, Room W454
P.O. Box 7083
Indianapolis, IN 46207-7083
Within state: (800) 545-7763
Contact: Geneva Shedd

REGIONAL AGENCIES

Area 2 Area Agency on Aging/ Real Services
622 North Michigan
P.O. Box 1835
South Bend, IN 46366
Within state: (800) 552-2916
Contact: Rebecca Zaseck

Area 4 Area Agency on Aging and Community Services
660 North Thirty-sixth Street
P.O. Box 4727
Lafayette, IN 47903
(800) 382-7556
Contact: Fay Elbrite

Area 5 Area Agency on Aging and Community Services, Inc.
3001 U.S. 24 East
Eastgate Plaza
Logansport, IN 46947
Fulton County: (219) 223-4213
Miami County: (317) 472-1979
Tipton County: (317) 675-4746
Howard County: (317) 457-4481
Wabash County: (219) 563-4475
Cass County: (219) 722-2424
Contact: Michael B. Meager

Area 6 Council on Aging, Inc.
2100 North Granville Avenue
Box 1919
Muncie, IN 47308
Within state: (800) 589-1121
Contact: William Boothe

Area 9 Area Agency on Aging
Indiana University East
303 South A Street
Richmond, IN 47374
(317) 966-1795
Contact: Tony Shepherd

Area 10 Area Agency on Aging
2129 Yost Avenue
Bloomington, IN 47403
(812) 334-3383
Contact: Jewel Echelbarger

Area 11 Area Agency on Aging
1635 North National Road
P.O. Box 904
Columbus, IN 47202-0904
(812) 372-6918
Contact: Diane Cantrell

Area 12 Council on Aging
12794 North Street
P.O. Box 97
Dillsboro, IN 47018
Within state: (800) 742-5001
Contact: Sally Beckley

Area 13A Area Agency on Aging
Older Hoosier Programs
1019 North Fourth Street
P.O. Box 314
Vincennes, IN 47591
Within state: (800) 742-9002
Contact: Anne N. Jacoby

Central Indiana Council on Aging, Inc.
4755 Kingsway Drive, Suite 200
Indianapolis, IN 46205-1560
Boone County: (317) 482-5220
Hamilton County: (317) 773-4322
Hancock County: (317) 462-3758
Hendricks County: (317) 745-4303
Johnson County: (317) 736-7736
Marion County: (317) 254-3600;
  (800) 432-2422
Morgan County: (317) 342-3007
Shelby County: (317) 398-0127
Contact: Duane J. Etienne

Hoosier Uplands Economic Development Area 15 Area Agency on Aging
521 West Main Street
Mitchell, IN 47466
(800) 333-2451
Contact: Barbara Tarr

LCEOC, Inc. Area 1 Area Agency on Aging
5518 Calumet Avenue
Hammond, IN 46320
Lake County: (800) 826-7871
Porter County: (219) 464-9736
Pulaski County: (219) 946-6500
Jasper County: (219) 866-8071
Starke County: (219) 772-9154
Newton County: (219) 285-2247
Contact: Reverend D. Schultz

Northeast Area III Council on Aging, Inc.
201 East Rudisill Boulevard, Suite 208
Fort Wayne, IN 46806-1738
Within state: (800) 552-3662
Out of state: (219) 745-1200
Contact: Diann Shappell

Southwestern Indiana Regional Council on Aging
7 Southeast Martin Luther King, Jr. Boulevard
Evansville, IN 47708
Gibson County: (812) 385-8818
South Spencer County (Rockport Senior Center): (812) 649-2606
North Spencer County (Santa Claus Senior Center): (812) 937-4410
Perry County: (812) 547-8115
Posey County: (812) 838-4656
Vanderburgh County: (812) 464-7800; (800) 253-2188
Warrick County: (812) 897-4437
Contact: Robert J. Patrow

South Central Indiana Council for the Aging and Aged, Inc.
134 East Main Street
New Albany, IN 47150
(812) 948-8330
Contact: Patricia Jewell

West Central Indiana Economic Development District
1718 Wabash Avenue
P.O. Box 359
Terre Haute, IN 47808
(800) 489-1561
Contact: Linda Ostermeier

Iowa

STATE AGENCY

Iowa Department of Elder Affairs
Jewett Building, Suite 236
914 Grand Avenue
Des Moines, IA 50319
(515) 281-5187
Contact: Betty Grandquist

REGIONAL AGENCIES

Area 1 Area Agency on Aging
808 River Street
Decorah, IA 52101
Within state: (800) 233-4603
Contact: Bruce Butters

Area 4 Area Agency on Aging
505 Fifth Street, Room 508
Sioux City, IA 51101
Woodbury, Plymouth, Cherokee,
  Ida,
and Monona Counties: (800) 798-
  6916
Contact: Richard Motz

Area 14 Area Agency on Aging
228 North Pine Street
Creston, IA 50801
Adair County: (515) 743-8907
Adams County: (515) 322-4608
Clarke County: (515) 342-6221
Decatur County: (515) 446-4433
Ringgold County: (515) 464-2190
Taylor County: (712) 523-3522
Union County: (515) 782-2447
Contact: Lois Houston

Crossroads of Iowa Area Agency on Aging
921 Sixth Avenue, Suite B
Des Moines, IA 50309
Boone County: (515) 432-5048
Dallas County: (515) 993-3158
Jasper County: (515) 792-1955
Madison County: (515) 462-1334
Marion County: (515) 828-8149
Polk County: (515) 286-3677;
  (515) 244-4046
Story County: (515) 233-2906
Warren County: (515) 961-1001
Contact: Dorothy E. Holland

Elderbridge Area Agency on Aging
22 North Georgia Street, Suite
  216
Mason City, IA 50401
Within state: (800) 243-0678
Contact: Lahoma Counts

Great River Bend Area 9—Area Agency on Aging
P.O. Box 3008
Davenport, IA 52808
Clinton County: (319) 243-7353
Muscatine County: (319) 263-
  7292
Scott County: (319) 386-7477
Contact: Marvin C. Webb

Hawkeye Valley Area Agency on Aging
404 East Fourth Street
P.O. Box 2576
Waterloo, IA 50704
Within state: (800) 779-8707
Contact: Donna Rhone

Heritage Area Agency on Aging
6301 Kirkwood Boulevard, SW
P.O. Box 2068
Cedar Rapids, IA 52406
Benton, Cedar, Iowa, Jones, Linn,
  and Washington Counties:
  (800) 332-8182
Iowa City and rural Johnson
  County: (319) 338-7823; (319)
  356-5217
Cedar Rapids and rural Linn
  County: (319) 398-3578
Contact: Tom Miskimen

Northwest Aging Association
2 Grand Avenue
P.O. Box 3010
Spence, IA 51301
Within state: (800) 242-5033
Contact: Greg Anliker

Scenic Valley Area 8 Area Agency on Aging
2013 Central
Dubuque, IA 52001
Delaware County: (319) 927-5037
Dubuque County: (319) 588-3970
Jackson County: (319) 652-6771
Contact: Linda McDonald

Seneca Area Agency on Aging
228 East Second
P.O. Box 1546
Ottumwa, IA 52501
Within state: (800) 642-6522
Contact: Peggy Amos

Southeast Iowa Area Agency on Aging, Inc.
509 Jefferson Street
Burlington, IA 52601-5427
Within state: (800) 292-1268
Contact: Dennis Zegarac

Southwest 8 Senior Services Inc.
3319 Nebraska Avenue
Council Bluffs, IA 51501
(800) 432-9209
Contact: Barbara Blocker

Kansas

STATE AGENCY

Department on Aging
Docking State Office Building, 122-S
915 Southwest Harrison
Topeka, KS 66612
Within state: (800) 432-3535
Out of state: (913) 296-4986
Contact: Joanne Hurst

REGIONAL AGENCIES

Central Plains Area Agency on Aging
510 North Main Street
Wichita, KS 67203
Butler County: (316) 321-5650
Harvey County: (316) 284-6880
Sedgwick County: (316) 383-7824
Wichita County: (316) 267-0250
Contact: Irene Hart

East Central Kansas Area Agency on Aging
132 South Main
Ottawa, KS 66067
(800) 633-5621
Contact: Beatrice Shisler

Jayhawk Area Agency on Aging, Inc.
1195 Buchanan, Suite 103
Topeka, KS 66604
Douglas County: (913) 842-0543
Jefferson County: (913) 597-5642
Shawnee County: (913) 232-9065
Contact: Donna J. Kidd

Johnson County Area Agency on Aging
301A South Clairbourne
Olathe, KS 66062
Within state: (800) 432-3535
Contact: Annice White

North Central—Flint Hills Area Agency on Aging
437 Houston Street
Manhattan, KS 66502
Within state: (800) 432-2703
Contact: Veryl Tiemeyer

Northeast Kansas Area Agency on Aging
P.O. Box 145
107 Oregon
Hiawatha, KS 66434
Atchison County: (913) 367-4655
Brown County: (913) 742-7881
Doniphan County: (913) 985-2380
Jackson County: (913) 364-3571
Marshall County: (913) 562-2020
Nemaha County: (913) 336-2714
Washington County: (913) 325-3231
Contact: Denise Clemonds

Northwest Kansas Area Agency on Aging
301 West Thirteenth Street
Hays, KS 67601
Within state: (800) 432-7422
Contact: Ellene Davis

South Central Kansas Area Agency on Aging
P.O. Box 1122
Arkansas City, KS 67005
Greenwood and Chautauqua Counties: (800) 362-0264
Elk County: (316) 374-2388
Reno County: (316) 665-2911
Rice County: (316) 257-5153
McPherson County: (316) 241-1848
Cowley County: (316) 442-3330
Sumner County: (316) 326-3933
Kingman County: (316) 532-5744
Harper County: (316) 842-5104
Contact: Betty Londeen

Southeast Kansas Area Agency on Aging
P.O. Box J
811 West Main
Chanute, KS 66720
Within state: (800) 794-2440
Contact: Jerry D. Williams

Southwest Kansas Area Agency on Aging
P.O. Box 1636
Dodge City, KS 67801
Within state: (800) 742-9531
Contact: David L. Geist

Wyandotte/Leavenworth Area Agency on Aging
9400 State Avenue
Kansas City, KS 66112
Wyandotte County: (913) 596-9231
Leavenworth County: (913) 684-0777
Contact: Arthur A. Collins

Kentucky

STATE AGENCY

Division of Aging Services
Cabinet for Human Resources
CHR Building, Fifth Floor West
275 East Main Street
Frankfort, KY 40621
(502) 564-6930
Contact: Sue Tuttle

REGIONAL AGENCIES

Barren River Area Development District
117 North Graham Avenue
P.O. Box 90005
Bowling Green, KY 42102-9005
(800) 598-2381
Contact: Debbie McCarty

Big Sandy Area Development District
HC 69, Box 266
Prestonburg, KY 41653
Johnson County: (606) 789-4830
Martin County: (606) 298-7033
Magofflin County: (606) 349-5152
Pike and Floyd Counties: (606) 886-2374
Contact: Bonnie Hale

Bluegrass Area Agency on Aging

3220 Nicholasville Road, Suite 11
Lexington, KY 40503-3382
Anderson County: (502) 839-7520
Bourbon County: (606) 987-7453
Boyle County: (606) 236-2070
Clark County: (606) 744-3235
Estill County: (606) 723-3315
Fayette County: (606) 278-6072
Franklin County: (502) 223-5794
Garrard County: (606) 792-3147
Harrison County: (606) 234-5801
Jessamine County: (606) 885-9102
Lincoln County: (606) 365-9016
Madison County: (606) 986-8350
Madison County: (606) 623-0474
Mercer County: (606) 734-5185
Nicholas County: (606) 289-2329
Powell County: (606) 663-5981
Scott County: (502) 863-4041
Woodford County: (606) 873-7290
Contact: Peggy Chadwick

Buffalo Trace Area Agency on Aging

327 West Second Street
Maysville, KY 41056
Bracken County: (606) 735-2948
Fleming County: (606) 845-1411
Lewis County: (606) 796-3893
Mason County: (606) 564-6954
Robertson County: (606) 724-5513
Contact: Linda Gabbard

Cumberland Valley Area Agency on Aging

CVADD Office Building
342 Old Whitley Road
P.O. Box 1740
London, KY 40743-1740
(606) 864-7391
Contact: Bernice Miracle

FIVCO Area Agency on Aging

3000 Louisa Street
P.O. Box 636
Catlettsburg, KY 41129
(606) 739-5191
Contact: J. David Salisbury

Gateway Area Development District

P.O. Box 1070
Owingsville, KY 40360
Within state: (606) 768-3502
Out of state: (606) 674-6355
Contact: Gail K. Wright

Green River Area Agency on Aging

3860 U.S. Highway 60 West
Owensboro, KY 42301
Davies County: (502) 926-0787
Hancock County: (502) 927-8313
Henderson County: (502) 827-2948
MacLean County: (502) 273-5412
Ohio County: (502) 298-7749
Union County: (502) 389-2062
Webster County: (502) 639-5394
Contact: Nelda Barnett

Kentucky Regional Planning and Development Agency

11520 Commonwealth Drive
Louisville, KY 40299
Jefferson County: (502) 589-4313
Bulitt, Shelby, and Spencer
  Counties: (502) 633-2218
Henry, Oldham, and Trimble
  Counties: (502) 222-9619
Contact: James Kimbrough

Kentucky River Area Agency on Aging

381 Perry County Park Road
Hazard, KY 41701

Breathitt County: (606) 666-2550
Knott County: (606) 672-3222
Letcher County: (606) 633-1021
Lee County: (606) 464-8005
Leslie County: (606) 593-5594
Owsley County: (606) 593-5594
Perry County: (606) 436-5095
Wolfe County: (606) 668-3954
Contact: Ruth Ann Miller

Lake Cumberland Area Agency on Aging

Lake Cumberland Area
    Development District
P.O. Box 1570
Russell Springs, KY 42642
Adair County: (502) 384-4026
Casey County: (606) 787-9919
Clinton County: (606) 387-7007
Cumberland County: (502) 864-2265
Green County: (502) 932-3246
McCreary County: (606) 376-8511
Bronston, Burnside, Sloan Valley,
    and Tateville: (606) 561-6306
Jamestown: (502) 343-4949
Russell Springs, Windsor, and
    Webb Cross Roads: (502) 866-5065
Somerset, W. Somerset, and
    Walnut Grove: (606) 679-7715
Taylor and Wayne Counties: (800)
    982-0392
Contact: Tony Agee

Lincoln Trail Area Agency on Aging

P.O. Box 604
Elizabeth, KY 42702
(502) 769-2393
Contact: Nancy Addington

North Kentucky Area Development District

16 Spiral Drive
Florence, KY 41042
(606) 291-4522
Contact: Carol Marek

Pennyrile Area Development District

300 Hammond Drive
Hopkinsville, KY 42240
Caldwell County: (502) 365-7446
Christian County: (502) 886-4516
Crittenden County: (502) 965-5229
Hopkins County: (502) 821-9173
Livingston County: (502) 928-2811
Lyon County: (502) 388-2171
Muhlenburg County: (502) 754-1350
Todd County: (502) 265-5935
Trigg County: (502) 522-8341
Contact: Agnes Davis

Purchase Area Agency on Aging

1002 Medical Drive
P.O. Box 588
Mayfield, KY 42066
Ballard County: (502) 334-3115
Carlisle County: (502) 628-5474
Calloway County: (502) 753-0929
Fulton County: (502) 472-2900
Graves County: (502) 247-2566
Hickman County: (502) 653-4314
Marshall County: (502) 527-9860
McCracken County: (502) 443-8579
Contact: Peggy Williams

Louisiana

STATE AGENCY

Governor's Office of Elderly Affairs
P.O. Box 80374
4550 North Boulevard, Second Floor
Baton Rouge, LA 70806
(504) 925-1700
Contact: Bobby Fontenot

REGIONAL AGENCIES

Beauregard Council on Aging, Inc.
104 Port Street
P.O. Drawer 534
Deridder, LA 70634
(318) 463-6578
Contact: Juanita LaBue

Bienville Area Agency on Aging
Courthouse, Room 112
Arcadia, LA 71001
(318) 263-8936
Contact: Elton A. Lamkin

Bossier Council on Aging/Area Agency on Aging
706 Bearkat Drive
P.O. Box 5606
Bossier City, LA 71171-5606
(318) 741-8302
Contact: Bill J. Davis

Caddo Council on Aging, Inc.
4015 Greenwood Road
Shreveport, LA 71109-6422
(318) 632-2090
Contact: Myrtle Pickering

Cajun Area Agency on Aging, Inc.
1304 Bertrand Drive, Suite F-6
Lafayette, LA 70506
Acadia Parish: (318) 788-1400
Allen Parish: (318) 335-3195
Evangeline Parish: (318) 363-5161
Iberia Parish: (318) 367-1556
Jefferson Davis Parish: (318) 824-5504
Lafayette Parish: (318) 262-5990
St. Landry Parish: (318) 942-6579
St. Martin Parish: (318) 332-3063
St. Mary Parish: (318) 828-4100
Vermillion Parish: (318) 893-2563
Contact: Shannon Mouton

Calcasieu Area Agency on Aging
P.O. Box 6403
Lake Charles, LA 70606
(318) 433-0630
Contact: Millie Woodel

Caldwell Parish Council on Aging
P.O. Box 1498
Corner of Pearl and Main
Columbia, LA 71418
(318) 649-2584
Contact: Angela Savoie

Cameron Council on Aging
P.O. Box 421
Cameron, LA 70631
(318) 775-5668
Contact: Dinah B. Nunez

Capital Area Agency on Aging
11861 Coursey Boulevard
P.O. Box 86430
Baton Rouge, LA 70896
Ascension Parish: (504) 473-3789
Assumption Parish: (504) 369-7961
East Feliciana Parish: (504) 683-9862
Iberville Parish: (504) 687-9682
Livingston Parish: (504) 664-9343
St. Helena Parish: (504) 222-6070
Point Coupe Parish: (504) 638-4402
Tangipahoa Parish: (504) 748-7486
Washington Parish: (504) 839-4535
West Baton Rouge Parish: (504) 383-0638
West Feliciana Parish: (504) 635-6719
Contact: James Blouin

Clairborne Voluntary Council on Aging
608 East Fourth Street
Homer, LA 71040
(318) 927-6922
Contact: Josephine Miller

DeSoto Area Agency on Aging/ Council on Aging
1004 Polk Street
Mansfield, LA 71052
(318) 872-2691; (318) 872-2699
Contact: Betty H. Walker

East Baton Rouge Council on Aging
5790 Florida Boulevard
Baton Rouge, LA 70806-0000
(504) 923-8012
Contact: Sharon LaFleur

Jefferson Council on Aging, Inc.
P.O. Box 6878
Metairie, LA 70009
(504) 888-5880
Contact: Thomas C. Laughlin

Kisatchie Delta Area Agency on Aging
P.O. Box 12248
Alexandria, LA 71315
(318) 487-5454
Contact: Kristin Duke

LaFourche Council on Aging/ Area Agency on Aging
710 Church Street
P.O. Box 187
Lockport, LA 70374
(504) 532-2381
Contact: Sondra N. Barrios

Lincoln Council on Aging
109 South Sparta
Ruston, LA 71270
(318) 255-5070
Contact: Deborah Pace

Madison Council on Aging
203 South Elm
P.O. Box 1229
Tallulah, LA 71282
(318) 574-4101
Contact: Audrey Ogden

Morehouse Council on Aging,
 Inc./Area Agency on Aging
East Madison Park, Elm Street
P.O. Box 1471
Bastrop, LA 71221-1471
Bastrop and Mer Rouge: (318)
 283-0845
Bonita, Collinston, Jones, and
 Oak Ridge: (800) 256-3006
Contact: R. D. DeFreese, Jr.

Natchitoches Parish Council on
 Aging
220 East Fifth Street
Natchitoches, LA 71457
(318) 357-3250
Contact: Norma M. Metoyer

New Orleans Council on Aging
2475 Canal Street, Suite 400
P.O. Box 19067
New Orleans, LA 70179-0067
(504) 821-4121
Contact: George Gates

North Delta Area Agency on
 Aging
2115 Justice Street
Monroe, LA 71201
East Carol Parish: (318) 559-2774
Franklin Parish: (800) 843-8676
Jackson Parish: (800) 256-3607
Richland Parish: (800) 794-5605
Union Parish: (800) 256-2846
Contact: Lanell Winston

Ouachita Council on Aging,
 Inc./Area Agency on Aging
1209 Oliver Road
P.O. Box 14363
Monroe, LA 14363
(318) 387-0535
Contact: Joseph Nastasi

Plaquemines Parish Area
 Agency on Aging
Highway 23 South
P.O. Box 189
Port Sulphur, LA 70083
(504) 564-3220
Contact: Connie Lincoln

Red River Council on Aging
1825 Front Street
P.O. Box 688
Coushatta, LA 71019
(318) 932-5721
Contact: Mary Wailes

Sabine Council on Aging
750 Railroad Avenue
P.O. Box 1678
Many, LA 71449
(800) 960-8808
Contact: Glen Starks

St. Bernard Council on Aging,
 Inc.
1818 Center Street
Arabi, LA 70032
(504) 278-7335
Contact: Alfreda Earhart

St. Charles Council on Aging
5940 Pine Street
Hahnville, LA 70057
(504) 783-6683
Contact: Margaret Powe

**St. James Parish Department of
    Human Resources**
Human Resources Building
5153 Canatella Street
P.O. Box 87
Convent, LA 70723
Convent and Hester: (504) 562-
    2299
Gramercy, Lutcher, and Paulina:
    (504) 869-5425
St. James: (504) 473-1035
Vacherie: (504) 265-6012
Contact: Dianne G. Brathwaite

St. John Area Agency on Aging
1805 West Airline Highway
LaPlace, LA 70084
(501) 652-3660
Contact: Barbara Gralapp

**St. Tammany Council on the
    Aging, Inc.**
P.O. Box 171
Covington, LA 70434-0171
Within state: (800) 256-2823
Contact: Gloria Sellars

Tensas Council on Aging
104 Panola
P.O. Box 726
St. Joseph, LA 71366
(318) 766-3770
Contact: Dorothy Morgan

Terrebonne Council on Aging
1706 East Main
Station 1, Box 10066
Houma, LA 70363
(504) 868-7701
Contact: Carol Matherne

Webster Area Agency on Aging
316 McIntyre
P.O. Box 913
Minden, LA 71058
(800) 256-2853
Contact: Dathene Brown

West Carroll Council on Aging
207 East Jefferson
P.O. Box 1058
Oak Grove, LA 71263
(318) 428-4217
Contact: Fay Long

Maine

STATE AGENCY

Bureau of Elder and Adult Services
Department of Human Services
State House, Station 11
35 Anthony Avenue
Augusta, ME 04333
(207) 626-5555
Contact: Christine Gianapoulos

REGIONAL AGENCIES

Aroostook Area Agency on Aging, Inc.
33 Davis Street
P.O. Box 1288
Presque Isle, ME 04769
Within state: (800) 439-1789
Contact: Stephen Farnham

Central Maine Area Agency on Aging
Senior Spectrum
51 Main Avenue
P.O. Box 248
Gardiner, ME 04345
Knox, Lincoln, and Sagadahoc
  Counties: (207) 563-1363
North Kennebec County: (207)
  873-4745
Somerset County: (207) 474-7501
South Kennebec County: (207)
  582-8643
Waldo County: (207) 338-1190
Contact: Muriel Scott

Eastern Agency on Aging
238 State Street, Twin City Plaza
Brewer, ME 04112
Within state: (800) 432-7812
Contact: Roberta Downey

Southern Maine Area Agency on Aging, Inc.
P.O. Box 10480
Portland, ME 04104
Within state: (800) 427-7411
Contact: Laurence W. Gross

Western Area Agency on Aging
P.O. Box 659
Lewiston, ME 04243-0659
(207) 795-4010
Contact: Eloise L. Moreau

Maryland

STATE AGENCY

Maryland Office on Aging
State Office Building
301 West Preston Street, Room 1004
Baltimore, MD 21201
Within state: (800) 243-3425
Contact: Rosalie Abrahms

REGIONAL AGENCIES

Allegany County Area Agency on Aging
19 Frederick Street
Cumberland, MD 21502
Bel Air, Corriganville,
  Cresaptown, Cumberland,
  Ellerslie, Flintstone, LaVale,
  Little Orleans, Oldtown, Pinto,
  Rawlings, and Spring Gap:
  (301) 724-8626
Eckhart Mines, Frostburg,
  Midlothian, and Mount
  Savage: (301) 689-5510
Barton, Lonaconing, and Midland:
  (301) 463-6215
Luke, McCoole, and Westernport:
  (301) 359-9930
Contact: Terry Froelich

Area Agency on Aging—Anne Arundel County
101 Crain Highway, NW
Glen Burnie, MD 21061
(800) 492-2499
Contact: Dr. Carol R. Baker

Baltimore City Commission on Aging
Retirement Education—CARE
118 North Howard Street,
  Seventh Floor
Baltimore, MD 21201
(410) 396-1341
Contact: Neetu Dhawan-Gray

Baltimore County Department of Aging
611 Central Avenue
Towson, MD 21204
(410) 887-2594
Contact: Dr. Philip H. Pushkin

Calvert County Office on Aging
450 West Dares Beach Road
Port Frederick, MD 20678
(410) 535-4606; (301) 885-1170
Contact: Bettina Dubas

Carroll County Bureau of Aging
7 Schoolhouse Avenue
Westminster, MD 21157
(410) 848-4049
Contact: Janet B. Flora

Cecil County Department of Aging
214 North Street
Elkton, MD 21921
(410) 996-5295
Contact: Lucie P. Neill

Charles County Department of Community Services, Aging Division
Star Route 1, Box 1144
Port Tobacco, MD 20677
(301) 934-5423
Contact: Karen L. Lehman

Frederick County Commission on Aging
520 North Market Street
Frederick, MD 21701
(301) 694-1604
Contact: Patricia B. Throne

Garrett County Area Agency on Aging
360 Liberty Street
P.O. Box 449
Oakland, MD 21550
(301) 334-5856
Contact: Adina Brode

Harford County Office on Aging
145 North Hickory Avenue
Bel Air, MD 21014
(410) 638-3025
Contact: James Macgill

Howard County Area Agency on Aging
9250 Rumsey Road
Columbia, MD 21045
(410) 313-7212; (410) 992-1923
Contact: Vivian Reid

MAC, Inc. Area Agency on Aging
1504 Riverside Drive
Salisbury, MD 21801
Dorchester County: (410) 221-1930
Somerset County: (410) 651-0020
Wicomico County: (410) 543-0388
Worcester County: (410) 632-1289
Contact: Margaret A. Bradford

Montgomery County Government
Division of Elder Affairs
101 Monroe Street
Rockville, MD 20850
(301) 468-4443
Contact: Elizabeth Boehner

Prince George's Bureau of Aging Department of Family Services
5012 Rhode Island Avenue
Hyattsville, MD 20781
(301) 699-2696
Contact: Sue Ward

Queen Anne's County Department of Aging
104 Powell Street
Centreville, MD 21617
(410) 758-0848
Contact: Sue E. Leager

St. Mary's County Office on Aging
P.O. Box 653
Leonardtown, MD 20650
(301) 475-4489
Contact: Gene Carter

Upper Shore Aging, Inc.
400 High Street
Chestertown, MD 21620
Caroline County: (410) 479-2535
Kent County: (410) 778-2564
Talbot County: (410) 822-6828
Contact: Gerald E. Webb

Washington County Commission on Aging
9 Public Square
Hagerstown, MD 21740
(301) 790-0275
Contact: Frederick Otto

Massachusetts

STATE AGENCY

Executive Office of Elder Affairs
One Ashburton Place, Fifth Floor
Boston, MA 02108
Within state: (800) 882-2003
Contact: Franklin Ollivierre

REGIONAL AGENCIES

**BayPath Senior Citizens
Services, Inc.**
31 Flagg Drive
P.O. Box 2625, Center Station
Framingham, MA 01701
(800) 287-7284
Contact: Jeanne McCann

**Boston Commission on Affairs
of Elderly**
Boston City Hall, Room 806
Boston, MA 02201
(617) 635-3993
Contact: Diane Watson

Bristol Elder Services, Inc.
182 North Main Street
Fall River, MA 02720
(508) 675-2101
Contact: J. Sumner Hoisington

**Central Massachusetts Agency
on Aging**
360 Boylston Street
Boylston, MA 01583
Ashburnham, Ashby, Ayer, Berlin,
 Bolton, Clinton, Fitchburg,
 Gardner, Groton, Hubbardston,
 Lancaster, Lunenburg,

Pepperell, Princeton, Shirley,
 Sterling, Templeton, Townsend,
 Westminster, and Wichendon:
 (508) 345-7312
Auburn, Barre, Boylston, Grafton,
 Hardwick, Holden, Leicester,
 Millbury, New Braintree,
 Oakham, Paxton, Rutland,
 Shrewsbury, West Boylston,
 and Worcester: (508) 756-1545
Bellingham, Blackstone,
 Brookfield, East Brookfield,
 Franklin, Hopedale, Medway,
 Mendon, Milford, Millville,
 North Brookfield, Northbridge,
 Oxford, Southbridge, Sutton,
 Upton, Uxbridge, Warren,
 Webster, and West Brookfield:
 (508) 764-2501
Contact: Catherine S. Fellenz

**Chelsea Revere Winthrop Elder
Services Area Agency on
Aging**
300 Broadway
P.O. Box 189
Revere, MA 02151
(617) 286-0550
Contact: James P. Cummingham, Jr.

Coastline Elderly Services, Inc.
1646 Purchase Street
New Bedford, MA 02740
Within state: (800) 243-4636
Contact: Charles Sisson

Elder Services of Berkshire
  County, Inc.
66 Wendell Avenue
Pittsfield, MA 01201
Within state: (800) 554-5242
Contact: Catherine May

Elder Services of Cape Cod and
  the Islands
68 Route 134
South Dennis, MA 02660
Within state: (800) 244-4630
Contact: Leslie E. Scheer

Elder Services of Merrimack
  Valley, Inc.
360 Merrimack Street
Building 5
Lawrence, MA 01843
Within state: (800) 892-0890
Contact: Roasanne J. DiStefano

Franklin County Home Care
  Corporation
58 Main Street
Turners Falls, MA 01376
Within state: (800) 732-4636
Contact: Patricia Kerrins

Greater Lynn Senior Services
8 Silsbee Street
Lynn, MA 01901
(617) 599-0110
Contact: Vincent Lique

Greater Springfield Senior
  Services, Inc.
66 Industry Avenue
Springfield, MA 01104
Within state: (800) 649-3641
Contact: Patricia Clark

Health and Social Services
  Consortium, Inc.
80 Carpenter Street
Foxborough, MA 02035
Within state: (800) 462-5221
Contact: Mary Jean McDermott

Highland Valley Elder Services
320 Riverside Drive
Northampton, MA 01060
Within state: (800) 332-0551
Contact: Robert Gallant

Minuteman Home Care
24 Third Avenue
Burlington, MA 01803
(617) 272-7177
Contact: Joan Butler-West

Mystic Valley Elder Services
19 Riverview Commercial Park
300 Commercial Street
Malden, MA 02148
(617) 324-1369
Contact: Marsha Webster

North Shore Elder Services, Inc.
152 Sylvan Street
Danvers, MA 01923
(508) 750-4540
Contact: Janet McAveeney

Old Colony Planning Council
  Area Agency on Aging
70 School Street
Brockton, MA 02401-4097
(508) 583-1833
Contact: Patricia Goggin

Senior Home Care Services
4 Blackburn Center
Black Industrial Park
Gloucester, MA 01930
(508) 281-1750
Contact: Guntis Licis

Somerville Cambridge Elder Services
20-40 Holland Street
P.O. Box 338
Somerville, MA 02144
(617) 628-2601
Contact: John O'Neill

South Shore Elder Services, Inc.
639 Granite Street

Braintree, MA 02184
(617) 848-3910
Contact: Edward J. Flynn, Jr.

West Suburban Elder Services, Inc.
124 Watertown Street
Watertown, MA 02172
(800) 243-4636
Contact: Carol Oram

WestMass Elder Care Inc.
4 Valley Mill Road
Holyoke, MA 01040-5855
Within state: (800) 462-2301
Contact: Priscilla Chalmers

Michigan

STATE AGENCY

Office of Services to the Aging
P.O. Box 30026
Lansing, MI 48909
(517) 373-8230
Contact: Carol Parr

REGIONAL AGENCIES

Area Agency on Aging 1B
400 Franklin Center
29100 Northwestern Highway
Southfield, MI 48034
Within state (Oakland, Macomb, Monroe, and Washtenaw
   Counties): (800) 852-7795
Contact: Sandra K. Reminga

Area Agency on Aging— Region 3
8135 Cox's Drive, Suite 1C
Portage, MI 49002
Barry County: (616) 948-4856
Branch County: (616) 279-7043
Calhoun County: (616) 965-0555
Kalamazoo County: (616) 382-0515

St. Joseph County: (616) 467-
4485
Contact: Dr. Joseph Ham

Area Agency on Aging of
Western Michigan, Inc,
1279 Cedar Street, NW
Grand Rapids, MI 49503
Allegan County: (800) 368-7856
Iona County: (616) 527-5365
Kent County: (616) 459-6019
Lake County: (616) 745-7201
Mason County: (616) 757-4705
Mecosta County: (800) 531-5381
Montcalm County: (517) 831-
5967
Newaygo County: (616) 689-7210
Osceola County: (616) 734-5559
Contact: Lawrence L. Murray, Jr.

Detroit Area Agency on Aging
1100 Michigan Building
220 Bagley
Detroit, MI 48226-1410
Detroit: (313) 567-8800
Grosse Pointes and Harper
Woods: (313) 882-9600
Highland Park: (313) 869-6217
Contact: Paul Bridgewater

Northeast Michigan
Community Services Area
Agency on Aging
2372 Gordon Road
Alpena, MI 49707
(517) 356-3474
Contact: Sue Schuler

Northwest Senior Resources,
Inc.
1609 Park Drive
P.O. Box 3010
Traverse City, MI 49685-2010
(616) 947-8920
Contact: Gregory Piaskowski

Region 2 Area Agency on
Aging
322 North Adrian Drive
P.O. Box 646
Adrian, MI 49221
Hillsdale County: (517) 437-3346
Jackson County: (517) 788-4364
Lenawee County: (517) 264-5280
Contact: Mary J. Marshall

Region 4 Area Agency on
Aging
2919 Division Street
St. Joseph, MI 49085
Within state: (800) 442-2803
Contact: Robert L. Dolsen

Region 7 Area Agency on
Aging
126 Washington
Bay City, MI 48708
(800) 858-1637
Contact: Mohammed Khan

Region 14 Area Agency on
Aging
255 West Sherman Boulevard
Muskegon Heights, MI 49444
Within state: (800) 442-0054
Contact: Dee Scott

The Senior Alliance, Area
Agency on Aging 1C
3850 Second Street, Suite 160
Wayne, MI 48184
(313) 282-7171
Contact: Nel Thompson

Tri-County Office on Aging
500 West Washtenaw
Lansing, MI 48933
Clinton County: (517) 224-7998
Easton County: (517) 543-6075
Ingham County: (517) 676-1081

Clinton, Eaton, and Ingham
  Counties (for Spanish-speaking
  persons only): (517) 372-4700
Lansing: (517) 483-4150
Contact: Roxanna Peterson

**Upper Peninsula Area Agency
  on Aging**
UPCAP
2501 Fourteenth Avenue South
P.O. Box 606
Escanaba, MI 49829
Within state: (800) 562-4806
Contact: Jonathan Mead

Valley Area Agency on Aging
711 North Saginaw Street, Room
  325
Flint, MI 48503
Genesee County: (313) 239-7671
Lapeer County: (313) 667-0231
Lapeer County: (313) 724-6030
Shiawassee County: (517) 723-
  8875
Contact: Valaria J. Conerly

Minnesota

STATE AGENCY

Board on Aging
444 Lafayette Road
St. Paul, MN 55155-3843
Within state: (800) 333-2433
Contact: Gerald Bloedow

REGIONAL AGENCIES

**Arrowhead Area Agency on
  Aging**
330 Canal Park Drive
Duluth, MN 55802
Within state: (800) 232-0707
Contact: Anne Tellett

**Central Minnesota Council on
  Aging**
600 Twenty-fifth Avenue South,
  Suite 206
St. Cloud, MN 56301
Within state: (800) 333-2433
Contact: Donna Domino Walberg

East Central Area Agency on Aging
East Central Regional
 Development Commission
100 South Park Street
P.O. Box 147
Mora, MN 55051
Onamia Isle: (612) 532-3885
Chicago County: (612) 257-2400
Isanti, Kanabec, Mille Lacs, and
 Pine Counties: (612) 679-4065
Contact: Herman E. Baker

Headwaters Area Agency on Aging
403 Fourth Street, NW
P.O. Box 906
Bemidji, MN 56601
(218) 755-4196
Contact: Alan Goldberg

Metropolitan Council Area Agency on Aging
230 East Fifth Street
St. Paul, MN 55101
Dakota, Ramsey, and Washington
 Counties: (612) 224-1133
Anoka, Carver, Hennepin, and
 Scott Counties: (612) 824-9999
Contact: Andrea Skolkin

Mid-Minnesota Area Agency on Aging
333 West Sixth Street
Willmar, MN 56201
Within state: (800) 450-8608
Contact: Lorraine Patton

Northwest Area Agency on Aging
525 Brook Avenue South
Thief River Falls, MN 56701
(800) 450-2637
Contact: Faith Rudd

Region 5 Area Agency on Aging
611 Iowa Avenue
Staples, MN 56479
(218) 894-2500
Contact: Barbara Card

Region 9 Area Agency on Aging
P.O. Box 3367
Mankato, MN 56002
Within state: (800) 722-2278
Contact: Bonnie Mertesdorf

Southeast Minnesota Area Agency on Aging
121 North Broadway, Room 302
Rochester, MN 55906
Within state: (800) 333-2433
Contact: Connie J. Bagley

Southwest Area Agency on Aging
2524 Broadway Avenue
Slayton, MN 56172
Within state: (800) 333-2433
Contact: Maddy Forsberg

Upper Minnesota Valley Area Agency on Aging
323 West Schileman Avenue
Appleton, MN 56208
Within state: (800) 752-1983
Contact: Connie Nygard

West Central Area Agency on Aging
1122 West Washington Avenue
P.O. Box 726
Fergus Falls, MN 56537-0726
Within state: (800) 333-2433
Contact: Virginia Smith

Mississippi

STATE AGENCY

Council on Aging
Division of Aging and Adult Services
455 North Lamar Street
Jackson, MS 39202
Within state: (800) 345-6347
Contact: James R. Johnson

REGIONAL AGENCIES

**Area Agency on Aging of
Southern Mississippi**
1020 Thirty-second Avenue
Gulfport, MS 39501
Within state: (800) 444-8014
Contact: Jane Kennedy

**Central Mississippi Area
Agency on Aging**
1170 Lakeland Drive
Jackson, MS 39296
(601) 981-1516
Contact: Bettye Burgess

**East Central Area Agency on
Aging**
410 Decatur Street
P.O. Box 499
Newton, MS 39345
Clarke, Jasper, Kemper,
Lauderdale, Leake, Neshoba,
Newton, Scott, and Smith
Counties: (800) 264-2007
Contact: Myrtle Burton

**Golden Triangle Area Agency
on Aging**
P.O. Drawer DN
Mississippi St., MS 39762
Choctaw, Clay, Lowndes,
Noxubee, Oktibbeha, Webster,
and Winston Counties: (601)
323-2636
Contact: Bobby Gann

**North Central Area Agency on
Aging**
P.O. Box 668
Highway 51 South
Winona, MS 38967
(601) 283-2675
Contact: Pat Brown

**North Delta Planning and
Development District Area
Agency on Aging**
P.O. Box 1244
Clarksdale, MS 38614
Within state: (800) 844-2433
Contact: MariKay Wilson

Northeast Mississippi Area
  Agency on Aging
P.O. Box 600
Booneville, MS 38829
Alcorn County: (601) 286-7747
Benton County: (601) 224-6319
Marshall County: (601) 252-2713
Prentiss County: (601) 728-2118
Tippah County: (601) 837-9262
Tishomingo County: (601) 423-
  7013
Contact: Jane Holbrook

South Delta Planning and
  Development District
P.O. Box 1776
Greenville, MS 38702
(601) 378-3831
Contact: Sylvia G. Jackson

Southwest Mississippi Area
  Agency on Aging
110 South Wall Street
Natchez, MS 39120
Within state: (800) 338-2049
Contact: Robert M. Maddox

Three Rivers Area Agency on
  Aging
75 South Main Street
P.O. Box B
Pontotoc, MS 38863
(601) 489-6911
Contact: Jane Mapp

Missouri

STATE AGENCY

Division of Aging
Department of Social Services
615 Howerton Court
P.O. Box 1337
Jefferson City, MO 65109
(800) 235-5503
Contact: Bryan Forbis

REGIONAL AGENCIES

Area Agency on Aging Region
  10
1710 East Thirty-second Street
P.O. Box 3990

Joplin, MO 64803
(417) 781-7562
Contact: Linda Carlson

Central Missouri Area Agency on Aging
601 Business Loop 70 West
Parkade Center, Suite 216B
Columbia, MO 65203
(314) 443-5823
Contact: Jean Leonatti

District 3 Area Agency on Aging
106 West Young Street
P.O. Box 1078
Warrensburg, MO 64093
(816) 747-3107
Contact: Ray Diekmeier

Mid-America Regional Council
Department of Aging Services
600 Broadway
300 Rivergate Center
Kansas City, MO 64105
(816) 421-4980
Contact: Jacquelyn C. Moore

Mid-East Area Agency on Aging
2510 South Brentwood Boulevard
St. Louis, MO 63144
Franklin County: (314) 583-8919
Jefferson County: (314) 962-7999
St. Charles County: (314) 946-1123
St. Louis County: (314) 962-0808
Contact: William R. Keel

Northeast Missouri Area Agency on Aging
312 South Elson
P.O. Box 1067
Kirksville, MO 63501
Adair County: (816) 665-9163
Clark County: (816) 727-2400
Knox County: (816) 397-2296
Lewis County: (314) 494-3339

Lincoln County: (314) 528-7000
Macon County: (816) 385-6560
Marion County: (314) 221-4488
Monroe County: (816) 327-5824
Montgomery County: (314) 564-3224
Pike County: (314) 754-6511
Ralls County: (314) 735-2131
Randolph County: (816) 456-7625
Schyler County: (816) 457-3066
Scotland County: (816) 465-7011
Shelby County: (314) 588-7669
Warren County: (314) 456-3379
Contact: Derik L. Shields

Northwest Missouri Area Agency on Aging
106 South Smith
P.O. Drawer G
Albany, MO 64402
Within state: (800) 365-7724
Contact: Ronald L. Rauch

St. Louis Area Agency on Aging
634 North Grand Avenue, Suite 721
St. Louis, MO 63103
(314) 658-1021
Contact: Barbara J. Selders

Southeast Missouri Area Agency on Aging
121 South Broadview, Suite 11
Cape Girardeau, MO 63701
Within state: (800) 392-8771
Contact: Glenda Hoffmeister

Southwest Missouri Office on Aging
317 Park Central East
P.O. Box 50805
Springfield, MO 65805
Barry County: (417) 847-4510;
(417) 235-3285

Christian County: (417) 725-2322; (417) 485-2538
Dade County: (417) 637-2626
Dallas County: (417) 345-8277
Douglas County: (417) 683-5712
Greene County: (417) 672-3826; (417) 862-0762; (417) 732-7672
Howell County: (417) 934-6504; (417) 256-4055; (417) 469-3892
Lawrence County: (417) 678-5383; (417) 466-2072
Oregon County: (417) 264-7354; (417) 778-7342

Osark County: (417) 679-4746
Polk County: (417) 326-5570
Shannon County: (314) 325-4636
Stone County: (417) 723-8110; (417) 739-5242
Taney County: (417) 335-4801; (417) 546-6100
Texas County: (417) 967-2013; (314) 674-3588; (417) 962-3860
Webster County: (417) 935-2211; (417) 468-5184
Wright County: (417) 926-5867
Contact: Winston Bledsoe

Montana

STATE AGENCY

The Governor's Office on Aging
State Capitol Building
Capitol Station, Room 219
Helena, MT 59620
Within state: (800) 332-2272
Contact: Hank Hudson

REGIONAL AGENCIES

Area Agency on Aging 9
723 Fifth Avenue East
Kalispell, MT 59901
(406) 756-5635
Contact: Jim Atkinson

Area 1 Area Agency on Aging
111 West Bell
Glendive, MT 59330

Carter County: (406) 775-8749
Custer County: (406) 232-2538
Daniels County: (406) 487-2434
Dawson County: (406) 365-3927
Fallon County: (406) 778-3595
Garfield County: (406) 557-2501
McCone County: (406) 485-2418
Phillips County: (406) 654-1056
Powder River County: (406) 436-2635

Prairie County: (406) 637-5736
Richland County: (406) 482-2651
Roosevelt County: (406) 525-3629
Rosebud County: (406) 365-3364
Sheridan County: (406) 765-2642
Treasure County: (406) 342-5252
Valley County: (406) 228-8221
Wibaux County: (406) 795-2601
Contact: Lori Brengle

Area 2 Area Agency on Aging
343 Main
Roundup, MT 59072
(406) 323-1320
Contact: Karen Erdie

Area 4 Area Agency on Aging
343 Main
P.O. Box 1717
Helena, MT 59624
Within state: (800) 356-6544
Contact: Charles W. Briggs

Area 5 Area Agency on Aging
115 East Pennsylvania Avenue
P.O. Box 608
Anaconda, MT 59711
(406) 563-3110
Contact: Jane Anderson

Area 7 Area Agency on Aging
1445 Avenue B
P.O. Box 21838
Billings, MT 59102
(800) 758-4812
Contact: Darrell La Merer

Area 8 Area Agency on Aging
2332 Smelter Avenue
Black Eagle, MT 59414
(406) 761-1919
Contact: Randy Barrett

Hill County Council on Aging
2 West Second Street
Havre, MT 59501
(406) 265-5464
Contact: Evelyn Havskjold

Missoula Aging Services
227 West Front
Missoula, MT 59802
(406) 728-7588
Contact: Susan Kohler-Hurd

**North Central Area Agency on
    Aging**
323 South Main
Conrad, MT 59425
Within state: (800) 332-2272
Contact: Rhonda Wisner

**Western Montana Area 4 Area
    Agency on Aging**
12 Fifth Avenue East #1
Polson, MT 59860-2127
(406) 883-6211, ext. 288
Contact: Duane Lutke

Nebraska

STATE AGENCY

Nebraska Department on Aging
P.O. Box 95044
301 Centennial Mall South
Lincoln, NE 68509
Within state: (800) 942-7830
Contact: Jacklyn Smith

REGIONAL AGENCIES

Aging Office of Western Nebraska
1517 Broadway, Suite 122
Scottsbuff, NE 69361
Within state: (800) 682-5140
Contact: Victor Walker

Blue Rivers Area Agency on Aging
Gage County Courthouse, Room 24
612 Grant Street
Beatrice, NE 68310
Gage, Johnson, Nemaha, Otoe, Pawnee, and Richardson Counties: (402) 223-1352
Thayer County: (402) 768-6052
Jefferson County: (402) 729-6475
Contact: Larry Ossowski

Eastern Nebraska Office on Aging
885 South Seventy-second
Omaha, NE 68114
(402) 444-6444
Contact: Beverly Griffith

Lincoln Area Agency on Aging
129 North Tenth Street, Room 241
Lincoln, NE 68508-3648
Within state: (800) 247-0938
Contact: James E. Zietlow

Midland Area Agency on Aging
P.O. Box 905
Hastings, NE 68902
Adams County: (402) 463-5681
Clay County: (402) 762-3226
Hall County: (308) 381-5308
Hamilton County: (402) 694-2176
Howard County: (308) 754-5452
Merrick County: (308) 946-3779
Nuckolls County: (402) 879-4679
Webster County: (402) 746-3708
Contact: Jerry Ryan

Northeast Nebraska Area Agency on Aging
White Stone Building
P.O. Box 1447
Norfolk, VA 68702
Within state: (800) 672-8368
Contact: Joann Forster

South Central Nebraska Area Agency on Aging
124 West Forty-sixth Street
Kearney, NE 68847
Blain, Buffalo, Custer, Franklin, Furnas, Garfield, Greeley, Harlan, Kearney, Loup, Phelps, Shreman, Valley, and Wheeler Counties: (800) 658-4320
Franklin County: (308) 425-3724
Harlan County: (308) 928-2149
Phelps County: (308) 995-5345
Contact: Donna Mayo

West Central Nebraska Area Agency on Aging
200 South Silber Avenue
North Platte, NE 69101
Within state: (800) 662-2961
Contact: Merlyn Haight

Nevada

STATE AGENCY

Department of Human Resources
Division for Aging Services
340 North Eleventh Street, Suite 114
Las Vegas, NV 89101
(702) 486-3545
Contact: Suzanne Ernst

New Hampshire

STATE AGENCY

Division of Elderly and Adult Services
6 Hazen Drive
Concord, NH 03301
Within state: (800) 351-1888
Contact: Richard Chevrefils

New Jersey

STATE AGENCY

Division of Aging
Department of Community Affairs
CN 807, South Broad and Front Streets
Trenton, NJ 08625-0807
Within state: (800) 792-8820
Out of state: (609) 984-6693
Contact: Lois Hull

REGIONAL AGENCIES

Atlantic County Division on Aging
1333 Atlantic Avenue, Third Floor
Atlantic City, NJ 08401
(609) 345-6700
Contact: John McLevnon

Bergen County Division on Aging
21 Main Street
Court Plaza South
West Wing #109W
Hackensack, NJ 07601
(201) 646-2625
Contact: Gloria Layne

Burlington County Office on Aging
County Office Building
Mt. Holly, NJ 08060
Within state: (800) 792-8890
Contact: Cecile Neidich

Camden County Office on Aging
120 White Horse Pike, Suite 103
Haddon Heights, NJ 08035
Within state: (609) 546-6404
Contact: Joy M. Merulla

Cape May County Department of Aging
3509 Route 9 South
Rio Grand, NJ 08242
(609) 886-2784
Contact: Margaret Spencer

Cumberland County Office on Aging
790 East Commerce Street
Bridgeton, NJ 08332
Within state: (800) 792-8820
Contact: Misono Miller

Essex County Division on Aging
15 South Munn Avenue
East Orange, NJ 07018
(201) 678-9700
Contact: Dolores Critchley

Gloucester County Department on Aging
Route 45 and Budd Boulevard
P.O. Box 337
Woodbury, NJ 08096
(609) 384-6910
Contact: Margaret C. Mendoza

Hudson County Office on Aging
Hudson County Department of Human Services
567 Pavonia Avenue
Jersey City, NJ 07306
(201) 915-1171
Contact: Carol Ann Wilson

Hunterdon County Office on Aging
6 Gauntt Place
Flemington, NJ 08822
Within state: (800) 792-8820
Contact: Rosemarie Doremus

Mercer County Office on Aging
640 South Broad Street
P.O. Box 8068
Trenton, NJ 08650-0068
Within state: (800) 792-8820
Contact: Carl F. West

Middlesex County Office on Aging
Hall of Records Annex
Freehold, NJ 07728
Monmouth County: (908) 431-7450
Long Branch, Monmouth Beach, Oceanport, and West Long Beach: (908) 571-6540
Asbury Park, Allenhurst, Bradley Beach, and Deal: (908) 988-5252

Adelphia, Farmingdale, and Howell: (908) 938-4500
Eatontown, Little Silver, Navesink, Red Back, and Shrewsbury: (908) 747-5204
Neptune, Neptune City, and Ocean Grove: (908) 988-8855
Belford, East Keansburg, Leonardo, Lincroft, Middletown, Navesink, and Port Monmouth: (908) 615-2265
Contact: Sister Mary Simon

Morris County Office on Aging
P.O. Box 900
Morristown, NJ 07960-0990
(201) 285-6868
Contact: Bonnie Kelly

Ocean County Office on Aging
3 Mott Place, CN2191
Toms River, NJ 08754
(908) 929-2091
Contact: Philip Rubenstein

Passaic County Office on Aging
675 Goffle Road
Hawthorne, NJ 07506
Within state: (800) 223-0556
Contact: John Stuart

Salem County Office on Aging
P.O. Box 276
Woodstown, NJ 08098
(609) 769-4150
Contact: Constance G. Undy

Somerset County Office on Aging
614 First Avenue
Washington School
Raritan, NJ 08869
(908) 231-7176
Contact: Ruth M. Reader

Sussex County Office on Aging
P.O. Box 709
Newton, NJ 07860
(201) 579-0557
Contact: Rosemarie C. Agostini

Union County Division on Aging
County Administration Building,
  Fourth Floor
Elizabeth, NJ 07207
(908) 527-4872
Contact: Philip H. Pearlman

Warren County Office on Aging
Dumont Administration Building
165 County Road 519S
Belvidere, NJ 07823
(908) 475-6591
Contact: Anne B. Schneider

New Mexico

STATE AGENCY

State Agency on Aging
La Villa Rivera Building
224 East Palace Avenue
Santa Fe, NM 87501
Within state: (800) 432-2080
Out of state: (505) 827-7640
Contact: Michelle Lujan Grisham

REGIONAL AGENCIES

City of Albuquerque Area Agency on Aging
714 Seventh Street, SW
Albuquerque, NM 87102
(505) 764-6400
Contact: Ronald Montoya

Eastern New Mexico Area Agency on Aging
901 West Thirteenth Street
Clovis, NM 88101
(505) 769-1613
Contact: Frank White

North Central New Mexico
Economic Development
District Area Agency on
Aging
P.O. Box 5115
Santa Fe, NM 87502
(505) 827-7313
Contact: Jenny Martinez

Southwestern New Mexico
Area Agency on Aging
Mesilla Community Center, Suite 6
P.O. Box 822
Mesilla, NM 88046
(800) 497-3646
Contact: Art Bardwell

New York

STATE AGENCY

New York State Office for the Aging
New York State Plaza
Agency Building 2
Albany, NY 12223
Within state: (800) 342-9871
Contact: Jane Gould

REGIONAL AGENCIES

Albany County Department for
the Aging
112 State Street, Room 710
Albany, NY 12207
(518) 447-7177
Contact: Richard D. Healy

Alleghany County Office for
the Aging
17 Court Street
Belmont, NY 14813
(716) 268-9390
Contact: Kimberley Toot

Broome County Office for the
Aging
County Building
Government Plaza
P.O. Box 1766
Binghamton, NY 13902
(607) 778-2411
Contact: George Tomaras

Cattaraugus County
Department of Aging
1701 Lincoln Avenue, Suite 7610
Olean, NY 14760
Within state: (800) 462-2901
Contact: John R. Searles

Cayuga County Office of the Aging
160 Genesee Street
Auburn, NY 13021
(315) 253-1226
Contact: Joan K. Gallo

Chautauqua County Office for the Aging
7 North Erie Street
Mayville, NY 14757
Ashville, Bemus Point, Celoron, Falconer, Frewsburg, Greenhurst, Jamestown, Kennedy, and Lakewood: (716) 664-2029
Brocton, Dunkirk, Forestville, Fredonia, Irving, Sheridan, Silver Creek, and Van Buren Point: (716) 366-4465
Chautauqua, Clymer, Dewittville, Findley Lake, Maple Springs, Mayville, Niobe, North Clymer, Panama Point, Portland, Ripley, Sherman, Stockton, Stow, and Westfield: (716) 753-4471
Ellington, Gerry, Lily Dale, Sinclairville, and South Dayton: (716) 962-8131
Contact: Mac McCoy

Chemung County Office for the Aging
Human Resource Center
425 Pennsylvania Avenue
Elmira, NY 14904
(607) 737-5520
Contact: Samuel A. David

Chenango County Area Agency on Aging
5 Court Street
Norwich, NY 13815
(607) 337-1770
Contact: Denise Newvine

Clinton County Office for the Aging
135 Margaret Street
Plattsburgh, NY 12901
(518) 565-4620
Contact: Katherine V. Felty

Columbia County Office for the Aging
71 North Third Street
Hudson, NY 12534
(518) 828-4258
Contact: Kit Ali

Cortland County Area Agency on Aging
60 Central Avenue
P.O. Box 5590
Cortland, NY 13045
(607) 753-5060
Contact: Nancy Hansen

Delaware County Office for the Aging
6 Court Street
Delhi, NY 13753
(607) 746-6333
Contact: Tom Briggs

Dutchess County Office for the Aging
488 Main Street
Poughkeepsie, NY 12601
(914) 431-2465
Contact: Douglas A. McHoul

Erie County Department of Senior Services
95 Franklin Street
Buffalo, NY 14202
(716) 858-8526
Contact: Robert A. Mendez

Essex County Office for the Aging
County Complex
Elizabethtown, NY 12932
Within state: (800) 562-3660
Contact: Grace L. Armstrong

Franklin County Office for the Aging
63 West Main Street
Malone, NY 12953
Within state: (800) 397-8686
Contact: Janice Henderson

Fulton County Office for the Aging
19 North William Street
Johnstown, NY 12095
(518) 762-0650
Contact: Kathryn Leitch

Genesee County Office for the Aging
2 Bank Street
Batavia, NY 14020
(716) 343-1611
Contact: Connie Boyd

Greene County Department for the Aging
19-A South Jefferson Avenue
Catskill, NY 12414
(518) 943-5332
Contact: Thomas A. Yandeau

Herkimer County Office for the Aging
109-111 Mary Street
P.O. Box 267
Herkimer, NY 13350
(315) 867-1121
Contact: Mary Scanlon

Jefferson County Office for the Aging
250 Arsenal Street
Watertown, NY 13601
(315) 785-3191
Contact: Anthony Bova

Lewis County Office for the Aging
Outer Stowe Street
P.O. Box 408
Lowville, NY 13367
(315) 376-5313
Contact: Thomas F. Kingston

Livingston County Office for the Aging
Livingston County Campus
  Building #8
Mt. Morris, NY 14510
(716) 243-7520
Contact: Karen Smith

Madison County Office for the Aging
43 East Main Street
P.O. Box 250
Morrisville, NY 13408
(315) 684-9424
Contact: Anthony Joseph

Metropolitan Commission on Aging
421 Montgomery Street
Syracuse, NY 13202
(315) 474-7011
Contact: Dale Parsons

Monroe County Office for the Aging
375 Westfall Road
Rochester, NY 14620
(716) 274-8151; (716) 275-5151
Contact: Lorraine Anderson

Montgomery County Office for the Aging
380 Guy Park Avenue
Amsterdam, NY 12010
(518) 843-2300
Contact: Lorraine Suliveres

Nassau County Department of Senior Citizens Affairs
400 County Seat Drive
Mineola, NY 11501
(516) 571-5814
Contact: Rena Iacono

New York City Department of Aging
2 Lafayette Street
New York, NY 10007
(212) 577-0800; (212) 577-0283
  (Hispanic Helpline)

Niagara County Office for the Aging
Switzer Building
100 Davison Road
Lockport, NY 14094
(716) 439-7833
Contact: Shirley Wayda

Oneida County Office for the Aging
800 Park Avenue
Utica, NY 13501
Within state: (800) 541-0151
Contact: Theresa L. Laper

Ontario County Office for the Aging
3871 County Road #46
Canandaigua, NY 14424
(716) 396-4040
Contact: James X. Kennedy

Orange County Office for the Aging
30 Matthews Street, Suite 201
Goshen, NY 10924
(914) 294-5151, ext. 1560
Contact: Nick Gerten

Orleans County Office for the Aging
14016 Route 31
Albion, NY 14411
(716) 589-7004
Contact: Carol T. Blake

Oswego County Office for the Aging
County Office Complex
70 Bunner Street
Oswego, NY 13126
(315) 349-3484
Contact: Mary R. Robbins

Otsego County Office for the Aging
197 Main Street
County Building Annex
Cooperstown, NY 13326-1129
(607) 547-4232; (607) 432-9501
Contact: Edward F. Bommer

Putnam County Office for the Aging
110 Old Route 6
Building A
Carmel, NY 10512
(914) 225-1034

Rensselaer County Department for the Aging
Ned Patterson Rensselaer County
  Government Center
1600 Seventh Avenue
Troy, NY 12180
(518) 270-2738
Contact: Paul J. Tazbir

Rockland County Office for the Aging
Dr. Robert Yeager Health Center
Building B
Pomona, NY 10970
(914) 364-2110
Contact: Virginia M. Weil

St. Lawrence County Office for the Aging
Sears Building
Canton, NY 13617
(315) 379-2282
Contact: John A. Karlberg

Saratoga County Office for the Aging
40 South Street
Ballston Spa, NY 12020
(518) 885-5381
Contact: Franklin DeMarinis

Schenectady County Office for the Aging
220 Nott Terrace
Schenectady, NY 12307-1026
(518) 382-8481
Contact: Nancy DeLisso

Schoharie County Office for the Aging
122 East Main Street
Cobleskill, NY 12043
(518) 234-4219
Contact: Ethel Benninger

Schuyler County Office for the Aging
336-338 West Main Street
P.O. Box J
Montour Falls, NY 14865
(607) 535-7100
Contact: Richard Cole

Seneca County Office for the Aging
1 DiPronio Drive
Waterloo, NY 13165
(315) 539-5655
Contact: Angela M. Marconi

Steuben County Office for the Aging
117 East Steuben Street
Bath, NY 14810
(607) 776-9631
Contact: Linda M. Tetor

Suffolk County Office for the Aging
395 Oser Avenue
Hauppauge, NY 11788-3631
(516) 853-3628
Contact: Patricia Lunetta

Sullivan County Office for the Aging
100 North Street
P.O. Box 5012
(914) 794-3000
Contact: James P. Galligan

Tioga County Area Agency on Aging
231 Main Street
Oswego, NY 13827
(607) 687-4120
Contact: Jean Hefft

Tompkins County Office for the Aging
309 North Tioga Street
Ithaca, NY 14850
(607) 227-0148
Contact: Irene W. Stein

Ulster County Office for the Aging
1 Albany Avenue
P.O. Box 1800
Kingston, NY 12401
(914) 331-9300
Contact: Patricia P. Pine

Warren/Hamilton Counties Office for the Aging
Warren County Municipal Center
Lake George, NY 12845
North Hamilton County: (518) 352-7719
South Hamilton County: (518) 548-8101
Warren County: (518) 761-6347
Contact: James A. Baker

Washington County Office for the Aging
Washington County Building
Upper Broadway
Fort Edward, NY 12828
Within state: (800) 848-3303
Contact: Muriel N. Eckhard

Wayne County Area Agency on Aging
16 William Street
Lyons, NY 14489
(315) 946-5624
Contact: Robert L. Linder

Westchester County Office for the Aging
214 Central Avenue
White Plains, NY 10606
(914) 682-3000
Contact: Mae Carpenter

Wyoming County Office for the Aging
76 North Main Street
Warsaw, NY 14569
Within state: (800) 724-7932
Contact: Martin D. Mucher

Yates County Area Agency on Aging
5 Collins Avenue
Penn Yan, NY 14527
(315) 536-2368
Contact: Julia K. Teahan

North Carolina

STATE AGENCY

Division on Aging
693 Palmer Drive
Caller Box 29531
Raleigh, NC 27626-0531
Within state: (800) 662-7030
Out of state: (919) 733-4261
Contact: Bonnie Cramer

REGIONAL AGENCIES

Albemarle Commission
512 Church Street
P.O. Box 646
Hertford, NC 27944
(919) 426-5753
Contact: Lee Riddick

**Centralina Area Agency on
Aging**
P.O. Box 35008
Charlotte, NC 28235
Cabarrus County: (704) 788-1156
Gaston County: (704) 866-3801
Iredell County: (704) 873-5171
Lincoln County: (704) 735-1496
Mecklenburg County: (704) 377-
1100
Rowan County: (704) 636-2344
Stanly County: (704) 983-7334
Union County: (704) 289-8102
Contact: Sue B. Archer

**Cape Fear Council of
Governments**
1480 Harbour Drive
Wilmington, NC 28401
(919) 395-4553
Contact: Carolyn Soders

**Isothermal Planning and
Development Commission**
101 West Court Street
P.O. Box 841
Rutherfordton, NC 28139
Cleveland County: (704) 482-
3488
Kings Mountain: (704) 734-0447
Rutherford County: (704) 245-
0515
Polk County: (704) 859-9707
McDowell County: (704) 652-
8953
Contact: Sybil Walker

**Kerr-Tar Regional Council of
Governments Area Agency
on Aging**
238 Orange Street
P.O. Box 709
Henderson, NC 27536
Franklin County: (919) 496-1131
Granville County: (919) 693-1930
Person County: (919) 599-7484
Vance County: (919) 430-0257
Warren County: (919) 257-3111
Contact: Stephen Y. Norwood

Land of Sky Regional Council
25 Heritage Drive
Asheville, NC 28806
(704) 254-8131
Contact: Joan Tuttle

**Lumber River Area Agency on
Aging**
4721 Fayetteville Road
Lumberton, NC 28358
(800) 253-9468
Contact: Betty Rising

**Mid-Carolina Area Agency on
Aging**
P.O. Drawer 1510
Fayetteville, NC 28302
Within state: (800) 662-7030
Contact: Margaret Hardee

**Mid-East Commission Area
Agency on Aging**
P.O. Box 1787
Washington, NC 27889
Beaufort County: (919) 975-5500
Bertie County: (919) 749-5315
Hertford County: (919) 358-7856
Martin County: (919) 792-1027
Pitt County: (919) 752-1717;
(919) 757-0303
Contact: Louisa Cox

Neuse River Council of Governments Area Agency on Aging
233 Middle Street
P.O. Box 1717
New Bern, NC 28563
Carteret County: (919) 728-7669
Craven County: (919) 636-6614
Duplin County: (919) 296-2140
Greene County: (919) 747-5436
Jones County: (919) 638-3800
Lenoir County: (919) 527-1342
Onslow County: (919) 455-2747
Pamlico County: (919) 745-7196
Wayne County: (919) 731-1588
Contact: Connie Winstead-Barnes

Northwest Piedmont Council of Governments Area Agency on Aging
280 South Liberty Street
Winston-Salem, NC 27101-5288
Davie County: (704) 634-0611
Forsyth County: (919) 727-8100
Stokes County: (919) 593-8156
Surry County: (919) 386-9400
Yadkin County: (919) 679-3596
Contact: Joyce Massey-Smith

Pee Dee Council of Governments
302 Leak Street
Rockingham, NC 28379
Anson County: (704) 694-6217
Montgomery County: (919) 572-3757
Moore County: (919) 947-2881
Richmond County: (919) 997-4491
Contact: Phyllis Bridgeman

Piedmont Triad Council of Governments Area Agency on Aging
2216 West Meadowview Road, Suite 201
Greensboro, NC 27407-3480

Alamance County: (919) 226-2488
Caswell County: (919) 694-6428
Davidson County: (704) 242-2290
Guilford County: (919) 333-6981
Randolph County: (919) 625-3389
Rockingham County: (919) 342-9999
Contact: Kimberly Dawkins-Berry

Region A Area Agency on Aging
P.O. Box 850
Bryson City, NC 28713
Cherokee County: (704) 837-2467
Clay County: (704) 389-9271
Graham County: (704) 479-3361
Jackson County: (704) 586-8562
Haywood County: (704) 452-1447
Macon County: (704) 524-6421
Swain County: (704) 488-3047
Contact: Mary P. Barker

Region D Area Agency on Aging
Executive Arts Building
Furman Road
P.O. Box 1820
Boone, NC 28607
Alleghany County: (919) 372-8840
Ashe County: (919) 246-2461
Avery County: (704) 733-8220
Mitchell County: (704) 688-3019
Watauga County: (704) 264-2060
Wilkes County: (919) 651-7811
Yancey County: (704) 682-6011
Contact: Barbara Barghothi

Region L Council of Government
1309 South Wesleyan Boulevard
P.O. Drawer 2748

Rocky Mount, NC 27802
(919) 446-0411
Contact: Lucretia Y. Hanks

Triangle J Council of
   Governments
P.O. Box 12276
Research Triangle Park, NC
   27709
Chatham County: (919) 542-4512
Durham County: (919) 688-8247
Johnson County: (919) 934-6066
Lee County: (919) 776-0501
Orange County: (919) 968-2080

Wake County: (919) 872-7933
Contact: David M. Moser

Western Piedmont Council of
   Governments
317 First Avenue, NW
Hickory, NC 28601
Alexander County: (704) 632-
   1080
Burke County: (704) 437-1201
Catawba County: (704) 328-2269
Caldwell County: (704) 758-2566
Contact: R. Douglas Taylor

North Dakota

STATE AGENCY

Aging Services Division
Department of Human Services
1929 North Washington Street
P.O. Box 7070
Bismarck, ND 58507-7070
Within state: (800) 472-2622
Contact: Linda Wright

Ohio

STATE AGENCY

Ohio Department of Aging
50 West Broad Street, 8th Floor
Columbus, OH 43266-0501
(614) 466-5500
Contact: Judith Brachman

REGIONAL AGENCIES

Area Agency on Aging 10B, Inc.
1550 Corporate Woods Parkway, Suite 100
Uniontown, OH 44685
Portage County: (216) 297-4636
Stark County: (216) 453-9172
Summit County: (216) 374-0333
Wayne County: (216) 264-9473
Contact: Joseph Ruby

Area Agency on Aging of Northwestern Ohio, Inc.
2155 Arlington Avenue
Toledo, OH 43609
Defiance County: (419) 782-3233
Erie County: (419) 626-2560
Henry County: (419) 599-5515
Paulding County: (419) 399-3650
Sandusky County: (419) 334-3218
Williams County: (419) 485-3218
Fulton, Lucas, Ottawa and Wood Counties: (419) 382-0624
Contact: Billie Johnson

Area Agency on Aging District 7, Inc.
University of Rio Grande
P.O. Box 978
Rio Grande, OH 45674
Adams County: (513) 544-3979
Brown County: (513) 378-6603
Gallia County: (614) 446-7000
Highland County: (513) 393-4745
Jackson County: (614) 286-6365
Lawrence County: (614) 894-7569
Pike County: (614) 947-5555
Ross County: (614) 773-3544
Scioto County: (614) 354-6672
Vinton County: (614) 596-4706
Contact: Pamela K. Matura

Area Agency on Aging, PSA #2
6 South Patterson Boulevard
Dayton, OH 45402
Champaign, Darke, Greene, Logan, Miami, Preble and Shelby Counties: (800) 258-7277
Clark County: (513) 323-4948
Montgomery County: (513) 223-2112
Contact: Douglas McGarry

Area Agency on Aging, PSA #3
311 East Market Street, Suite 201
Lima, OH 45801
Allen County: (419) 228-5135
Auglaize County: (419) 394-4217
Hancock County: (419) 423-8496
Hardin County: (419) 673-1102
Mercer County: (419) 586-1644
Putnam County: (419) 523-4121
Van Wert County: (419) 238-5011
Contact: Harold K. Dahill

Area Agency on Aging Region 9, Inc.
Southgate Office Center
60788 Southgate Road
Byesville, OH 43722
Belmont Contact: (614) 695-4142
Carrol County: (216) 627-7017
Cishicton County: (614) 622-4852
Guernsey County: (614) 439-6681
Harrison County: (614) 942-3238
Holmes County: (216) 674-0580
Jefferson County: (614) 283-7470
Muskingum County: (614) 454-9761
Contact: Shirley Blackledge

Buckeye Hills-Hocking Valley Regional Development District
Route 1, Box 20
Marietta, OH 45750
Within state: (800) 331-2644
Contact: Cindy L. Farson

Central Ohio Area Agency on Aging
272 South Gift Street
Columbus, OH 43215
Franklin County: (614) 462-6200
Delaware, Fairfield, Fayette,
   Licking, Madison, Pickaway
   and Union Counties: (614)
   645-7250
Delaware County: (614) 369-9628
Fairfield County: (614) 687-6655
Fayette County: (614) 335-4144
Licking County: (614) 345-6064
Madison County: (614) 852-3001
Pickaway County: (614) 474-8831
Contact: Larke Recchie

Council on Aging, Cincinnati Area
Holiday Office Park, Suite 1100
644 Linn Street
Cincinnati, OH 45203
Butler and Hamilton Counties:
   (513) 895-6978
Clermont County: (513) 724-1268
Clinton County: (513) 382-7170
Hamilton County: (513) 474-
   3100; (513) 984-1234
Middletown: (513) 425-0492
Oxford: (513) 523-8100
Warren County: (513) 381-6173
Contact: Robert D. Logan

District 11 Area Agency on Aging, Inc.
25 East Boardman Street

Youngtown, OH 44503
Ashtabula County: (216) 988-
   6750
Columbiana County: (216) 332-
   1163
Mahoning County: (216) 744-
   5071
Trumbull County: (216) 399-8846
Contact: Donald J. Medd

Ohio District 5 Area Agency on Aging
235 Marion Avenue
P.O. Box 1978
Mansfield, OH 44901
Ashland County: (419) 281-1477
Crawford County: (419) 562-3050
Huron County: (800) 826-1306
Knox County: (614) 397-2417
Marion County: (614) 387-6100
Morrow County: (419) 946-4191
Richland County: (419) 524-2133
Seneca County: (419) 447-5792
Wyandot County: (419) 294-5733
Contact: Patricia Brammer

Western Reserve Area Agency on Aging
1030 Euclid Avenue, Suite 318
Cleveland, OH 44115
Central Lake County: (216) 357-
   2741
Cuyahoga County: (216) 391-
   5800
Eastern Lake County: (216) 428-
   7581 Ext. 2741
Geauga County: (216) 258-2222
   Ext. 5522
Lorain County: (216) 329-5132
Medina County: (216) 723-3641
Western Lake County: (216) 975-
   4111
Contact: Ron Hill

Oklahoma

STATE AGENCY

Aging Services Division
Department of Human Services
312 North East 28th Street
P.O. Box 25352
Oklahoma, OK 73125
(405) 521-2281
Contact: Roy Keen

REGIONAL AGENCIES

Area Agency on Aging EODD
215 North State #408
P.O. Box 1367
Muskogee, OK 74402
(918) 682-7891
Contact: Patricia Burks

Areawide Aging Agency, Inc.
3200 Northwest 48th, Suite 104
Oklahoma City, OK 73112
Canadian, Cleveland, Logan and
  Oklahoma Counties: (405)
  943-4344
Cleveland County: (405) 321-
  3200
Canadian County: (405) 262-7121
Logan County: (405) 282-1803
Contact: Don Hudman

ASCOG Area Agency on Aging
802 Main Street
P.O. Box 1647
Duncan, OK 73534
(800) 658-1466
Contact: Jim Vanzant

COEDD Area Agency on Aging
P.O. Box 3398
Shawnee, OK 74802
Hughes, Seminole and Okfuskee
  Counties: (405) 379-5404
Lincoln, Pawnee, Payne and
  Pottawatomie Counties: (405)
  258-2044
Contact: Cathy Manuel

**Grand Gateway Area Agency
  on Aging**
320 South Wilson
P.O. Box 330
Vinita, OK 74301
Within state: (800) 482-4594
Contact: Judy Branscum

KEDDO Area Agency on Aging
P.O. Box 638
Wilburton, OK 74578
Within state: (800) 722-8180
Contact: Toni Enis

NODA Area Agency on Aging
1216 West Willow, Suite A
Enid, OK 73703
(800) 749-1149
Contact: Rick Billings

OEDA Area Agency on Aging
P.O. Box 668
Beaver, OK 73932
Within state: (800) 658-2844
Contact: Richard Adams

SODA Area Agency on Aging
15 First Avenue Southeast
P.O. Box 848
Ardmore, OK 73402
Within state: (800) 371-7032
Contact: Perry G. Anderson

SWODA Area Agency on Aging
420 Sooner Drive
Box 569
Burns Flat, OK 73624
(800) 627-4882
Contact: James Boyd

Tulsa Area Agency on Aging
110 South Hartford
Tulsa, OK 74120-1820
Creek County: (918) 367-5400
Osage County: (918) 287-1064
Tulsa County: (918) 832-9999
Contact: Paul Stabler

Oregon

STATE AGENCY

Senior and Disabled Services Division
500 Summer Street Northeast
2nd Floor North
Salem, OR 97310-1015
(800) 282-8096
Contact: James C. Wilson

REGIONAL AGENCIES

Area Agency on Aging District 7
1160 Newport
P.O. Box 1118
Coos Bay, OR 97420
(503) 269-2013
Contact: Connie Croy

Central Oregon Council on Aging
2303 Southwest First Street
Redmond, OR 97756
Crook County: (503) 447-1177
Deschutes County: (800) 262-7488

Jefferson County: (503) 475-6494
Contact: Veronica C. Zecchini

**Clackamas County Area
Agency on Aging**
P.O. Box 68369
Oak Grove, OR 97268-0369
(503) 655-8860
Contact: Pat Lyon

**Clatsop-Tillamook
Intergovernmental Council**
1065 South Hemlock Street
P.O. Box 488
Cannon Beach, OR 97110
Arch Cape, Cannon Beach,
    Seaside, Elsie, Jewell and
    Tolovana Park Counties: (503)
    738-7393
Astoria, Hammond and
    Warrenton Counties: (503)
    325-0123
Beaver, Cloverdale, Hebo,
    Nehalem, Netarts, Pacific City,
    Rockaway Beach and
    Tillamook Counties: (503) 842-
    7988
Knappa and Svensen Counties:
    (503) 458-6888
Contact: Donald Fields

**Columbia County Area Agency
on Aging**
c/o CTIC-District One Area
    Agency on Aging
P.O. Box 488
Cannon Beach, OR 97110
(503) 397-4000
Contact: Don Fields

**District 12, Area Agency on
Aging**
17 Southwest Frazier, Suite 20

P.O. Box 1207
Pendelton, OR 97801
Gillian, Grant, Morrow, Umatilla
    and Wheeler Counties: (503)
    276-6732
Contact: Charles Briggs

**Douglas County Senior Services
Division**
621 West Madrone Street
Roseburg, OR 97470
(503) 440-3580
Contact: G. John DeGroot

**Harney County Senior Center,
Inc.**
17 South Alder
Burns, OR 97720
(503) 573-6024
Contact: Theresa Mingus

HELP, Inc.
104 Elm Street
La Grande, OR 97850
(503) 963-7532
Contact: Dwight Hopkins

**Klamath Basin Senior Citizen's
Council**
2045 Arthur Street
Klamath Falls, OR 97603-4675
(503) 889-7171
Contact: Helen M. Baltazor

Lane Council of Governments
Senior Services Division
1025 Williamette Street, Suite 200
Eugene, OR 97401
Oakridge and Westfir: (503) 782-
    4726
Blue River, Dexter, Lowell,
    Pleasant Hill, Springfield,
    Waterville and Vida: (503) 726-
    4361

Lorane and Saginaw: (503) 942-5577
Eugene: (800) 441-4038
Elmira, Noti, Veneta and Walton: (503) 935-2262
Cheshire and Junction City: (503) 998-8445
Blachly, Deadwood, Florence, Mapleton, Swisshome and Westlake: (503) 997-8251
Contact: Ted Stevens

Malheur Council on Aging
842 Southeast First Avenue
P.O. Box 937
Ontario, OR 97914
(503) 889-7651

Mid-Columbia Senior and Disabled Services
700 Union, Room 214
The Dalles, OR 97058
Within state: (800) 452-2333
Contact: Sally Zuck

Mid-Willamette Valley Senior Services
P.O. Box 12189
Salem, OR 97309
South Marion County: (503) 371-1313
Polk County: (503) 623-2301
North Marion County: (503) 981-5138
Yamhill County: (503) 472-9441
Slayton County: (503) 769-6174
Sheridan County: (503) 843-3133
Contact: Barry Donenfeld

Multnomah County Aging Services Division
421 Southwest Fifth Avenue, 3rd Floor
Portland, OR 97204
(503) 248-3656
Contact: James McConnell

Oregon Cascades West Council of Governments—Senior Services
408 Southwest Monroe
Corvallis, OR 97333
Benton and Linn Counties: (800) 638-0510
Lincoln County: (800) 282-6194
Contact: Tom Hyder

Rogue Valley Council of Governments—Senior and Disabled Services
155 South Second Street
P.O. Box 3275
Central Point, OR 97502
Jackson County: (503) 779-6691
Josephine County: (503) 474-5440
Contact: Donald O. Bruland

Washington County Department of Aging Services
133 Southeast Second Avenue
Hillsboro, OR 97123
(503) 640-3489
Contact: Mary Lou Ritter

Pennsylvania

STATE AGENCY

Department of Aging
Market Street State Office Building, Seventh Floor
400 Market Street
Harrisburg, PA 17101-2301
(717) 783-1550
Contact: Linda Rhodes

REGIONAL AGENCIES

Active Aging, Inc.
1034 Park Avenue
Meadville, PA 16335
Within state: (800) 321-7705
Contact: Pauline Mooney

Adams County Office for the Aging, Inc.
220 Baltimore Street
Gettysburg, PA 17325
Within state: (800) 548-3240
Contact: Steven D. Niebler

Aging Services, Inc.
1005 Oak Street
P.O. Box 519
Indiana, PA 15701-0519
Within state: (800) 442-8016
Contact: Carole A. Ling

Allegheny County Department of Aging
441 Smithfield Street, Third Floor
Pittsburgh, PA 15222
(412) 355-4232
Contact: Thomas D. O'Shea

Area Agency on Aging of Somerset County
132 East Catherine Street
P.O. Box 960
Somerset, PA 15501
Within state: (800) 452-0825
Contact: Arthur DiLoreto

Armstrong Area Agency on Aging
125 Queen Street
Kittanning, PA 16201
Within state: (800) 368-1066
Contact: Janet D. Crissman

Beaver County Office on Aging
Stone Point Landing, Suite 202
500 Market Street
Beaver, PA 15009
(412) 728-7707
Contact: R. Brandon James

Berks County Office of Aging
County Services Center
633 Court Street
Reading, PA 19601-4303
(215) 478-6500
Contact: Barbara Coffin

Blair Senior Services, Inc.
1320 Twelfth Avenue
Altoona, PA 16601
Within state: (800) 245-3282
Contact: David M. Slat

**Bradford—Sullivan—
Susquehana—Tioga Area
Agency on Aging**
701 Main Street
Towanda, PA 18848
Within state: (800) 982-4346
Contact: William Farley

**Bucks County Area Agency on
Aging**
30 East Oakland Avenue
Doylestown, PA 18901
(215) 348-0510
Contact: Margaret O'Neill

**Butler County Area Agency on
Aging**
111 Sunnyview Circle, Suite 101
Butler, PA 16001-3547
(412) 283-8865
Contact: William L. Patterson

**Cambria County Area Agency
on Aging**
P.O. Box 88
Ebensburg, PA 15931
(814) 472-5580
Contact: James Kudel

**Carbon County Area Agency
on Aging**
1122 North Street
P.O. Box 251
Jim Thorpe, PA 18229
(717) 325-2726
Contact: Rodney G. Jones

Centre County Office on Aging
Willowbank Building
420 Holmes Street
Bellefonte, PA 16823
Within state: (800) 242-4247
Contact: Jane G. Taylor

Chester County Office of Aging
Government Services Building
601 Westtown Road
West Chester, PA 19382
Within state: (800) 692-1100, ext.
6353
Contact: Monda M. Spool

**Clarion County Area Agency
on Aging**
12 Grant Street
Clarion, PA 16214
Within state: (800) 672-7116
Contact: Stephanie Wilshire

**Clearfield County Area Agency
on Aging**
103 North Front Street
P.O. Box 550
Clearfield, PA 16830
(800) 225-8571
Contact: John Kordish

**Columbia—Montour Area
Agency on Aging**
15 Perry Avenue
Bloomsburg, PA 17815
(800) 598-5001
Contact: Kathleen Lynn

Cumberland County Office of Aging
Room 111—East Wing
1 Courthouse Square
Carlisle, PA 17013
(717) 240-6110
Contact: Judith F. Shuey

Dauphin County Area Agency on Aging
25 South Front Street
Harrisburg, PA 17101-2025
(800) 328-0058
Contact: Ralph Moyer

Delaware County Services for the Aging
Government Center Building
Second and Orange Streets
Media, PA 19063
(215) 891-4455
Contact: John Bauer

Experience, Inc., Area Agency on Aging
905 Fourth Avenue West
Warren, PA 16365
Forest County: (800) 222-1706
Warren County: (814) 723-1706
Contact: Allen R. Roberts

Franklin County Area Agency on Aging
425 Franklin Farm Lane
Chambersburg, PA 17201
(717) 263-2153
Contact: Kimberly Murdaugh

Greater Erie Community Action Committee
18 West Ninth Street
Erie, PA 16501
(814) 459-4581, ext. 400
Contact: Carolyn Chester

Huntingdon/Bedford/Fulton Area Agency on Aging
240 Wood Street
P.O. Box 46
Bedford, PA 15522
Bedford County: (814) 623-8148
Fulton County: (717) 485-5151
Huntingdon County: (814) 643-5115
Contact: Alan Smith

Jefferson County Area Agency on Aging
RD #5, Box 47
Brookville, PA 15825
(800) 852-8036
Contact: Laura Mae Baker

Lackawanna County Agency on Aging
200 Adams Avenue, Suite 300
Scranton, PA 18503
(717) 963-6740
Contact: Kevin Russin

Lancaster County Office of Aging
50 North Duke Street
P.O. Box 3480
Lancaster, PA 17603-1881
(717) 299-7979
Contact: Patricia Mann

Lawrence County Area Agency on Aging
15 West Washington Street
Olde Post Office Complex, Suite 201
New Castle, PA 16101
(412) 658-3729
Contact: Roberta M. Taylor

Lebanon County Area Agency on Aging
710 Maple Street
Lebanon, PA 17042
(717) 273-9262
🐖 Contact: Michael G. Kristovensky

Lehigh County Area Agency on Aging
523 Hamilton Street
Allentown, PA 18101
(215) 820-3034
Contact: Peter D. Johnstone

Luzerne/Wyoming Bureau for the Aging
111 North Pennsylvania Boulevard
Wilkes Barre, PA 18701
Within state: (800) 252-1512
Contact: Carole J. Lewis

Lycoming/Clinton Office of Aging
352 East Water Street
P.O. Box 770
Lock Haven, PA 17745
(717) 748-8665
Contact: Patricia Essip

Mercer County Area Agency on Aging, Inc.
404 Mercer County Courthouse
Mercer, PA 16137
(412) 662-3800
Contact: Ann Marie Spiardi

Mifflin—Juniata Area Agency on Aging, Inc.
P.O. Box 750
Lewiston, PA 17044
(717) 242-0315
Contact: Carlene S. Hack

Monroe County Area Agency on Aging
62 Analomink Street
P.O. Box 384
East Stroudsburg, PA 18301
(717) 424-5290
Contact: Dorothy Kaufman

Montgomery County Aging and Adult Services
Courthouse
Norristown, PA 19404
(215) 278-3601
Contact: Edward Keenan

Northampton County Area Agency on Aging
Governor Wolf Building, Third Floor
45 North Second Street
Easton, PA 18042
(215) 559-3270
Contact: John R. Mehler

Northumberland County Area Agency on Aging
R.D. #1, Box 943
Shamokin, PA 17872
Within state: (800) 479-2626
Contact: Patricia M. Crone

Office of Human Services, Inc.
108 Center Street
P.O. Box A
Ridgeway, PA 15853
Within state: (800) 672-7145
Contact: Bill Orzechowski

Perry County Office on Aging
Center Square
P.O. Box 596
New Bloomfield, PA 17068
(717) 582-2131
Contact: Joan L. Brodisch

Pike County Area Agency on Aging
106 Broad Street
Milford, PA 18337
(717) 296-7813
Contact: Linda Peifer

Philadelphia Corporation for the Aging
642 North Broad Street
Philadelphia, PA 19130-3409
(215) 765-9040
Contact: Rodney D. Williams

Potter County Area Agency on Aging
Mapleview Complex
R.D. 3, Box 107A
Couderport, PA 16915
Within state: (800) 327-5419
Contact: Kathleen A. Wilson

Schuykill County Area Agency on Aging
112 South Claude A. Lord Boulevard
Pottsville, PA 17901
Within state: (800) 832-3313
Contact: Marie Beauchamp

Southwestern Pennsylvania Area Agency on Aging, Inc.
Eastgate 8
Monessen, PA 15062-1399
Fayette County: (412) 430-4603
Greene County: (412) 852-1510
Washington County: (412) 228-7080
Contact: Bob Willison

Union—Snyder Area Agency on Aging
116 North Second Street
Lewisburg, PA 17837
(717) 524-2100
Contact: Farida Zaid

Venango County Area Agency on Aging
1283 Liberty Street
P.O. Box 1130
Franklin, PA 16323
(814) 437-6871, ext. 264
Contact: Gary Dittman

Wayne County Area Agency on Aging
323 Tenth Street
Honesdale, PA 18431
(717) 253-4262
Contact: Andrea C. Whyte

Westmoreland County Area Agency on Aging
2482 South Grande Boulevard
Greensburgh, PA 15601-8904
Within state: (800) 442-8000
Contact: Ray DuCoeur

York County Area Agency on Aging
141 West Market Street
York, PA 17401
Within state: (800) 632-9073
Contact: Mary Daniels Levy

Puerto Rico

STATE AGENCY

Governor's Office of Elderly Affairs
Cobian Plaza Stop 23, U.M. Floor, Office C
Ponce de Leon Avenue #1603
Santurce, PR 00908
(809) 721-4560
Contact: Celia E. Cintrøn

REGIONAL AGENCIES

**Area Agency on Aging—
Metropolitan**
Call Box 11874
Fernandez Juncos Station
San Juan, PR 00910-1874
(809) 724-7253
Contact: Osvaldo Berrios

**Area Agency on Aging—
Northern I**
No. 4 Dr. Ferrer Street
Bayamon, PR 00956
(809) 780-1815
Contact: Hector M. Rivera

**Area Agency on Aging—
Northern II**
160 Juan Rosado Avenue
Ferrocarril, Mall Station Building
Arecibo, PR 00612
(809) 878-4095
Contact: Olga Rodriguez

**Area Agency on Aging—
Central Region**
No. 76 Celis Aguilera Street
Tapia Corner

Caguas, PR 00725
(809) 850-0040; (809) 258-1691
Contact: Alma Pagan

**Area Agency on Aging—
Eastern Region**
Bernardo Garcia Street #7
Domingo Caseres Corner
Carolina, PR 00985
(809) 752-6142
Contact: Wanda Aquino

**Area Agency on Aging—
Southern Region**
7-B Office Michelle Plaza Building
Bucana Industrial-Mercedita
Sector
Ponce, PR 00715
(809) 841-1180
Contact: Geneva Rojas Sierra

**Area Agency on Aging—
Western Region**
Medical Center Plaza, 314 Office
P.O. Box 2721
Mayaguez, PR 00681
(809) 833-4536
Contact: Eneida Zayas

Rhode Island

STATE AGENCY

Department of Elderly Affairs
160 Pine Street
Providence, RI 02903-3708
Within state: (800) 322-2880
Contact: Maureen Maigret

South Carolina

STATE AGENCY

South Carolina Commission on Aging
400 Arbor Lake Drive, Suite B-500
Columbia, SC 29223
(803) 735-0210
Contact: Ruth Seigler

REGIONAL AGENCIES

Catawba Area Agency on
  Aging
157 East Main Street, Suite 403
P.O. Box 4618
Rock Hill, SC 29732
York County: (803) 327-6694
Chester County: (803) 385-3838
Lancaster County: (803) 285-6956
Union County: (803) 429-1684
Contact: Sherron Marshall

Central Midlands Regional
  Planning Council Area
  Agency on Aging
236 Stoneridge Drive
Columbia, SC 29210
Fairfield County: (803) 635-3015
Lexington County: (803) 359-
  4048
Newberry County: (803) 276-
  8266
Richland County: (803) 252-7734;
  (803) 254-1248
Contact: Sherri Craft

ElderLink, Incorporated, Trident Area Agency on Aging
4500 Leeds Avenue, Suite 210
North Charleston, SC 29405
Berkeley County: (803) 761-6900
Charleston County: (803) 745-1710
Dorchester County: (803) 871-5053
Contact: Christine T. Harrison

Lower Country Council of Governments Area Agency on Aging
Interstate 95, U.S. 17
P.O. Box 98
Yemassee, SC 29945
Beaufort County: (803) 524-8609
Colleton County: (803) 549-5331
Hampton County: (803) 943-7555
Jasper County: (803) 726-5601
Contact: Corona Harrigan

Lower Savannah Area Agency on Aging
P.O. Box 850
Aiken, SC 29802
Aiken County: (803) 648-5447
Allendale County: (803) 584-4350
Bamberg County: (803) 245-3021
Carnwell County: (803) 259-3738
Calhoun County: (803) 874-1270
Orangeburg County: (803) 531-4663
Contact: Linda H. Holmes

Pee-Dee Community Health Services, Inc.
P.O. Box 238
Society Hill, SC 29593
Chesterfield County: (803) 623-2280
Darlington County: (803) 393-8521

Dillon County: (803) 774-0055
Florence County: (803) 669-6761
Marion County: (803) 423-4391
Marlboro County: (803) 479-9951
Contact: Ann Morgan

Santee—Lynches/COG Area Agency on Aging
P.O. Drawer 1837
Sumter, SC 29151
(803) 773-6628
Contact: Connie D. Munn

South Carolina Appalachian Council of Governments Area Agency on Aging
500 Grand Avenue
P.O. Drawer 6668
Greenville, SC 29606
Anderson County: (803) 225-3370
Cherokee County: (803) 489-3868
Greenville County: (803) 467-3660
Oconec County: (803) 885-1509
Pickents County: (803) 843-2275
Spartanburg County: (803) 596-3910
Contact: Michael J. Stogner

Upper Savannah Council of Governments Area Agency on Aging
P.O. Box 1366
Greenwood, SC 29648
Abbeville County: (803) 459-9666
Edgefield County: (803) 637-5326
Greenwood County: (803) 223-0164
Laurens County: (803) 984-4572
McCormick County: (803) 465-2626
Saluda County: (803) 445-2175
Contact: Patricia Edmonds

**Waccamaw Area Agency on
  Aging**
USC Coastal Carolina College
P.O. Box 1954
Conway, SC 29526
Georgetown County: (803) 546-
  8539

Horry County: (803) 248-5523
Williamsburg County: (803) 354-
  5496
Contact: Linda P. Lyerly

South Dakota

STATE AGENCY

Office of Adult Services and Aging
700 Governors Drive
Pierre, SD 57501
(605) 773-3656
Contact: Gail Ferris

Tennessee

STATE AGENCY

Tennessee Commission on Aging
706 Church Street, Suite 201
Nashville, TN 37243-0860
(615) 741-2056
Contact: Emily Wiseman

REGIONAL AGENCIES

Delta Area Agency on Aging
City Hall—Penthouse
125 North Mid-America Mall
Memphis, TN 38103
(901) 576-6600
Contact: Robert McFalls

**East Tennessee Human
  Resource Agency Area
  Agency on Aging**
408 North Cedar Bluff Road,
  Suite 150
Knoxville, TN 37923

Anderson County: (615) 457-3259
Blount County: (615) 983-8411
Campbell County: (615) 562-2948
Claiborne County: (615) 626-9471
Cocke County: (615) 623-1400
Grainger County: (615) 828-5397
Hamblen County: (615) 581-5166
Jefferson County: (615) 475-2222
Knox County: (615) 546-6262;
(615) 524-2786
Loudon County: (615) 458-5445
Monroe County: (615) 442-2022
Morgan County: (615) 346-6651
Roane County: (615) 354-0450
Scott County: (615) 569-5972
Sevier County: (615) 453-8080
Union County: (615) 992-3292
Contact: Aaron Bradley

First Tennessee Area Agency on Aging
207 North Boone Street, Suite 800
Johnson City, TN 37604
(615) 929-3328
Contact: Patricia Brown

Greater Nashville Area Agency on Aging
211 Union Street
Box 233
Nashville, TN 37201
Davison County, Nashville: (615) 259-7491
Cheatham County: (615) 792-3629
Dickson County: (615) 446-9350
Humphreys County: (615) 296-2979
Houston County: (615) 289-3848
Montgomery County: (615) 648-1645
Robertson County: (615) 384-6367

Rutherford County: (615) 890-8877
Steward County: (615) 232-7663
Sumner County: (615) 451-1531
Trousdale County: (615) 374-3311
East Wilson County, Lebanon, and Watertown: (615) 449-4600
West Wilson County: (615) 758-9114
Contact: Rick Fowlkes

Northwest Tennessee Area Agency on Aging
124 Weldon Drive
P.O. Box 963
Martin, TN 38237
Benton County: (901) 584-4101
Bradford and Gibson Counties: (901) 742-2891
Carroll County: (901) 986-5943
Crockett County: (901) 696-4637
Dyer County: (901) 286-7820
Henry County: (901) 642-2919
Humbolt County: (901) 784-1137
Lake County: (901) 253-7607
Milan County: (901) 686-0851
Martin: (901) 587-3900
Obion County: (901) 885-1246
Obion: (901) 538-9970
Sharon: (901) 456-2213
Ridgely: (901) 264-9929
Weakley County: (901) 364-3581
Contact: Paul D. Steele

South Central Tennessee Development District Area Agency on Aging
815 South Main
P.O. Box 1346
Columbia, TN 38402
Bedford County: (615) 684-0019

Coffee County: (615) 455-1787
Franklin County: (615) 967-0741
Giles County: (615) 363-6610
Hickman County: (615) 729-2115
Lawrence County: (615) 762-9259
Lewis County: (615) 796-5558
Lincoln County: (615) 433-7271
Marshall County: (615) 359-1463
Maury County: (615) 388-9595
Moore County: (615) 759-7317
Perry County: (615) 589-5111
Wayne County: (615) 722-3514
Contact: Bob Lundquist

Southeast Area Agency on Aging—Southeast Tennessee Development District
25 Cherokee Boulevard
P.O. Box 4757-0757
Chattanooga, TN 37405
Hamilton County: (615) 755-5173
Grandview, Spring City, and Watts
  Bar Dam: (615) 365-5173
Bradley County: (615) 479-4111
Bledsoe County: (615) 447-6111
Dayton, Evansville, and
  Graysville: (615) 775-6776
Grundy County: (615) 779-5494
Meigs County: (615) 334-3242
Polk County: (615) 496-7113
McMinn County: (615) 745-6830
Sequatchie County: (615) 949-
  2228
Marion County: (615) 658-5000
Contact: Phyllis Casarant

Southwest Tennessee Development District Area Agency on Aging
27 Conrad Drive, Suite 150
Jackson, TN 38305-2850
Chester County: (901) 989-7434
Decatur County: (901) 847-7212

Denmark and Mercer Counties:
  (901) 427-9658
Hardeman County: (901) 658-
  2887
Hardin County: (901) 925-2210
Haywood County: (901) 772-
  2438
Henderson County: (901) 968-
  4222
Jackson and Madison Counties:
  (901) 424-5191
McNairy County: (901) 632-0302
Whiteville: (901) 254-8011
Contact: Wanda Simmons

Upper Cumberland Area Agency on Aging
1225 Burgess Falls Road
Cookeville, TN 38501
Cannon County: (615) 563-5304
Clay County: (615) 243-3467
Cumberland County: (615) 484-
  9235
Alexandria: (615) 529-2928
Dowellton and Liberty: (615) 536-
  5422
Fentress County: (615) 879-749
Gainsboro: (615) 268-0837
Granville and Whitleyville: (615)
  653-4647
Macon County: (615) 666-3780
Overton County: (615) 823-1268
Pickett County: (615) 864-3652
Putnam County: (615) 526-9318
Smith County: (615) 735-0476
Smithville: (615) 597-4504
Van Buren County: (615) 946-
  7151
Warren County: (615) 473-6550
White County: (615) 836-3663
Contact: Nancy Peace

Texas

STATE AGENCY

Department of Aging
1949 Interstate Highway 35 South
P.O. Box 12786
Austin, TX 78711-3072
Within state: (800) 252-9240
Contact: Mary Sapp

REGIONAL AGENCIES

Alamo Area Agency on Aging
118 Broadway, Suite 400
San Antonio, TX 78205
(210) 222-1845
Contact: Frank Adamo

**Area Agency on Aging of
  Southeast Texas**
3501 Turtle Creek Drive #108
Port Arthur, TX 77642
Within state: (800) 395-5465
Contact: Joyce Philen

**Ark-Tex Council of
  Governments Area Agency
  on Aging**
911 North Bishop Road
Building A Centre West
P.O. Box 5307
Texarkana, TX 75505
(903) 832-8636
Contact: Martha Hall Smith

**Bexar County Area Agency on
  Aging**
118 Broadway, Suite 400
San Antonio, TX 78205
(210) 222-1845
Contact: Minnie R. Williams

**Brazos Valley Area Agency on
  Aging**
3006 East Twenty-ninth Street
Bryan, TX 77805
(409) 776-2277
Contact: Roberta Linquist

**Capital Area Planning Council/
  Area Agency on Aging**
2520 Interstate Highway 35
  South, Suite 100
Austin, TX 78704
Bastrop County: (512) 237-3950
Blanco County: (512) 833-5206
Bertram, Briggs, and Burnett:
  (512) 756-4945
Caldwell County: (512) 398-6660
Fayette County: (409) 968-6424
Hays County: (512) 353-5018

Lee County: (409) 542-0215
Llano County: (915) 247-4662
Marble Falls and Spicewood:
(512) 693-3109
Travis County: (512) 451-0106
Williamson County: (512) 255-
4970
Contact: Delma Juarez

Central Texas Council of Governments/Area Agency on Aging
302 East Central
P.O. Box 729
Belton, TX 76513
Within state: (800) 447-7169
Contact: H. Richard McGhee

Coastal Bend Area Agency on Aging
2910 Leopard Street
P.O. Box 9909
Corpus Christi, TX 78469
Within state: (800) 421-4636
Contact: Betty Lamb

Concho Valley Area Agency on Aging
P.O. Box 60050
San Angelo, TX 76906
Within state: (800) 728-2592
Contact: Betty Ford

Dallas Area Agency on Aging
212 Main Street, Suite 500
Dallas, TX 75201
(214) 741-5244
Contact: Norman L. Moorhead

Deep East Texas Council of Governments
274 East Lamar
Jasper, TX 75951
Within state: (800) 435-3377
Contact: Holly Anderson

East Texas Area Agency on Aging
3800 Stone Road
Kilgore, TX 75662
(903) 984-8641
Contact: Claude I. Andrews

Golden Crescent Area Agency on Aging
P.O. Box 2028
Victoria, TX 77902
Calhoun County: (512) 552-3350
Dewitt County: (512) 275-6371
Goliad County: (512) 645-2144
Gonzales County: (512) 672-6469
Jackson County: (512) 782-5511
Lavaca County: (512) 798-5971
Victoria County: (512) 576-2189
Contact: Cindy Cornish

Heart of Texas Council of Governments
300 Franklin Avenue
Waco, TX 76701
(817) 752-3240
Contact: John McCue

Houston—Galveston Area Agency on Aging
3555 Timmons Lane, Suite 500
P.O. Box 22777
Houston, TX 77027
Austin County: (409) 885-4188
Bay City, Cedar Lane, Markham,
Pledger, Van Vleck, and
Wadsworth: (409) 245-6901
Blessing, Collegeport, Elmaton,
Midfield, and Palacios: (512)
972-2715
Brazoria County: (713) 331-6101
Chambers County: (409) 267-
3559
Colorado and Wharton Counties:
(409) 532-5617

Fort Bend County: (713) 342-8970
Galveston County: (409) 762-8621
Liberty County: (713) 592-1174; (409) 336-7265
Montgomery County: (409) 539-2981
Waller County: (713) 342-8970
Contact: Don Smith

Houston—Harris County Area Agency on Aging
800 North Stadium Drive, Eighth Floor
Houston, TX 77054
(713) 794-9001
Contact: Charlene Hunter James

Lower Rio Grande Valley Area Agency on Aging
4900 North Twenty-third Street
McAllen, TX 78504
Within state: (800) 365-6131
Contact: Jose L. Gonzales

Middle Rio Grande Area Agency on Aging
1904 North First Street
P.O. Box 1199
Carrizo Springs, TX 78834
(512) 876-3533
Contact: Martha A. Duerksen

North Central Texas Area Agency on Aging
616 Six Flags Drive
Arlington, TX 76005-5888
Collin County: (800) 371-0955
Denton County: (817) 382-2224
Ellis County: (214) 937-7023
Erath and Somervell Counties: (817) 897-2319

Hood, Palo Pinto, Parker, and Wise Counties: (800) 222-8696
Hunt and Rockwell Counties: (903) 454-1444
Johnson County: (817) 641-7895
Kaufman: (214) 563-1421
Navarro: (903) 872-2404
Contact: Nelda Davis

North Texas Area Agency on Aging
4309 Jacksboro Highway, Suite 200
P.O. Box 5144
Wichita Falls, TX 76307
(817) 322-5281
Contact: Rhonda Pogue

Panhandle Area Agency on Aging
2736 Tenth Street
P.O. Box 9257
Amarillo, TX 79105
(800) 642-6008
Contact: Mike McQueen

Permian Basin Area Agency on Aging
2910 La Force Boulevard
P.O. Box 60660
Midland, TX 79711-0660
(915) 563-1061
Contact: William E. Smith

Rio Grande Area Agency on Aging
1014 North Stanton, Suite 100
El Paso, TX 79902
(800) 333-7082
Contact: Andrea G. Carrillo

South Plains Association of Governments
1323 Fifty-eighth Street

P.O. Box 3730
Lubbock, TX 79412
(800) 858-1809
Contact: Robert V. Marshall

South Texas Area Agency on Aging
600 South Sandman
P.O. Box 2187
Laredo, TX 78044
(800) 292-5426
Contact: Andy Smith, Jr.

Tarrant County Area Agency on Aging
210 East Ninth Street
Fort Worth, TX 76102

(817) 878-0100
Contact: Patricia Cheong

Texoma Area Agency on Aging
10000 Grayson Drive
Denison, TX 75020
Within state: (800) 677-8264
Contact: Janis Gray

West Central Texas Council of Governments
1025 East North Tenth Street
P.O. Box 3195
Abilene, TX 79604
(915) 672-8544
Contact: Dr. Lewis E. Lemmond

Utah

STATE AGENCY

Division of Aging and Adult Services
Department of Human Services
P.O. Box 45500
Salt Lake City, UT 84145-0500
(801) 538-3910
Contact: Robin Arnold-Williams

REGIONAL AGENCIES

Bear River Area Agency on Aging
170 North Main
Logan, UT 84321
(801) 752-7242
Contact: Susan Amman Raymond

Davis County Council on Aging
50 East State Street
P.O. Box 618
Farmington, UT 84025
(801) 295-6600
Contact: Joyce Smith

Five County Area Agency on Aging
906 North 1400 West
St. George, UT 84770
Beaver County: (801) 438-5313
Garfield County: (801) 826-4317
Iron County: (801) 477-8925
Kane County: (801) 644-5250
Washington County: (801) 634-5716
Contact: Bob Rasmussen

Mountainland Association of Governments
2545 North Canyon Road
Provo, UT 84604
(801) 377-2262
Contact: Ted Livingston

Salt Lake County Aging Services
2001 South State Street
Salt Lake City, UT 84190-2300
(801) 468-2480
Contact: Shauna O'Neil

San Juan Area Agency on Aging
117 South Main Street
P.O. Box 9
Monticello, UT 84535
(801) 587-3225
Contact: Frank Morrell

Six County Area Agency on Aging
P.O. Box 820
Richfield, UT 84701
(801) 896-9222
Contact: Ross Bumgardner

Southeastern Utah Area Agency on Aging
145 West 3450 South
P.O. Drawer 1106
Price, UT 84501
Carbon, Emery, and Grand Counties: (801) 637-4268
San Juan County: (801) 587-3225
Contact: Maughan Guymon

Tooele County Aging and Adult Services
59 East Vince Street
Tooele, UT 84074
(801) 884-3446
Contact: Joyce Rigby

Uintah Basin Area Agency on Aging
120 South 100 East #43-4
Roosevelt, UT 84066
(801) 722-4518
Contact: Anna Maria Whitmore

Uintah Basin Area Agency on Aging
155 South 100 West
Vernal, UT 84078
(801) 789-2169
Contact: Joan Janes

Weber–Morgan Area Agency on Aging
2650 Lincoln Avenue, Room 134
Ogden, UT 84401
Morgan County: (801) 829-6811
Weber County: (801) 625-3780
Contact: Harold L. Morrill

Vermont

STATE AGENCY

Department of Aging and Disabilities
103 South Main Street
Waterbury, VT 05671-2301
Within state: (800) 642-5119
Contact: Lawrence G. Crist

REGIONAL AGENCIES

**Area Agency on Aging for
   Northeastern Vermont**
12 Western Avenue
Box 4070
St. Johnsbury, VT 05819
Within state: (800) 639-1543
Contact: Jean Dedam

**Central Vermont Council on
   Aging**
18 South Main Street
Barre, VT 05641
(802) 479-0531
Contact: Charles Castle

**Champlain Valley Area Agency
   on Aging**
Chase Mill - 1 Mill Street
P.O. Box 158
Burlington, VT 05404
Within state: (800) 642-5119
Contact: John Barbour

**Council on Aging for
   Southeastern Vermont**
139 Main Street
P.O. Box 818
Brattleboro, VT 05301
(802) 254-4446
Contact: Sally Fuller

**Southwestern Vermont Council
   on Aging**
142 Merchants Row
Rutland, VT 05701
Bennington County: (802) 442-
   5436
Rutland County: (802) 775-3223
Contact: John G. Campbell

Virginia

STATE AGENCY

Virginia Department for the Aging
700 East Franklin Street, Tenth Floor
Richmond, VA 23219-2327
Within state: (800) 552-4464
Contact: Thelma Bland

REGIONAL AGENCIES

Alexandria Agency on Aging
2525 Mount Vernon Avenue, Unit #5
Alexandria, VA 22301-1159
(703) 838-0920
Contact: Moya Atkinson

Appalachian Agency for Senior Services
P.O. Box 765
Cedar Bluff, VA 24609
(703) 964-0400
Contact: Diana Wallace

Arlington Area Agency on Aging
1801 North George Mason Drive
Arlington, VA 22207
(703) 358-5030
Contact: Terri Lynch

Capital Area Agency on Aging
24 East Cary Street
Richmond, VA 23219-3796
Within state: (800) 989-2286
Contact: Mary C. Payne

Central Virginia Area Agency on Aging
2511 Memorial Avenue, Suite 301
Lynchburg, VA 24501
(804) 846-1326
Contact: Jo K. Nelson

Crater District Area Agency on Aging
23 Seyler Drive
Petersburg, VA 23805
(804) 732-7020
Contact: David Sadowski

District Three Governmental Cooperative
305 South Park Street
Marion, VA 24354
(800) 541-0933
Contact: Mike Guy

Eastern Shore Area Agency on Aging
Community Action Agency
49 Market Street
P.O. Box 8
Onanock, VA 23417
(800) 452-5977
Contact: George V. Podelco, Ph.D.

Fairfax Area Agency on Aging
12011 Government Center
  Parkway, Suite 720
Fairfax, VA 22035
Within state: (800) 552-4464
Contact: Carla B. Pitman

Jefferson Area Board for Aging
2300 Commonwealth Drive, Suite
  B-1
Charlottesville, VA 22901
(804) 978-3644
Contact: Gordon Walker
(804) 978-3644

Lake Country Area Agency on
  Aging
1105 West Danville Street
South Hill, VA 23970
Within state: (800) 252-4464
Contact: Gay S. Currie

League of Older Americans,
  Inc.
706 Campbell Avenue, SW
P.O. Box 14205
Roanoke, VA 24038
(703) 345-0451
Contact: Susan Williams

Loudoun County Area Agency
  on Aging
751 Miller Drive, SE, Suite D2
Leesburg, VA 22075
(800) 552-4464
Contact: Anne H. Edwards

Mountain Empire Older
  Citizens, Inc.
Box 888
Big Stone Gap Industrial Park
Big Stone Gap, VA 24219
Within state: (800) 252-6362
Contact: Marilyn Maxwell

New River Valley Agency on
  Aging
141 East Main Street
Pulaski, VA 24301
(703) 639-9677
Contact: Debbie H. Palmer

Northern Neck—Middle
  Peninsula Area Agency on
  Aging, Inc.
Route 602
Urban Professional Center
P.O. Box 610
Urbanna, VA 23175
(804) 758-2386
Contact: Callyn W. Gemerek

Peninsula Agency on Aging,
  Inc.
739 Thimble Shoals Boulevard,
  Suite 1006
Newport News, VA 23606-3562
(804) 873-0541
Contact: William S. Massey

Piedmont Senior Resource Area
  Agency on Aging
Route 624
P.O. Box 398
Burkeville, VA 23922
(804) 767-5588
Contact: Ronald Dunn

Prince William Area Agency on
  Aging
7987 Ashton Avenue, Suite 204
Manassas, VA 22110
(703) 792-6400
Contact: Lin D. Wagener

Rappahannock Area Agency on Aging
204 Thompson Avenue
Fredericksburg, VA 22405
(703) 371-3375
Contact: Carol Davis

Rappahannock–Rapidan Area Agency
401 South Main Street
Culpeper, VA 22701
(703) 825-3100
Contact: Sallie Morgan

Shenandoah Area Agency on Aging, Inc.
15 North Royal Avenue
Front Royal, VA 22630
(703) 635-7141
Contact: Catherine Galvin

Southeast Virginia Areawide Model Program
7 Koger Executive Center, Suite 100
York Building
Norfolk, VA 23502
(804) 461-9481
Contact: John Skirven

Southern Area Agency on Aging, Inc.
433 Commonwealth Boulevard
Marinsville, VA 24112
Within state: (800) 255-3337
Contact: Teresa N. Carter

Valley Program for Aging Services, Inc.
325 Pine Avenue
P.O. Box 817
Waynesboro, VA 22980-0603
Within state: (800) 868-8727
Contact: Ann Bender

Washington

STATE AGENCY

Aging and Adult Services Administration
Department of Social and Health Services
P.O. Box 45600
Olympia, WA 98504-5600
Within state: (800) 422-3263
Contact: Charles Reed

REGIONAL AGENCIES

Columbia River Area Agency on Aging
230 North Georgia
East Wenatchee, WA 98802
Within state: (800) 572-4459
Contact: John Cottrell

Eastern Washington Area Agency on Aging
West 1101 College Avenue, Room 365
Spokane, WA 99201
Ferry County: (509) 775-3329
Ferry, Pend Oreille, and Stevens Counties: (509) 684-3932
Spokane County: (509) 458-7450
Whitman County: (509) 397-4305
Contact: Nick Beamer

Kitsap County Area Agency on Aging
614 Division Street, MS-5
Port Orchard, WA 98366
Within state: (800) 562-6418
Contact: Gail S. Hiestand

Lewis/Mason/Thurston Area Agency on Aging
503 West Fourth Avenue
Olympia, WA 98501
East Lewis County: (800) 247-5872
Lewis County: (800) 843-3053
Mason County: (206) 426-9612
Thurston County: (206) 943-6188
Contact: Dennis W. Mahar

Northwest Washington Area Agency on Aging 1
1800 James Street
Bellingham, WA 98225
Island County: (206) 321-1600
San Juan County: (206) 378-2677
Skagit County: (206) 336-9345
Whatcom County: (206) 733-4030
Contact: Dewey G. Desler

Olympic Area Agency on Aging
423 Washington Street
P.O. Box 1072
Port Townsend, WA 98368
Bay Center, Lebam, Menlo, Raymond, South Bend, and Tokeland: (206) 972-2177
Beaver, Clallam Bay, Forks, La Push, Neah Bay, and Sekieu: (206) 374-9496
Carlsborg, Joyce, Port Angeles, and Sequim: (206) 452-3221
Chinook, Ilwaco, Long Beach, Naselle, Ocean Park, Oysterville, and Grays Harbour Counties: (206) 532-0520
Jefferson County: (206) 385-3552
Seaview: (206) 642-3634
Contact: Debra Bergthold

Pierce County Aging and Long-Term Care
8811 South Tacoma Way #210
Tacoma, WA 98499-4591
Within state: (800) 642-5769

Seattle–King County Division of Aging
618 Second Avenue, Suite 1020
Seattle, WA 98104-2232
(206) 448-3110
Contact: Frank Jose

Southeast Washington Office of Aging and Long-Term Care
2009 South Sixty-fourth Avenue
Yakima, WA 98903
Asotin County: (509) 758-2355
Benton County: (509) 735-0315
Columbia County: (509) 382-4787
Franklin County: (509) 545-3459
Garfield County: (509) 843-3008
Kittitas County: (509) 925-1928
Walla Walla County: (509) 529-6470
Yakima County: (509) 454-5475
Contact: Greg Heartburg

Southwest Washington Agency on Aging
7414 Northeast Hazel Dell Avenue

P.O. Box 425
Vancouver, WA 98666-0425
Clark County: (800) 752-9422
Cowlitz and Wahkiakum
   Counties: (800) 962-6468
Klickitat County: (800) 447-7858
Skamania County: (509) 427-5166
Contact: Kamala Bremer

Snohomish County Division of Aging
2722 Colby, Suite 104
Everett, WA 98201
(206) 259-7113
Contact: Michael T. Manley

West Virginia

STATE AGENCY

Commission on Aging
Holly Grove
1900 Kanawha Boulevard East
Charleston, WV 25305-0160
(304) 558-3317
Contact: William E. Lytton, Jr.

REGIONAL AGENCIES

Appalachian Area Agency on Aging
701 Mercer Street
P.O. Box 1432
Princeton, WV 24740

Braxton County: (304) 587-2468
Clay County: (304) 587-2468
Fayette County: (304) 465-8484
Greenbrier County: (304) 392-5138

McDowell County: (304) 436-6588

Mercer County: (304) 425-3480

Monroe County: (304) 753-4384

Nicholas County: (304) 872-1162

Pocahontas County: (304) 799-6337

Raleigh County: (304) 255-1397

Summers County: (304) 466-4019

Webster County: (304) 847-5252

Wyoming County: (304) 294-8800

Contact: Ramona McNeely

Northwestern Area Agency on Aging

2177 National Road

P.O. Box 2086

Wheeling, WV 26003

Brooke County: (304) 527-3410

Calhoun County: (304) 354-7822

Doddridge County: (304) 878-2061

Gilmer County: (304) 462-5761

Hancock County: (304) 564-3801

Harrison County: (304) 623-6795

Marion County: (304) 366-8779

Marshall County: (304) 845-8200

Monongalia County: (304) 296-9812

Ohio County: (304) 232-6730

Pleasants County: (304) 684-9243

Ritchie County: (304) 643-4941

Tyler County: (304) 652-3364

Wetzel County: (304) 455-3220

Wirt County: (304) 275-3158

Wood County: (304) 485-6748

Contact: Gaylene Miller

Upper Potomac Area Agency on Aging

Airport Road

P.O. Box 869

Petersburg, WV 26847

Barbour County: (304) 457-4545

Berkeley County: (304) 263-8873

Grant County: (304) 257-1166

Hampshire County: (304) 822-4097

Hardy County: (304) 538-2256; (304) 538-6987

Jefferson County: (304) 725-4044

Lewis County: (304) 269-5738

Mineral County: (304) 788-5467

Morgan County: (304) 258-3096

Pendleton County: (304) 358-2421

Preston County: (304) 329-0464

Randolph County: (304) 636-4747

Taylor County: (304) 265-4555

Tucker County: (304) 478-2423

Upshur County: (304) 472-0528

Contact: Raymond Gaudet

West Virginia State College Metro Area Agency on Aging

West Virginia State College

Wallace Hall

P.O. Box 518

Institute, WV 25112

Boone County: (304) 949-3673

Cabell County: (304) 529-4952

Jackson County: (304) 372-2406

Kanawha County: (304) 348-0707

Lincoln County: (304) 824-3448

Logan County: (304) 752-6868

Mason County: (304) 675-2369

Mingo County: (304) 235-1701

Putnam County: (304) 757-2656

Roane County: (304) 927-1997

Wayne County: (304) 272-5112

Contact: James D. Recco

Wisconsin

STATE AGENCY

Bureau on Aging
Division of Community Services
P.O. Box 7851
Madison, WI 53707
(608) 266-2536
Contact: Donna McDowell

REGIONAL AGENCIES

**Lake Michigan–Winnebago
   Area Agency on Aging**
850 C. Lombardi Avenue
Green Bay, WI 54304
Brown County: (414) 432-9235
Calumet County: (414) 849-2361
Door County: (414) 743-3083
Fond du Lac County: (800) 242-4928
Green Lake County: (414) 294-4070
Kewaunee County: (414) 388-0626
Outagamie County: (414) 832-5145
Manitowaoc County: (414) 683-4180
Marquette County: (608) 297-9108
Marinette County: (715) 854-7453
Oconto County: (414) 834-4332
Shawano County: (715) 526-9344
Sheboygan County: (414) 459-3095
Waupaca County: (715) 258-6275
Waushara County: (414) 787-4631

Winnebago County: (414) 236-4668
Menominee County: (715) 799-3341
Contact: Barbara Mamerow

**Milwaukee County Department
   on Aging**
235 West Galema Street, Suite 180
Milwaukee, WI 53212-3925
(414) 289-6874
Stephanie Stein

**New Ventures of Wisconsin,
   Inc., Area Agency on Aging**
3601 Memorial Drive
Madison, WI 53704
Columbia County: (608) 742-9208
Dane County: (608) 266-9063
Dodge County: (414) 386-3582
Grant County: (608) 723-6113
Green County: (608) 328-9396
Iowa County: (608) 935-2577
Jefferson County: (414) 674-3105
Juneau County: (608) 847-9366
Lafayette County: (608) 776-4888

Richland County: (608) 647-6226
Rock County: (608) 757-5472
Sauk County: (608) 356-5581
Contact: Arthur M. Hendrick

Northern Area Agency on Aging

1853 North Stevens Street
P.O. Box 1028
Rhinelander, WI 54501
Adams County: (608) 339-4281
Ashland County: (715) 682-4414
Bayfield County: (715) 373-6127
Douglas County: (715) 394-3611
Florence County: (715) 528-4890
Forest County: (715) 478-3256
Iron County: (715) 561-2108
Lac du Flambeau: (715) 865-3379
Sawyer Area: (715) 634-3000
Langlade County: (715) 627-6230
Lincoln County: (715) 536-0311
Marathon County: (715) 847-5505
Oneida County: (715) 369-6170
Portage County: (715) 346-1401
Price County: (715) 339-3943
Taylor County: (715) 748-1491
Vilas County: (715) 479-3625
Wood County: (715) 421-8900
Contact: Richard Sicchio

Southeastern Wisconsin Area Agency on Aging

125 North Executive Drive, Suite 102
Brookfield, WI 23005
Kenosha County: (414) 653-6646
Ozaukee County: (414) 238-8120

Racine County: (800) 924-5137
Walworth County: (800) 365-1587
Washington County: (414) 335-4494
Waukesha County: (414) 335-4494
Contact: Helen A. Ramon

Western Wisconsin Area Agency on Aging

1316 Fairfax Street #106
Eau Claire, WI 54701
Barron County: (715) 537-6225
Buffalo County: (608) 685-4412
Burnett County: (715) 349-2557
Chippewa County: (715) 726-7777
Clark County: (715) 743-5144
Crawford County: (608) 326-0235
Dunn County: (715) 232-4066
Eau Claire County: (715) 839-4735
Jackson County: (715) 284-0219
LaCrosse County: (608) 785-9900
Monroe County: (608) 269-8690
Pepin County: (715) 672-8936
Pierce County: (715) 273-3531
Polk County: (715) 485-3161
Rusk County: (715) 532-2157
St. Croix County: (715) 796-5221
Trempealeau County: (715) 538-2311
Vernon County: (608) 637-2736
Washburn County: (715) 468-7335
Contact: Pamela Halter

Wyoming

STATE AGENCY

Wyoming Division on Aging
Wyoming Department of Health
Hathaway Building, Room 129
Cheyenne, WY 82002-0480
(800) 442-2766
Crowheart, Fort Washakie, and
   Shoshoni: (307) 857-2570
Albany County: (307) 745-5116
Deaver, Cowley, Byron, Lovell,
   Frannie, Shell, and Burlington:
   (307) 548-6556
Greybull, Hyattville, Basin, Otto,
Manderson, and Emblem: (307)
   765-4488
Campbell County: (307) 686-0804
Carbon County: (307) 328-0320
Converse County: (307) 358-4348
Crook County: (307) 283-1710
Riverton, Hudson, and Saint
   Stephens: (307) 856-6332
Pavillion and Jeffery City: (307)
   332-2746
Dubois: (307) 455-2990

Goshen County: (307) 532-7445
Hot Springs County: (307) 864-
   2151
Johnson County: (307) 684-9552
Laramie County: (307) 635-2435
Lincoln County: (307) 877-3806
Natrona County: (307) 265-4678
Niobrara County: (307) 334-2561
Park County: (307) 587-6221
Platte County: (307) 332-3424
Sheridan County: (307) 674-9343
Big Piney and Daniel: (307) 276-
   3249
Pinedale, Cora, Boulder, and
   Bondurant: (307) 367-2881
Green River: (307) 875-2286
Sweet Water (except Green River):
   (307) 362-2440
Teton County: (307) 733-7300
Uinta County: (307) 789-9833
Washakie County: (307) 347-3208
West County: (307) 468-2576
Contact: Morris Gardner

Bibliography

Blum, Laurie. *The Complete Guide to Getting a Grant,* New York: Poseidon Press, 1993.

Blum, Laurie. *Free Money for Diseases of Aging,* New York: Simon & Schuster, 1992.

Blum, Laurie. *Free Money for Health Care,* Gaithersburg, MD: Aspen Publishers, 1993.

Blum, Laurie. *Free Money for Heart Disease and Cancer Care,* New York: Simon & Schuster, 1992.

Cross, Wilbur. *The Henry Holt Retirement Sourcebook: An Information Guide for Planning and Managing Your Affairs,* New York: Henry Holt, 1991.

Directory of Biomedical and Health Grants, 6th ed., Phoenix, AZ: Oryx Press, 1991.

National Guide to Funding in Aging, 3d ed., New York: The Foundation Center, 1992.

National Guide to Funding in Health, 3d ed., New York: The Foundation Center, 1993.

Rob, Caroline, with Janet Reynolds. *The Caregiver's Guide,* Boston: Houghton Mifflin, 1991.

Silverstone, Barbara. *Growing Older Together: A Couple's Guide to Understanding and Coping with the Challenges of Later Life,* New York: Pantheon Books, 1992.

Index